Emotions and Aggressive Behavior

Edited by

Georges Steffgen
Department of Psychology
University of Luxembourg
Luxembourg

Mario Gollwitzer
Department of Psychology
University of Koblenz-Landau
Germany

Library of Congress Cataloging in Publication

is available via the Library of Congress Marc Database under the
LC Control Number 2007926690

Library and Archives Canada Cataloguing in Publication

Emotions and aggressive behavior / edited by Georges Steffgen, Mario Gollwitzer.
Includes bibliographical references.
ISBN 978-0-88937-343-3
    1. Aggressiveness. 2. Emotions. 3. Anger. I. Steffgen, Georges II. Gollwitzer,
Mario
BF575.A3E46 2007   155.2'32   C2007-902459-9

PUBLISHING OFFICES
USA: Hogrefe & Huber Publishers, 875 Massachusetts Avenue, 7th Floor,
                Cambridge, MA 02139
                Phone (866) 823-4726, Fax (617) 354-6875; E-mail info@hhpub.com
EUROPE: Hogrefe & Huber Publishers, Rohnsweg 25, 37085 Göttingen, Germany
                Phone +49 551 49609-0, Fax +49 551 49609-88, E-mail hh@hhpub.com

SALES & DISTRIBUTION
USA: Hogrefe & Huber Publishers, Customer Services Department,
                30 Amberwood Parkway, Ashland, OH 44805
                Phone (800) 228-3749, Fax (419) 281-6883, E-mail custserv@hhpub.com
EUROPE: Hogrefe & Huber Publishers, Rohnsweg 25, 37085 Göttingen, Germany
                Phone +49 551 49609-0, Fax +49 551 49609-88, E-mail hh@hhpub.com

OTHER OFFICES
CANADA: Hogrefe & Huber Publishers, 1543 Bayview Avenue, Toronto, Ontario M4G 3B5
SWITZERLAND: Hogrefe & Huber Publishers, Länggass-Strasse 76, CH-3000 Bern 9

Hogrefe & Huber Publishers
Incorporated and registered in the State of Washington, USA, and in Göttingen, Lower Saxony, Germany

ISBN 978-0-88937-343-3

Publication of this work was supported by:

Preface

Emotions play an important role in aggressive behavioral tendencies and responses. Emotions are not merely epiphenomena of aggression; they can be triggers, amplifiers, moderators, even ultimate goals of aggressive behavior. Insights concerning the functional relationship between emotions and aggression are not only of theoretical relevance; they are also crucial for finding solutions for efficient control, prevention, and reduction of aggression.

Although most researchers on aggression would probably not deny that emotions and aggression are strongly interrelated, the number of publications focusing explicitly on this relationship is relatively sparse. The present book therefore aims to fill this gap and to provide a compilation of papers that focus on theoretical elaborations and empirical findings on the emotion-aggression link.

The first glimmers of the present book were born in the autumn of 2005 at the X. Workshop Aggression, which we had the pleasure to organize at the University of Luxembourg. Most of the speakers who gave talks at this workshop were willing to contribute to this book project. Thus, the book brings together leading experts from fields such as social, personality, developmental, and physiological psychology presenting state-of-the-art research on the emotion-aggression link. The book describes assessment and treatment approaches, as well as theoretical concepts and research findings, and it presents an interdisciplinary perspective.

The book is roughly divided into five sections or parts. Part 1 deals with bibliometric analyses of psychological research on emotions and aggression. Part 2 deals with emotion-based motives and measures of aggression. Part 3 focuses on the relationship between anger and aggression. Part 4 investigates the emotion-aggression link in intergroup contexts. Finally, Part 5 deals with emotions and aggression from a developmental perspective.

Part 1: Historiography of Research on Emotions and Aggression

Part 1 consists of a single chapter by Gabriel Schui and Günter Krampen. Based on bibliometric analyses, Schui and Krampen investigate the development of psychological research on aggression and emotion between 1977 and 2003. Two findings are noteworthy: First, literature on the explicit relationship between aggression and emotion is hard to find; such publications cover only one tenth of a percent of the total psychological literature. Second, their analyses illustrate many similarities in the development of aggression and emotion research in the Anglo-American and German-speaking communities in the examined time span.

Part 2: Emotion-Based Motives and Measures of Aggression

Part 2 consists of two chapters. Leo Montada investigates the role of emotion-based motives for aggressive behavior. He begins with the provocative notion that understanding the individual and social functions of aggressive behavior is crucial for attempting to prevent or reduce such behavior. Such a model perceives humans to be principally responsible for their actions, whereas merely investigating the "determinants" of aggression does not allow for responsibility ascriptions. Montada proposes an action-theoretical (or human-psychological) approach to understanding aggression, in which emotions can be understood (a) as indicators of the aggressor's goals and motives, and (b) as the central key to aggression reduction.

Matthias Bluemke and Joerg Zumbach deal with the question of whether playing violent computer games increases both explicit and implicit aggression. This implies two research questions. The first question asks whether playing violent computer games is positively correlated with aggression, hostility, and anger proneness. The second question asks whether the effects are stronger on an implicit level (assessing automatic and spontaneous aspects of attitudes and dispositions) than on an explicit level (assessing controlled and deliberate aspects of attitudes and dispositions). The authors (a) highlight the advantages of implicit measures, (b) suggest that aggression research might profit from measuring (automatic) affective reactions and predicting behavior, and (c) describe two aggression-related Implicit Association Tests (IATs). Interestingly, they find reliable differences with regard to explicit and implicit aggression between "ordinary" PC users and users that frequently play (violent and nonviolent) computer games. However, they did not find any differences between players of violent and of nonviolent games.

Part 3: Anger and Aggression

Part 3 consists of four chapters. Roy F. Baumeister and Brad J. Bushman discuss theoretical perspectives on emotion and aggression and review the research on the role of anger on aggression. They argue that whereas the frustration-aggression hypothesis (including its derivatives) and catharsis theory have been dominating subjective (and even scientific) theories for a long time, recent research points to other theoretical contributions such as loss of self-control, self-regulation, and mood regulation. Baumeister and Bushman also discuss emotions that restrain and prevent aggression, such as guilt.

Sylvia Richter, Kirsten Jordan, and Torsten Wüstenberg review findings on the functional neuroanatomy of anger and aggression. These authors convincingly observe that recent research in cognitive neuroscience has already created new possibilities for investigating the physiological basis of anger and aggression. This chapter offers a very good introduction to research in neuroscience and one of its primary methods, functional Magnetic Resonance Imaging (fMRI). The authors also report findings from their own research group regarding the neurophysiological correlates of individual anger expression styles.

Georges Steffgen and Jan Pfetsch argue that anger and aggression are strongly interdependent and intertwined with each other. Very often, anger intervention programs also aim to directly or indirectly change aggressive behavior. Vice versa, trainings for aggression prevention or reduction often aim to reduce or change the experience of anger. A basic question is whether anger treatment necessarily reduces aggressive behavior. Steffgen and Pfetsch investigate the theoretical relationship between these two concepts and refer to comparative and meta-analytic studies in order to assess the specific effectiveness of anger intervention programs. The chapter concludes with a summary of principles for anger treatments that should be considered in aggression reduction interventions.

Mario Gollwitzer questions the notion found in many popular and philosophical writings that vengeful reactions are irrational, limitless, affective, and unconnected to general principles of fairness or proportionality. First, he assesses the dimensionality of different goals and functions underlying vengeful reactions. Second, he investigates the relationship between revenge goals and the likelihood of actually engaging in particular vengeful behavior. Interestingly, participants were unlikely to take revenge if the particular action was likely to do harm to the offender. More importantly, anger about a particular provocation did not predict vengeful behavior. On the other hand, people are more likely to take revenge when they consider the revenge option to be instrumental for demonstrating powerfulness, for restoring social identity, for reestablishing justice, and for reducing anger. These findings suggest that revenge cannot simply be conceived of as irrational and purely affective.

Part 4: Emotions and Aggression in Intergroup Contexts

Part 4 consists of two chapters. Ulrich Wagner and Oliver Christ investigate extreme forms of violence and aggression between groups. The authors review research on intergroup aggression and suggest a heuristic model that combines different levels of explanations. Furthermore, they present data from two representative surveys and a panel of German adult respondents. They show that intergroup aggression against foreigners living in Germany is predicted by prejudice, and that this relationship is both mediated and moderated by intergroup emotions, especially anger.

Kerstin Schütte and Thomas Kessler focus on intergroup aggression as well as outgroup derogation. They agree that group-based emotions can explain negative behavior toward outgroup members, but they also distinguish between outgroup derogation and other forms of intergroup bias. Preliminary results support their notion that group-based anger constitutes an affective route to outgroup derogation. Cognitive appraisals of intergroup relationships such as outgroup threat increase as a consequence of group-based anger.

Part 5: Emotions and Aggression in a Developmental Perspective

Part 5 consists of four chapters. Angela Ittel examines the validity of mediating pathways in a longitudinal study predicting adolescent aggression by social anxiety, depression, self-esteem, loneliness, and perceived social integration. The mediator model was supported for girls only. Thus, the assumption that social integration serves as a protective factor against the aggression-evoking effects of a negative emotional disposition is only true for girls. Ittel discusses her findings in the context of gender-specific prevention approaches for adolescent aggression.

Tina Malti reviews research on guilt and aggression among children. She empirically shows that self-attributed moral emotions and gender have an interactional effect on aggression. Her results suggest that the manner in which moral emotions are associated with aggressive responses is different for boys and girls, which might be due to gender-specific interactions.

Florian Juen, Doris Peham, Barbara Juen, and Cord Benecke discuss the prevention of aggressive behavior in early childhood. They consider aggressive behavior to be the result of a dynamic mental process caused by insecure or chaotic family environments in early childhood, and they highlight the role of affect and self-regulation for such attachment-related developmental effects. Finally, they also discuss the consequences of their approach for the intervention and prevention of aggression.

In the final chapter, Johannes Bach discusses aspects of the prevention of emotional-social disorders, which include both externalizing behaviors (such as aggression and violence) and internalizing behaviors (such as anxiety and depression) in childhood and adolescence. Bach describes a general approach for treating emotional-social disorders as well as a particular program, the PESS (prevention of emotional-social disorders for children with special needs), which addresses children with cognitive and linguistic deficits. PESS particularly concentrates on emotional expression, perception, and regulation. Bach emphasizes that there is a large need for further development and evaluation of programs for children with special needs.

Acknowledgments

We hope that most of the readers of this book will share our excitement and satisfaction with what has come out of it. We are indebted to many people who have contributed to this work. First of all, we wish to thank all the contributors who participated in this project and thus shared their expertise with the readers. Furthermore, we would like to thank Anna Baumert for preparing a translation of Montada's chapter into English. Jan Pfetsch and Judith Götz have done the enormous job of checking formal aspects of the manuscripts, such as orthography, citations, and references. Jane Thompson agreed to proofread each and every chapter with regard to language, grammar, and expressions; she has contributed immensely to the improvement of the manuscripts.

We also would like to thank Robert Dimbleby of Hogrefe & Huber Publishers in Göttingen for supporting the progress of our project during the last year.

Finally, we express our thanks to the Fonds National de la Recherche in Luxembourg and the University of Luxembourg for generously funding this project.

Luxembourg and Landau, July 2007   Georges Steffgen
                                                          Mario Gollwitzer

List of Contributors

Johannes Bach
Department of Pedagogy and
Rehabilitation
Ludwig-Maximilians-University Munich
Germany

Roy F. Baumeister
Department of Psychology
Florida State University
USA

Cord Benecke
Department of Psychology
University of Innsbruck
Austria

Matthias Bluemke
Psychological Institute
University of Heidelberg
Germany

Brad J. Bushman
Institute for Social Research
University of Michigan
USA
Vrije Universiteit Amsterdam
The Netherlands

Oliver Christ
Department of Psychology
Philipps-University Marburg
University of Bielefeld
Germany

Mario Gollwitzer
Department of Psychology
University of Koblenz-Landau
Germany

Angela Ittel
Department of Education
University of the Bundeswehr, Munich
Germany

Kirsten Jordan
Department of Psychology
Otto-von-Guericke-University Magdeburg
Department of Medical Psychology
Georg-August-University Göttingen
Germany

Barbara Juen
Department of Psychology
University of Innsbruck
Austria

Florian Juen
Department of Psychology
University of Innsbruck
Austria

Thomas Kessler
Department of Psychology
Friedrich-Schiller-University Jena
Germany

Günter Krampen
Institute for Psychology Information
(ZPID)
University of Trier
Germany

Tina Malti
Jacobs Center for Productive Youth
Development
University of Zurich
Switzerland

Leo Montada
Department of Psychology
University of Trier
Germany

Doris Peham
Department of Psychology
University of Innsbruck
Austria

Jan Pfetsch
Department of Psychology
University of Luxembourg
Luxembourg

Sylvia Richter
Department of Psychology
Otto-von-Guericke-University Magdeburg
Department of Neurochemistry and
Molecular Biology
Leibniz Institute for Neurobiology
Magdeburg
Germany

Gabriel Schui
Institute for Psychology Information
(ZPID)
University of Trier
Germany

Kerstin Schütte
Department of Psychology
Friedrich-Schiller-University Jena
Germany

Georges Steffgen
Department of Psychology
University of Luxembourg
Luxembourg

Ulrich Wagner
Department of Psychology
Philipps-University Marburg
Germany

Torsten Wüstenberg
Department of Psychology
Otto-von-Guericke-University Magdeburg
Department of Medical Psychology
Georg-August-University Göttingen
Germany

Joerg Zumbach
Department of Science Education and
Teacher Training
University of Salzburg
Austria

Table of Contents

Part 1

Historiography of Research on Aggression and Emotion

1 Historiography of Research on Aggression and Emotion and Their Intersection in the Last Quarter of the 20th Century:
Bibliometric Analyses of Psychological Research in German-Speaking and Anglo-American Research

Gabriel Schui and Günter Krampen

Aggression – i.e., aggressive and antisocial behavior as well as aggressiveness and antisocial personality (disorders) – has been a classic issue in basic and applied psychological research since the foundational period of psychology. In introductory texts (e.g., Heckhausen, 1989; Selg, Mees, & Berg, 1997), the respective research traditions focusing on aggression are mostly categorized into psychoanalytic (Freud, 1905, 1930) or ethological (Lorenz, 1963) instinct theories, frustration-aggression models (McDougall, 1908; Dollard, Doob, Miller, Mowrer, & Sears, 1939), and social learning theories (Berkowitz, 1962; Bandura, 1973) as they are described from the turn of the 20th century until the 1960s and 1970s.

Even as early as the first half of the 20th century, personality – as well as social-psychology – centered theoretical foci could already be distinguished. This became more distinct with attempts to measure interindividual differences in different aspects of aggression, initially using projective tests, e.g., the Thematic Apperception Test, TAT, and the Rosenzweig Picture Frustration Tests (for an overview see Feshbach, 1970), at the end of the 1950s. Later, there were questionnaires with their explicit focus on differential psychology on the one hand, and the boom of experimental aggression research initiated by Buss (1961), Berkowitz (1962), and Taylor (1967) in the 1960s, on the other.

Starting in the 1970s, attribution and emotion-based approaches related to anger started to emerge (see Heckhausen, 1989, for an overview). Also, since the 1970s, these and the older approaches were flanked by sociobiological, neurobiological, and neurochemical aspects (natural sciences background) as well as socio-normative aspects (social sciences background, e.g., concerning responsibility, justice, retaliation, and justification) in literature reviews and integrative models.

Thus, there has been a diversification of aggression research since the 1970s that reaches beyond the classic contributions from social psychology and differential psychology and their application in (mostly) criminology as well as clinical psychology. This is already discussed in the literature review by Mummendey (1983) and more so in more recent ones (e.g., Geen, 1998; Krahé, 2001; Krahé & Greve, 2002).

Theoretical and empirical diversifications in basic aggression research encompass approaches from developmental, biopsychological, victimological, and emotion-theory based perspectives. Diversification in applied disciplines incorporates research concerning topics like child abuse, sexual abuse, bullying, mass media influences (educational psychology), mobbing and bossing (organizational psychology), aggressive behavior, and its treatment in the context of certain disorders and with hospitalized patients (clinical psychology), anger reactions, and health (health psychology).

These recent diversifications in aggression research of the past 20–30 years led to a considerable increase in aggression-related descriptors in the "Thesaurus of psychological index terms" (Gallagher, 2004) published by the American Psychological Association (APA) (see Table 1). Presumably, they also contributed to the success of the "Workshop Aggression," which has well-established itself as an informal meeting (without any formal institutional or organizational connection, similar to the "TeaP") in the German-speaking community during the past ten years. Taking all of this into account, it is a worthwhile endeavour to empirically assess the developmental trends in aggression research in the last quarter of the 20th century using a bibliometric approach. Referring to the article by Wallbott (1991) on the "survey of a neglected borderzone" of social- and emotion-related psychological research, namely "das Emotionale in der Sozialpsychologie und das Soziale in der Emotionspsychologie" (Wallbott, 1991, p. 53), we also want to address the question of the development of literature in the intersection of research on aggression and emotion since the 1970s.

To accomplish these goals, we conducted a bibliometric survey of aggression and emotion-related literature published in the past 30 years, tracing developments in research and also possible thematic differences between the Anglo-American and German-speaking scientific communities. Specifically, we wanted to address three questions:

1. How many publications exist in the field of aggression research in the examined time-period?
2. How many publications exist in the field of emotion research in the examined time period?
3. How does the aggression-related literature intersect with that containing emotion-theory-based approaches?

Method

We used the psychological databases PsycINFO (Anglo-American focus) and PSYN-DEX (focus on literature from the German-speaking countries) which have little intersection (PsycINFO contains approximately 4% of literature from the German-speaking countries which is mostly limited to journal articles). For collecting the bibliometric data, we compared different automated search strategies, such as simple free text searches, searches in publication titles or descriptors and also specific searches for literature reviews and meta-analyses, regarding their efficacy and efficiency. The same search strategies, spanning the publication years from 1977 to 2003, for which complete literature documentation is to be expected, are applied to both databases.

Due to considerable variations in absolute publication counts of aggression/emotion-related literature per year (showing a clear overall increase) and the difference of PsycINFO and PSYNDEX in total document volumes (PsycINFO is approximately eight times larger, see Tables 1 and 2), the absolute aggression/emotion-related publication counts per year are standardized with respect to the total number of publications per year, in order to compare them. We applied (time of analysis: May 2005) different auto-mated search strategies to compare their efficacy and efficiency. These were:

1. Free text search on aggression and emotion in all fields of the databases.
2. Search on aggression and emotion limited to the title field.
3. Search for the subject fields *aggression* and *emotion* limited to the descriptor field.
4. Combination ("and") of Strategy 3 with the descriptor *literature review*.
5. Combination ("and") of Strategy 3 with the descriptor and methodology fields (PsycINFO) respectively the publication-type field (PSYNDEX) containing *meta-analysis*.

(detailed in Table 3)

Table 1. Descriptors Constituting the Subject Field "Aggression," their Year of Introduction to the APA Thesaurus, Absolute Literature Frequencies, and Percentages in Relation to the Total Subject Field in PsycINFO and PSYNDEX[1]

Date of inclusion	PsycINFO			PSYNDEX		
	Index Term (DE)	f	%	Deskriptor (DG)	f	%
1967	aggressive behavior	9392	13.7	Aggressions-verhalten	1684	19.6
1967	hostility	2160	3.2	Feindseligkeit	284	3.3
1967	war	3785	5.5	Krieg	782	9.1
1967	crime	7049	10.3	Straftat	1567	18.2
1971	antisocial behavior	3451	5.0	dissoziales Verhalten	574	6.7
1971	child abuse	13197	19.3	Kindesmisshand-lung	1155	13.4
1973	aggressiveness	1715	2.5	Aggressivität (Persönl.)	651	7.6
1973	antisocial personality disorder	2036	3.0	dissoziale Persön-lichkeit	158	1.8
1973	animal aggressive behavior	4580	6.7	Aggressionsverhalten bei Tieren	55	0.6
1973	attack behavior	680	1.0	Angriffsverhalten	16	0.2
1973	cruelty	77	0.1	Grausamkeit	18	0.2
1973	persecution	151	0.2	Verfolgung	118	1.4
1973	violence	14123	20.7	Gewalt	2262	26.3
1973	rape	2931	4.3	Vergewaltigung	236	2.7
1973	victimization	7444	10.9	Viktimisierung	1067	12.4
1978	vandalism	114	0.2	Vandalismus	39	0.5
1982	family violence	4216	6.2	Gewalt in der Familie	297	3.5
1982	terrorism	1162	1.7	Terrorismus	82	1.0
1982	sex offenses	2860	4.2	Sexualdelikte	403	4.7

Table 1 (continued)

Date of inclusion	PsycINFO			PSYNDEX		
	Index Term (DE)	f	%	Deskriptor (DG)	f	%
1985	nuclear war	550	0.8	Atomkrieg	67	0.8
1985	sexual harassment	1171	1.7	sexuelle Belästigung	104	1.2
1988	torture	365	0.5	Folter	160	1.9
1988	elder abuse	482	0.7	Misshandlung alter Menschen	47	0.5
1988	sexual abuse	9241	13.5	sexueller Missbrauch	1341	15.6
1988	kidnapping	116	0.2	Entführung	6	0.1
1991	retaliation	169	0.2	Vergeltung	16	0.2
1991	emotional abuse	936	1.4	psychische Miss-handlung	42	0.5
1991	partner abuse	2228	3.3	Partnermisshand-lung	57	0.7
1991	patient abuse	104	0.2	Patientenmiss-brauch	138	1.6
1991	physical abuse	2661	3.9	körperliche Misshandlung	167	1.9
1991	acquaintance rape	313	0.5	Vergewaltigung d. Bekannten	13	0.2
1994	coercion	493	0.7	Zwangsausübung	48	0.6
1994	involuntary treatment	427	0.6	Zwangsbehandlung	137	1.6
1994	patient violence	505	0.7	Patientengewalt-tätigkeit	83	1.0
1994	professional client sexual relations	348	0.5	sex. Bez. zu Klienten	121	1.4
2001	harassment	1281	1.9	Belästigung	123	1.4
2001	stalking	160	0.2	Stalking	14	0.2
2003	bullying	418	0.6	Mobbing	80	0.9
2003	school violence	168	0.2	Gewalt an Schulen	16	0.2
2003	criminal behavior	332	0.5	kriminelles Verhalten	37	0.4
2003	verbal abuse	25	0.0	verbale Misshand-lung	1	0.0
2003	violent crime	141	0.2	Gewaltverbrechen	49	0.6
2003	hate crimes	67	0.1	hassmotivierte Straf-taten	1	0.0
2004	aggressive driving behavior	29	0.0	aggressives Fahrver-halten	0	0.0

Note: Total percentages may be more than 100% because of multiple descriptor use.

To define the subject fields *aggression* and *emotion*, we used the standardized index terms of the "Thesaurus of psychological index terms" (Gallagher, 2004), for which an English-German/German-English translation (PSYNDEX Terms, Zentrum für Psychologische Information und Dokumentation, 2005) also exists. The terms relevant to the subject field aggression can be found in Table 1. These are 44 index terms, that are mostly nested in the form of narrower terms or broader terms and that also include (through "used for") terms designated for outward aggression, such as agonistic behavior, fighting, assault, sociopathology, and deviant behavior. The starting point of this considerable diversion of terms since the 1960s and 1970s were the terms: aggressive behavior, hostility, war, crime, antisocial behavior, child abuse, and aggressiveness (see Table 1).

It must be noted that the subject field "aggression" would be even wider if it was expanded with aspects of auto-aggression (i.e., "suicide," "attempted suicide," "trichotillomania," "self-destructive behavior," etc.). Because of the considerable scope and clear clinical orientation of the subject field of auto-aggression, which calls for fur-

Table 2. Descriptors Constituting the Core Subject Field "Emotion," their Year of Introduction to the APA Thesaurus, Absolute Literature Frequencies, and Percentages in Relation to the Total Subject Field in PsycINFO and PSYNDEX[1]

Date of inclusion	PsycINFO			PSYNDEX		
	Index Term (DE)	f	%	Deskriptor (DG)	f	%
1967	emotions	9527	20.85	Emotionen	2689	41.14
1967	emotional responses	7461	16.33	Emotionale Reaktionen	820	12.55
1973	emotional states	13164	28.81	Emotionale Zustände	1886	28.86
1973	emotional control	1157	2.53	Emotionale Kontrolle	178	2.72
1973	emotional development	2883	6.31	Emotionale Entwicklung	520	7.96
1973	emotional instability	195	0.43	Emotionale Labilität	60	0.92
1973	emotional stability	396	0.87	Emotionale Stabilität	98	1.50
1973	emotional adjustment	9301	20.35	Emotionale Bewältigung	685	10.48
1973	emotional content	1845	4.04	Emotionaler Inhalt	255	3.90
1973	emotionality (personality)	1585	3.47	Emotionalität	189	2.89
1978	animal emotionality	1108	2.42	Emotionalität bei Tieren	19	0.29

Note: Total percentages may be more than 100% because of multiple descriptor use.

ther differentiation, it is deliberately left out here and has to be examined in further studies.

Concerning the subject field "emotion," because of the wide scope of the concept of emotions, the definition of the corresponding subject field has to be kept more focused than for the aggression-field to keep the definition from getting too blurry around the edges. Looking at the related terms of the descriptors directly tied to emotional topics, one quickly sees the enormous breadth and heterogeneity of the field. To keep the focus on emotion research, we decided to limit our subject field to descriptors containing the term "emotion," without going into too specific subfields at the same time (subsequently we refer to this definition as the "core" subject field "emotion").

Results

Tables 1 and 2 show the definition of the subject fields "aggression" and "emotion," and compare the absolute and relative literature frequencies (standardized in relation to the publication totals of the subject field) for all related index terms in the databases PsycINFO and PSYNDEX for the time period from 1977 to 2003.

In both PsycINFO and PSYNDEX, with percentages of over 10% up to 26%, the topics "violence," "aggressive behavior," "crime," "child abuse," "sexual abuse," and "victimization" are the six most prominent domains within aggression research. Compared to these social psychology oriented, forensic, and systemic strands of research, the absolute and relative frequencies of all other index terms are considerably lower, which is especially true for personality psychology oriented aggression research. At the same time, the data suggest some differences between the Anglo-American and German-speaking scientific communities. In PsycINFO, literature related to "animal aggressive behavior," "attack behavior," "child abuse," "rape," "partner abuse," "family violence," "physical abuse," "stalking," and "antisocial personality disorder" is more frequent. Conversely, the topics "crime," "aggressive behavior (human)," "aggressiveness," "violence," "sexual abuse," "victimization, torture," "patient abuse," "involuntary treatment," and "professional client sexual relations" are more frequent in PSYNDEX (see Table 1).

In the core subject field "emotion," alongside the broad descriptor "emotion," the terms "emotional responses," "emotional states," and "emotional adjustment" are predominant. A notable difference between PsycINFO and PSYNDEX is found in the frequency of the term "emotions," which is twice as frequent in PSYNDEX. Within the narrower descriptors, the German-speaking community has somewhat higher percentages for publications on "emotional development" and "emotional stability," and "emotional instability". In the Anglo-American literature, publications concerned with "emotional responses," "emotional adjustment," and "animal emotionality" are more frequent (see Table 2).

The detailed versus narrow definitions of the subject fields "aggression" and "emotion" also interact with the effects of the different search strategies. The word "aggression" is not necessarily present in all the literature concerned with it. Thus, the free text search on aggression yields 31,271 (2.2%) hits in PsycINFO and 5,247 (2.8%) hits in

PSYNDEX, the title search on aggression only 9,236 (0.6%) in PsycINFO and 1,149 (0.6%) in PSYNDEX. The very detailed subject field "aggression" works to actually produce more hits (PsycINFO: 69,064, 4.8%; PSYNDEX: 8,886, 4.8%) which is closer to the actual percentage of research concerned with themes of aggression (see Table 3).

At the same time, the free text search on emotion produces a large number of documents (PsycINFO: 122,254; 8.5%; PSYNDEX: 20,219; 10.5%), indicating that the word "emotion" is much too generic to be used as a free text search term. The title search for emotion produces a much smaller number of hits (PsycINFO: 18,843; 1.3%; PSYNDEX: 2,676; 1.4%), while the descriptor search in the core subject field "emotion" yields a medium number of hits (PsycINFO: 45,698; 3.2%; PSYNDEX: 6,536; 3.5%; see Table 3).

Table 3. Absolute and Relative Frequencies of Literature in Subject Fields "Aggression" and "Emotion" Using Different Search Strategies in PsycINFO and PSYNDEX (1977–2003)

Search strategies	PsycINFO (1977–2003)		PSYNDEX (1977–2003)	
	f	%	f	%
Total number of documents	1444331	100	186087	100
Free text search on aggression (aggress*)	31271	2.2	5247	2.8
aggression in document title (aggress* in TI)	9236	0.6	1149	0.6
Subject field "aggression"[1] in descriptor field (DE)	69064	4.8	8886	4.8
Free text search on emotion (emoti*)	122254	8.5	20219	10.9
emotion in document title (emoti* in TI)	18843	1.3	2676	1.4
Subject field "emotion"[2] in descriptor field (DE)	45698	3.2	6536	3.5
Literature review[3]	40605	100	3414	100
Subject field "aggression" in DE and literature review[3]	2295	5.7	151	4.4
Subject field "emotion" in DE and literature review[3]	1198	3	139	4.1
Meta Analysis[4]	4288	100	401	100
Subject field "aggression" in DE and meta analysis[4]	188	4.4	16	4
Subject field "emotion" in DE and meta analysis[4]	116	2.7	10	2.5

[1] see Table 1; [2] see Table 2; [3] PsycINFO: Term "literature-review" in fields *methodology (MD)*, *descriptors (DE)* OR'ed together. PSYNDEX: Term "literature-review in" in fields *descriptors (DE) and publication type (PT)* OR'ed together; [4] PsycINFO: Term "meta-analysis" in fields *methodology (MD)*, *descriptors (DE), and key concepts (KC)* OR'ed together. PSYNDEX: Term "meta-analysis" in fields *descriptors (DE) and publication type (PT)* OR'ed together.

Only the combined descriptor search utilizes a unique selling point of the psychology databases (the index terms), which allow the user to tailor searches exactly to his/her needs. The results of the free text search are expected to overestimate the valid number of matching documents (but as the subject field "aggression" demonstrates, may also underestimate it), while the title search greatly underestimates it in most cases.

However, looking at whole subject fields, only the combination of the descriptor field search with the publication types of "literature review" or "meta-analysis" results in a reduced number of hits that can be efficiently processed (see Table 3, lower part), but it also comes with the risk of overlooking relevant theoretical or methodological publications (and also empirical original publications), thus being less effective in the end. A more effective and efficient approach is the search using single descriptors, and if necessary, combining them (using "and") with other index terms related to the research problem at hand.

International and Historiographic Comparison of the Relative Frequency of Aggression- and Emotion-Related Literature

The percentages of literature on aggression and emotion research, identified with the descriptor field search, amount to 4.8 % (aggression, identical in both databases), 3.2% (emotion, PsycINFO), and 3.5% (emotion, PSYNDEX) of the total literature in the corresponding databases. When compared to other ("classic") domains of psychological research, these are high percentages that are only markedly surpassed by broader research topics (e.g., attitudes or traits in general). The percentage of aggression-related literature within the total number of publications is considerably higher than the relative frequencies of topics such as social cognition, altruism, intelligence, creativity, extraversion, neuroticism, and also emotion (see Krampen & Schui, 2006, p. 118). As an interim result, it can be concluded that aggression-related publications are comparatively frequent in the last quarter of the 20th century, and thus, that the subject field is boldly represented in the documented psychological literature in both the Anglo-American and German-speaking scientific communities. The percentage of literature related to emotion is probably higher than indicated by our core subject field and probably surpasses that of aggression. This is also hinted at by the different hit ratios of the free text search vs. descriptor field searches on aggression and emotion (see Table 3).

However, the following questions remain: How did the percentages of literature on aggression and emotion develop during the past 25 years? And are these developments convergent or divergent in the two scientific communities? Figure 1 shows the corresponding developmental trends for the subject field "aggression." Figure 2 shows the same data for the core subject field "emotion."

In aggression research, there is a consistent marked increase from around 3% towards the end of the 1970s up to approximately 5–6% since the end of the 1990s. Thus, the relative frequency of aggression-related publications has more than doubled during the last quarter of the 20th century. This is equally true for PsycINFO and PSYNDEX, as is confirmed by a statistically significant rank correlation of both trends ($\rho = .86$; $p <$ .01). Hence, the presence of aggression-related literature has been continuously increas-

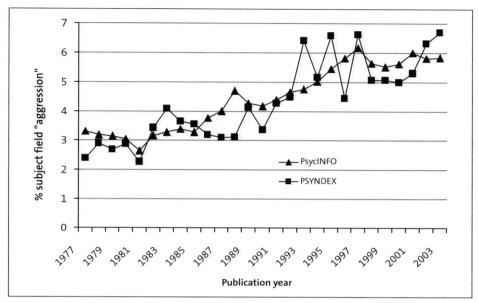

Figure 1. Relative frequency of documents in the subject field "aggression" (PsycINFO vs. PSYNDEX, 1977–2003).

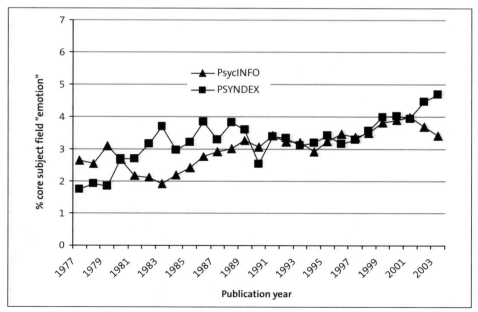

Figure 2. Relative frequency of documents in the subject field "emotion" (PsycINFO vs. PSYNDEX, 1977–2003).

ing since the 1980s. The more "jittery" graph for PSYNDEX in comparison to Psy-cINFO (showing more variation between years) is a typical result for smaller databases, in which the publication of thematically centred editions or special issues with multiple contributions have a greater effect on relative frequencies (remember that PsycINFO is approximately eight times the size of PSYNDEX).

In the core subject field "emotion," literature has also been increasing from 2–3% at the end of the 1970s to around 4% at the turn of the century. While PSYNDEX contains more emotion-related literature published in the 1980s, both databases contain nearly identical percentages of emotion-related literature published from 1991 to 2001, since when the percentages diverge again, increasing in PSYNDEX and decreasing in PsycINFO (see Figure 2). Despite these differences, the overall development is reasonably similar in both databases, which is also supported by a significant rank correlation between the two trends ($\rho = .58; p < .01$).

International and Historiographic Comparison of the Literature in Different Subfields of Aggression Research

In a previous bibliometric study, Krampen and Schui (2006) clustered the aggression-specific descriptors shown in Table 1 into different subfields of aggression research in order to analyze trends within aggression research (see Krampen & Schui 2006, p. 119). The clusters, based on the thesaurus systematic as well as on research traditions and domains, are (a) behaviorally-oriented aggression research, (b) personality psychology oriented aggression research, (c) research related to aggression in micro-, meso-, and macro-systems, (d) research related to aggressive crimes, (e) victimization research, and (f) research related to violence and aggression in clinical contexts. The observed developmental trends within the clusters in the last quarter of the 20th century show considerable changes in the foci of aggression research towards the end of the century and beyond, which are highly consistent in both databases.

The frequency of basic research publications from social- and personality psychology oriented traditions has noticeably decreased since the beginning of the 1980s, while simultaneously, the frequency of contributions on violence and aggression in micro-, meso-, and macro-systems has increased (up to 40–50% of aggression-related literature) in PsycINFO as well as PSYNDEX. Also continuously increasing in both databases is the relative frequency of aggression-related publications that are from an applied perspective.

The high number of similarities in the developments and foci of aggression research in the Anglo-American and German-speaking scientific communities are confirmed by significant, numerically high rank correlations ($.52 \leq \rho \leq .85, p < .01$). Furthermore, high negative and significant correlation coefficients between the publication trends in social- and personality psychology oriented aggression research and the four other clusters ($-.36 \leq \rho \leq -.90; p < .05$) consistently show that the decrease of basic research publications in the last quarter of the 20th century is accompanied by an increase in contributions from the applied perspective (see Krampen & Schui 2006, p. 120).

The Intersection of Research on Aggression and Emotion: Bibliometric Findings

Returning to Wallbott (1991) and his critique of the widespread disregard of the "emotional in social psychology" and the "social in emotion psychology," we analyzed the publications in the intersection of research on aggression and emotion and their development since the 1970s, which would indicate whether Wallbott's work had any influence.

Table 4 shows that in our analysis, emotion research has a lower percentage of the total psychological literature from 1977–2003 than aggression research. Also, the percentage is somewhat higher in the German-speaking community (3.5%) than in the Anglo-American community (3.2%). The lower percentage of emotion research is caused by our narrow definition of the core subject field "emotion." In reality, the number of – in a wider sense – emotion-related publications should be much larger, as the results of the free text and title searches (see Table 3) suggest.

The intersection of emotion and aggression research is very small and the amount of literature is in the one-tenth of a percent range with an identical average of 0.18% in both databases (equivalent to 100–200 publications per year in PsycINFO and 10–20 publications per year in PSYNDEX in the 1990s).

The historiographic trend-analysis shows seemingly dramatic variations in the relative frequencies of publications in combined emotion and aggression research in the German-speaking countries (see Figure 3). Especially the "peak value" of over 0.3 % in the year 1986 is irritating, but can be explained by the publication of an edited book containing 14 contributions concerning different possibilities of diagnosing aggression and emotion utilizing the Gottschalk-Gleser Content Analysis Scales in 1986. This is a good example of the effect that the publication of special issues or edited books can have on bibliometric results in subject fields with very small basic frequencies. When subtracting these 14 contributions, eight publications remain, which is well within the average. Similar circumstances apply to the other outlier values in Figure 3. Again, the data in Figure 3 show that the developmental trend in PsycINFO runs much smoother (because of the higher basic frequencies) and that it has a steady increase towards the end of the

Table 4. Absolute and Relative Frequencies of Literature in the Subject Fields "Aggression" and "Emotion" and Their Intersection in PsycINFO and PSYNDEX (1977–2003)

Search strategy	PsycINFO (1977–2003)		PSYNDEX (1977–2003)	
	f	%	f	%
Total documents	1444331	100	186087	100
Subject field "aggression" in descriptor field (DE)	69064	4.8	8886	4.8
Subject field "emotion" in descriptor field (DE)	45698	3.2	6536	3.5
Subject fields "aggression" AND "emotion" in descriptor field (DE)	2645	0.18	328	0.18

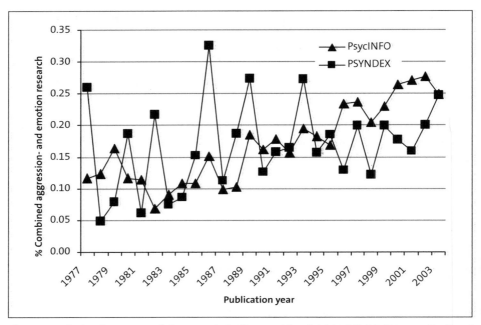

Figure 3. Relative frequency of documents in the combined subject fields "aggression" and "emotion" (PsycINFO vs. PSYNDEX, 1977–2003).

1990s, that – to a lesser extent and despite the large variations – can also be found in PSYNDEX. In summary, the results show a rise in the number of publications combining aggression and emotion research in psychology in both research communities. The increasing research efforts in this albeit very small field represent the indications given by Wallbott in 1991 rather well.

Conclusion

The presented historiographic results for the last quarter of the 20th century and the beginning of the 21st century clearly indicate that with percentages around 5% of the total literature in psychology, the subject of aggression research is well-positioned. Likewise, this is true for the Anglo-American PsycINFO as well as the German-speaking PSYNDEX. Also consistent in both databases is a marked increase of aggression-related publications starting around 3% towards the end of the 1970s up to approximately 5–6% since the 1990s. This level persists until 2003, the last year examined in this analysis. Thus, aggression-related publications are rather frequent and account for an increasing presence in the total literature of both scientific communities since the last quarter of the past century.

The analyses of the core field of emotion research show a similar picture with amounts around 2–4% of the total literature and a slight increase over time. In the

1980s PSYNDEX shows higher percentages of emotion-related literature (3–4%) than PsycINFO (2–3%), from 1991 to 2001 both databases show nearly identical values (3–4%) and since 2002 PSYNDEX increases, approaching the 5% mark, while PsycINFO decreases toward 3%. Again, it must be noted that the percentage of research somehow related to emotion probably is much larger, but is not analyzed here because of its heterogeneity.

Looking at the development of different foci of aggression research in the last quarter of the 20th century, there is empirical evidence for a reorientation of aggression research in a more application-oriented direction, as demanded by Selg (1982). This can be found in both psychological databases, PsycINFO and PSYNDEX. Aggression-related contributions from an applied research perspective and for practical application have clearly increased, while basic research contributions have decreased. The former even constitute the main focus of aggression-related literature in the time period from 1977 to 2003.

The identification of systematic literature reviews and meta-analyses in aggression and emotion research clarifies the efficacy and efficiency of differentiated search strategies in conjunction with specialized databases. Noticeable is the fact that since the 1980s, there have been hardly any contributions reviewing the whole field of aggression research (such as Mummendey, 1983), but only those limited to subfields (e.g., development of aggression during infancy, deviant behavior in adolescents, mobbing in organizations, sexual aggressive behavior, genetic epidemiology of aggressive behavior, etc.).

The intersection between aggression and emotion research is very small and contains only one tenth of a percent of the total psychological literature. Nevertheless, that amount has been climbing slowly since the 1970s and 1980s in the German as well as the Anglo-American research communities and today has more than doubled in comparison, indicating that Wallbott's position was probably adopted by some researchers working in these areas.

The bibliometric analyses in PsycINFO and PSYNDEX show large resemblances in the development of aggression and emotion research in the Anglo-American and German-speaking communities in the examined time span. This suggests – exemplary for these two research domains – that research from the German-speaking countries is aimed at and connected to the international state of the art, to which it also contributes. Specific differences in developments and foci between the communities can only be spotted on a more detailed level (e.g., various descriptors, see Tables 1 and 2).

References

Bandura, A. (1973). *Aggression: A social learning analysis*. Englewood Cliffs, NJ: Prentice-Hall.

Berkowitz, L. (1962). *Aggression: A social psychological analysis*. New York: McGraw-Hill.

Buss, A. H. (1961). *The psychology of aggression*. New York: Wiley.

Dollard, J., Doob, L., Miller, N. E., Mowrer, H. O., & Sears, R. R. (1939). *Frustration and aggression*. New Haven, NJ: Yale University Press.

Feshbach, S. (1970). Aggression. In P. H. Musen (Ed.), *Carmichael's manual of child psychology* (Rev. ed., pp. 159–259). New York: Wiley.

Freud, S. (1905/1961). *Gesammelte Werke: Vol. 5. Drei Abhandlungen zur Sexualtheorie* [Three Essays on the Theory of Sexuality] (3rd ed.). Frankfurt/Main, Germany: Fischer.

Freud, S. (1930/1963). *Gesammelte Werke: Vol. 14. Das Unbehagen in der Kultur* [Civilization and its discontents] (3rd ed.). Frankfurt/Main, Germany: Fischer.

Gallagher, L. A. (Ed.). (2004). *Thesaurus of psychological index terms* (10th ed.). Washington, DC: American Psychological Association.

Geen, R. G. (1998). Aggression and antisocial behavior. In D. T. Gilbert, S. T. Fiske, & G. Linzey (Eds.), *The handbook of social psychology* (4th ed., Vol. 2, pp. 317–356). New York: Mc-Graw-Hill.

Heckhausen, H. (1989). *Motivation und Handeln* [Motivation and action] (2nd ed.). Berlin, Germany: Springer.

Krahé, B. (2001). *The social psychology of aggression.* Hove, UK: Psychology Press.

Krahé, B., & Greve, W. (2002). Aggression und Gewalt: Aktueller Erkenntnisstand und Perspektiven künftiger Forschung [Aggression and violence: State of the art and perspectives for future research]. *Zeitschrift für Sozialpsychologie, 33,* 123–143.

Krampen, G., & Schui, G. (2006). Entwicklungslinien der Aggressionsforschung im letzten Viertel des 20. Jahrhunderts. Komparative bibliometrische Analysen für die psychologische Forschung im deutschsprachigen und angloamerikanischen Bereich [Historiography of research on aggression in the last quarter of the 20th century: Comparative bibliometrical analyses of psychological research in the German-speaking and Anglo-American research community]. *Zeitschrift für Sozialpsychologie, 37*(2), 113–123.

Lorenz, K. (1963). *Das sogenannte Böse: Zur Naturgeschichte der Aggression* [The so-called evil: About the natural history of aggression]. Vienna: Borotha-Schoeler.

McDougall, W. (1908). *An introduction to social psychology.* London: Methuen.

Mummendey, A. (1983). Aggression research in German-speaking countries. *German Journal of Psychology, 7,* 313–339.

Selg, H. (1982). Aggressionsdefinitionen – und kein Ende? [Defining aggression – a never-ending story?]. In R. K. Hilke (Ed.), *Aggression* (pp. 351–354). Bern, Switzerland: Huber.

Selg, H., Mees, U., & Berg, D. (1997). *Psychologie der Aggressivität* [Psychology of aggressiveness] (2nd ed.). Göttingen, Germany: Hogrefe.

Taylor, S. T. (1967). Aggressive behavior and physiological arousal as a function of provocation and the tendency to inhibit aggression. *Journal of Personality, 35,* 297–310.

Wallbott, H. G. (1991). Das Emotionale in der Sozialpsychologie und das Soziale in der Emotionspsychologie: Versuch einer Bestandsaufnahme eines vernachlässigten Grenzbereichs [The emotional in social psychology and the social in emotion psychology: An overview concerning the intersection between social psychology and emotion psychology]. *Zeitschrift für Sozialpsychologie, 22,* 53–65.

Zentrum für Psychologische Information und Dokumentation (Ed.). (2005). *PSYNDEX Terms: Deskriptoren / Subject Terms zur Datenbank PSYNDEX* [PSYNDEX Terms: Descriptors / Subject terms for the databank PSYNDEX] (7th ed.). Trier, Germany: ZPID, Universität Trier.

Part 2
Emotion-Based Motives and Measures of Aggression

Emotion-Based Aggression Motives

Leo Montada

For the analysis of aggression, two approaches in research and practice are to be distinguished: an action theoretical approach and an approach focusing on determinants of aggressive behavior. The important defining elements of both will be roughly contrasted, but controversies about definitions will be omitted (cf. Greve, 1994; Straub & Werbik, 1999). Both approaches imply distinct anthropological presumptions and provide distinct knowledge that allow for the generation of distinct options for preventing aggression.

Aggression as an Action

Aggression as an action (cf. Gollwitzer, 2005) implies the presumption that humans have freedom of decision for which they are accountable. Consequently, actors can be considered responsible for their own behavior. (In this chapter the terms actor and agent are used synonymously for individuals who supposedly have freedom of decision and control of their actions.) Actions are understandable if their motives and goals are known. In this context, understanding means to grasp the reason for the behavior. Accordingly, one goal of research is to identify the variety of motives and goals of aggressive actions to provide motivational hypotheses for the understanding of single cases of aggressive behavior.

Using the usual explanatory approach, aggression is conceived of as behavior that is explainable by antecedent variables which are theoretically conceived of as conditions. Research in this vein serves to establish empirical laws specifying such conditions or "determinants." In this approach, responsibility or guilt cannot be attributed.

This chapter considers the motivational impact of emotions on aggressive actions. It begins with the basic assumption that some emotions motivate aggressive behavior. This can be understood when we consider an emotional response to be a function of subjective appraisals of an incident (cf. Lazarus, 2001; Reisenzein, Meyer, & Schützzwohl, 2003). "Incident" is a term for any event, person, behavior, thought, imagination, story, memory, etc. "eliciting or evoking" an emotion. "Eliciting or evoking" is put in quotation marks because a subject's emotions are not caused by the incident. An emotion expresses a specific personal significance that a subject attributes to the incident.

For each specific or discrete category of emotion – e.g., fear, resentment, shame, or envy – a model can be conceptualized depicting the specific significance or meaning that subjects attribute to an incident. These models provide hypotheses about which motives may be evoked by a specific or discrete category of emotion. As many emotions are experienced as aversive, subjects are motivated to avoid them, to reduce their intensity, or to get rid of them. For some emotions, aggressive actions subjectively seem to function as an option to satisfy these motives. Thus, aggressive actions can be understood by looking at the aggressor's emotions.

In this chapter, I will not attempt to explain aggressive behavior from objectively definable and assessable preconditions. Instead, I intend to outline a basis for the interpretation of (or for grasping the reason for) the subjective functionality of aggression.

This concern does not correspond to a conception of psychology as a natural science. Rather, it corresponds to a human-psychological program that focuses on the psychological particularities of homo sapiens (Jüttemann, 2004). By its nature, homo sapiens generates theories, beliefs, and convictions – about the self, other humans, social relationships, about the world and beyond. It is also innate to humans to build cultures and to create normative standards for the evaluation of behavior and of all facets of social life and social relationships (Montada, 2004).

All of the theories, beliefs, and opinions, which are mostly culturally shaped, hold the key for understanding actions and their motives (cf. Lenk, 1987). Nota bene: To understand them does not imply to approve of them as right or justified. Whether theories and convictions are right or wrong, whether normative standards are wise or dumb, and whether cultures and organizations hinder or promote the unfolding of potentials and good development: We need to know these theories, beliefs, and opinions in order to be able to understand humans and their behavior, to provide options for solving problems, and to generate options for better cooperative living. This is the approach proposed to clarify the relationship between emotions and aggressive behavior.

An exhaustive literature review would go beyond the scope of this chapter. Instead, this chapter is conceived as a framework of analysis that can be used as a heuristic for understanding emotions and emotion-based aggression.

What Does Aggression Mean?

The variety of different forms of aggressive behavior is large: physical violence, psychological coercion, rape, imprisonment, torture, blackmailing, robbery, humiliation, accusation, derogation, irony, threat, ignorance, exclusion, defamation, etc. Equally large is the variety of resources that can be threatened, harmed, injured, or impaired: life, health, property, social status, social reputation, self-esteem, freedom, autonomy, religious beliefs, trust, cultural assets, and many more. Targets of aggression can be individuals or social groups like a family, a youth group, an ethnic or religious group, social categories like foreigners, and legal entities like corporations, institutions, or states.

On a purely behavioral level, aggression can only be defined as harm or impairment of a target (Tedeschi & Felson, 1994). However, this definition does not correspond to the usual (culturally shared) meaning of aggression (Jüttemann, 1978), which conceives aggression as intentional harm or injury, illegitimate, unjustified, or carelessly caused harm. Thus, aggression is perceived as an action. Even aggressive intentions that were not successful or whishes that were not carried out are included. Additionally, aggression is normatively evaluated.

Whether a specific case is aggressive or not can be questioned and disputed, e.g., cases of assault in courts. Was anybody harmed or impaired? Was the behavior an intentional action or an uncontrollable reaction to a provocation? Was the harm or impairment – if there has been any – intended? Was it illegitimate or justified? Was it merely subjectively justified or is it also justifiable according to commonly accepted normative standards?

One and the same action can be divergently appraised. An aggressive action can be condemned, justified, or even admired depending on how the underlying motives and goals are evaluated. For instance, politically motivated violence may be conceived of as terrorism, or rather as a struggle for freedom and just retaliation. Punishment can be criticized as repressive or as righteously deserved; depending on the attitude towards the target, the punishment may be condemned or legitimized. Aggression can be justified as retaliation for injustice. Depending on particular appraisals, aggression can be considered antisocial or prosocial.

Assumptions about the aggressor's motives and goals are crucial for these appraisals. This is a fact that calls into question whether aggression can be properly conceived or "reconstructed" at the behavioral level at all. In order to identify and evaluate motives, goals, intentions, expectancies, responsibilities, and guilt, it is necessary to conceive of aggression as an action.

The list of possible motives and goals is long, but each of them should be considered. Furthermore, the motives and goals mentioned here are not mutually exclusive, but may overlap.

– Defense of legitimate entitlements and rights, for instance the right to be respected, property, or autonomy. This also includes subjectively legitimized claims like obedience, approval of leadership, or protection of privileges.
– Retaliation for suffered injustice, insult, or disrespect.
– Compensation for suffered humiliation, defeat, or inferiority. One example is the attempt to compensate poor achievements in school by demonstrating "virile toughness."
– Defending religious or ethnic "oughts" or "holy" symbols and persons, and retaliating against their violation or defamation.
– Defending admired characters against attacks and debasement.
– Gaining self-esteem by ideologically based violence, e.g., in cases of xenophobic action and interethnic conflicts.
– Struggle for power and status, e.g., for status in a group, for leadership of a team, for authority.
– Protection of personal interests.
– Sadistic lust for the suffering of defenseless victims, sexual sadism.
– Satisfaction of sexual needs.
– Obedience to leaders, fear of exclusion (for example, in gangs or sects).
– Group conformity, group pressure (by joining group-based aggression).
– Self-defense against attacks, defense of third persons.
– Struggle for survival in catastrophes.
– Dutiful action, e.g., interventions by the police in order to protect citizens, interventions of teachers in order to protect pupils against violence or sexual harassment in school.
– Solidarity, e.g., against authorities.
– Emancipation from patronizing and paternalism.

- Demonstrating courage as self-affirmation.
- Compensation for perceived personal inferiority in cases of envy and jealousy.

The large number of hypotheses about possible motives serves to demonstrate that aggression is not a homogeneous psychological construct.

By considering such hypotheses, each case of aggression can be understood as an action having a specific function or goal for the aggressor, rather than an involuntary reaction to "determinants." It is necessary to understand the aggressor's motives and goals, and the function that the aggressive action had from his point of view.

Considering aggression as an action implies the attribution of responsibility to the actor. A person who acts is free to choose another action or at least, to refrain from that action. However, attribution of responsibility does not yet imply an evaluation of the action. Aggressive acting may be condemned or justified. Typical justifications include:

- Defense of legitimate personal interests.
- Struggling for survival.
- Self-defense.
- Defense of one's honor or the honor of one's family, country, religion, etc.
- Retaliation of injustice.
- Dutiful "prosocial" violence, e.g., protecting a threatened person or goods, national defense, enforcing legal order, punishing the violation of legal or moral norms in educations, etc.
- Legitimate violence in martial arts.

Possibilities for Aggression Prevention

Based on the understanding of a case of aggression, one can construe possibilities for preventing further aggression. Here are some examples:

- If an aggressive action in a particular conflict situation is understood as an attempt to push through personal interests, to defend personal values, or to retaliate against an insult, the underlying conflict should be discussed and may be settled, e.g., by mediation (Montada & Kals, 2007).
- It might be possible to eliminate the underlying motive: For instance, when an offensive remark or statement is reinterpreted, or when an offense can be interpreted as justified given the aggressor's prior provoking behavior. Likewise, accounts and apologies can eliminate motives for retaliation and punishment (Goffman, 1971; Montada & Kirchhoff, 2000).
- When aggression is a means to compensate for shame, one might help the aggressor to think of alternative, socially more acceptable means to regain honor and status.
- When aggression is a means for gaining social recognition and respect, as in many cases of adolescent delinquency (Streng, 1995), one might help the aggressor to think of alternative strategies to gain recognition according to his abilities and the opportunities, and according to the social context in which he lives in.

Conceiving of aggression as an action has further consequences. The actor is seen as having decisional control and freedom of choice. He decides between committing versus not committing an aggressive action or committing an alternative action. The decision to commit an aggressive action is based on the motive to act aggressively, despite existing reasons that speak against an aggressive action (like legal or other social norms, perceived risks, unintended consequences for oneself or for others, fines, revenge, disapproval by important others, long-term loss of life chances, etc.). One can assume that the aggressor considered, but eventually discarded such reasons. A complete understanding of the aggressive action requires knowledge of the motives and goals underlying the aggressive behavior, but also of the reasons against the aggressive action that the aggressor has considered. Moreover, it is important to know how he evaluates and justifies his actions. Such knowledge allows to interpret and evaluate his behavior, and to generate adequate responses:

- Possibly the actor's motive was based on erroneous perceptions and interpretations.
- Possibly the subjective importance of the motive can be qualified.
- Reasons against the aggressive act can be brought forward.
- Alternative ways to satisfy the actor's motives can be taken into consideration.

Understanding the subjective meaning of an aggressive act and the more or less restricted scope of predecisional deliberation provides the key for an internal control of aggression. Acts of violence have to be treated differently when they are understood as revenge for mortification or as a compensation for shameful humiliation, than when they are quasi-sportive fights (like in the case of hooligans) or when they aim to harm a person because of envy or jealousy. Interventions against aggression are advisory since the actor's freedom of decision is respected. Interventions can make the aggressor aware of his relevant motives and introduce new arguments and points of view. In cases in which the aggressor regrets his behavior but doubts whether he will ever be able to control his aggressive impulses, he can be advised to engage in a self-control training.

The analysis of actions also brings up questions about preconditions. Why was a specific motive aroused? Why, for instance, does an agent feel provoked by a verbal offense that other people would simply ignore? Why did the actor react aggressively in one case of provocation and not in another? Why did the agent not control the aggression-evoking motive? Was he not able to resist the desire to harm the provocateur or was he not willing to resist this desire? Why did he decide to satisfy his motive – e.g., envying a competitor's higher achievement – by behaving aggressively and not by behaving otherwise? The mere knowledge of the actor's motives does not answer these questions. Analyses of preconditions may provide answers. However, it would be misleading to think that these answers are the most important ones for the explanation and control of aggression.

Investigating Preconditions for Aggression and Violence

One can try to explain aggressive behavior from determining preconditions. Empirical research suggests several categories of hypotheses.

Situational Variables. Situational variables include, for example, frustration, provocation, humiliation, or peer pressure. First, it is important to note that these "conditions" cannot be objectively assessed because their effects depend on subjective interpretations. This is a core assumption in human-psychological theory. The hypothesis that frustration causes aggression and that each aggressive act is preceded by frustration (Dollard, Doob, Miller, Mowrer, & Sears, 1939) may serve as an example. This hypothesis is still prevalent, but does not fit the data. First of all, only those frustrations which are appraised as unjustified predispose individuals to aggressive behavior (Pastore, 1952). Aggression is mediated by anger (Berkowitz, 1990; Bierhoff, 1998), and anger results from subjective convictions that will be discussed in detail later. Second, what is appraised as unjustified differs from culture to culture, from person to person, and from case to case.

The same argument applies to provocations, mortification, group pressure, and further situational conditions of aggression. Objectively similar situational conditions have varying effects depending on cultural and individual differences and context-specific subjective expectations. For example, humans differ in how dependent they are on the prevalent opinions of their group, and they have different competencies in how to assert themselves within their group. For this reason, research has focused on person characteristics as mediating or moderating conditions, conceptualized as predispositions to aggressive behavior.

Personal Dispositions. One category of personal dispositions are psychological *states* such as emotions that facilitate aggressive behavior, or alcohol abuse that reduces moral self-control. Other categories are stable person characteristics – *traits* – like aggressiveness, authoritarianism, negative attitudes (against individuals or social categories, e.g., foreigners), vulnerabilities like low self-esteem (that leads a person to misinterpret harmless expressions as mortifications, e.g., Wahner, 1998), high justice sensitivity (that leads to frequent feelings of being treated unfairly, cf. Schmitt, Neumann, & Montada, 1995), lack of empathy, attitudes like xenophobia, or lack of competence to control problematic needs and affects (cf. Greve & Montada, in press). Nota bene: Assessment scales of such trait variables ask for subjective theories and convictions. The theoretical interpretation – or the effort to make sense – of empirical correlations between person characteristics and aggressive behavior regularly refers to subjective theories and convictions of actors as well.

Developmental Conditions. Another important set of preconditions for aggression are determinants of the development of relevant person characteristics, such as genetic predispositions, characteristics of the learning environment (e.g., deficits in moral socialization) or specific experiences (like suffered violence in childhood). A long list of contextual correlates of the development of aggression has been compiled, e.g., prevalence of consumed violence in the media, justifications of violence in subcultures (as revenge for befallen injustice, as a means to achieve one's goals, or as defense of personal or family honor), poverty and unemployment, discrimination of minorities perceived as unjust by the affected, poor achievement in school, professional training, and occupation, affiliation with violent groups, etc. (e.g., Farrington & West, 1990). Delinquency research focused on risk factors presumed to shape stable person characteristics that mediate aggression. Again, the theoretical interpretations of empirical findings rely on human-psychological concepts in order to make the effects plausible.

Hypotheses about developmental conditions of aggression may serve to derive measures for prevention or correction of aggressive behavior supposed that preconditions can be changed, suppressed or compensated. Knowledge of mediating person variables is necessary because these dispositions and deficits in competencies might prevail and trigger aggressive behavior while the previously effective conditions of their formation cannot be influenced anymore. (Therefore, conditions of formation of aggression and mainting of conditions have to be distinguished.) In this case, educational or therapeutic measures can be considered for changing problematic dispositions and for developing necessary competencies (e.g., self-control).

In principle, hypotheses about all categories of conditions can be used for the prevention of violence, when preconditions are controllable, for instance, when violence against children in their families can be reduced, when cultural justifications for aggressive behavior are questioned, or when violence in the media could be cut back.

However, knowledge about determinants of aggressive behavior is uncertain when based on empirical correlations with unclear theoretical status (Greve & Montada, in press), for instance the correlation between aggressiveness and hostile/punitive parental behavior: Is aggressiveness the effect of parental hostility during childhood, is it inherited, or is parental punitiveness a reaction to the child's aggressiveness? Moreover, as most of these correlations are not strong, it has yet to be determined which moderator variables strengthen or weaken the effects of the presumed conditions. Therefore, investments in preventive measures which aim to change the presumed antecedent conditions bear the risk of being ineffective or superfluous, as long as the moderator variables are unknown.

Above all, when thinking about intervention measures, it is crucial to reflect on whether the targets of these measures are perceived and treated as passive objects of the intervention or as subjects who are free and able to make their own decisions. In the latter case, addressees have to be convinced through arguments and to be motivated to reflect upon their convictions, their subjective theories, and their actions.

After these preliminary notes, we finally turn to the main issue of this chapter, emotion-based aggressions. How can they be understood and how can they be avoided?

Emotion: A Syndrome With Five Components

As already stated, emotions are subjective appraisals of an incident expressing the specific significance a subject attributes to the incident (Graumann, 1984). Although subjects may have the impression that their emotions are aroused by the incident – that they experience their emotions passively – the appraisals of the incident reflect subjects' needs, hopes, goals, values, beliefs, attitudes, normative expectations, their self-concepts, their world views, etc. Therefore, emotions are not caused or determined by an incident, but result from subjects' appraisals of the incidents (Lazarus, 2001). In principle, these appraisals are malleable. Usually, five components of emotions are distinguished (cf. Reisenzein et al., 2003):

1. A specific experienced quality that can be distinguished through introspection: Being proud, angry, or jealous, or feeling guilty – each experience has a specific subjective quality that is not easily denoted.
2. Appraisals of the emotion-evoking incident and its specific subjective significance: First of all, the incident triggering the emotion is appraised as significant,

as relevant for the subject. Second, it is appraised as positive or negative. The significance for the subject is specific for each category of emotion: Fear implies the appraisal that there is a risk or danger and that the subject is not sure whether the risk can be mastered or avoided; outrage implies the perception that another agent has violated a normative expectation or entitlement.

3. Some emotions have specific patterns of expression in face, posture, tonicity, intonation of speech, etc.
4. A pattern of physiological or biochemical changes (e.g., arousal).
5. Dispositions or motives to act. For instance, fear predisposes the subject to avoid the danger or to flee; outrage predisposes the subject to reproach, retaliate, or to punish; shame predisposes the subject to avoid the public or to engage in a "heroic activity", hoping for being able to compensate the shameful incident. The respective motive underlying fear is gaining security. The respective motive underlying outrage is to change or to punish the norm-violating behavior. The respective motive underlying shame is to avoid critique or to reestablish social recognition.

Most important for the understanding as well as for the (self-) control of emotions are the appraisals of an incident (Lazarus, 2001) and the aroused motives or dispositions to take action (Frijda, 1987). Emotions can only be described and distinguished properly by the cognitions and appraisals involved.

Using appraisals and motives models of discrete categories of emotions can be constructed. These models have heuristic value for the understanding and clarification of specific instances. The analysis and self-analysis of emotions aims to explore and reflect subjects' appraisals. Fear implies the subjective recognition of a threat. What exactly the subject believes to be threatened or what exactly the threat is needs to be clarified. The subjective appraisals may be false, but in the experience of intense emotions, the subjects believe that they are true. Control and self-control of emotions begins with reflecting the validity of appraisals: The subject has to recognize:

– That his or her subjective views are hypotheses rather than valid knowledge.
– That the appraisals depend on the perspective taken, and that other perspectives are possible.
– That the significance the subject has attributed to the incident may be reflected upon and changed as well.

The subject experiences his emotions spontaneously and immediately and usually as caused by external factors (including other persons that can evoke emotional reactions). Thus, emotions are generally perceived as befallen; a fact reflected in descriptions of emotions such as "panic-stricken" (Montada, 1989). One is usually not aware of one's own internal contributions to an emotional experience nor is one aware of one's own predispositions to emotional reactions (personal concerns, personality characteristics, attitudes, normative beliefs, etc., Montada, 1992). In contrast, as reflected by the actor-observer-bias (cf. Jones & Nisbett, 1972), humans tend to attribute emotional reactions of others to personal flaws, traits, and attitudes.

Repeated strong emotional reactions to one and the same incident indicate that the subject tends to "nurture" his emotions by ruminating about the incident, by repeating his appraisals, and by repeatedly stressing the personal significance of the incident. Emotions can also be reinforced when communication is preferred with persons who confirm one's own views and appraisals instead of attenuating them by motivating thoughtful and wise reflection.

Emotions That Motivate Aggressive and Conflict-Prone Behavior

Before we analyze specific emotions that predispose aggressive behavior, it should be stressed that there are also emotion-based motives that prevent aggressive behavior against others. Feelings of guilt about one's own aggression, for instance, can inhibit further aggression and motivate honest apologies. Anger and outrage about a norm violation, on the other hand, can dispose agents to punish the perpetrator. On the other hand, anger and moral outrage can be reduced when the subject sees that the perpetrator admits his blameworthiness. Likewise, humor can reduce anger.

In the following section, models of some specific emotions that predispose individuals to behave aggressively will be presented. These models serve as heuristics for deriving hypotheses about how aggression-related motives are evoked and how such predispositions can be prevented or reduced.

Outrage and Resentment

Outrage has several structural components (Bernhardt, 2000; Montada & Boll, 1988; Montada & Kals, 2007):

– A subjective entitlement or a subjectively valid norm is perceived to be violated, e.g., when the distribution of benefits and costs is seen as unfair; when the right to respect or to obedience is violated; when one's own authority or expertise is disregarded; when a "holy" symbol is perceived to be disparaged; or when a duty is perceived to be neglected. One can see from these examples that the incidents that trigger outrage are as manifold as subjects' normative convictions are.

– The person who supposedly violated a norm is held responsible for his or her behavior. Accordingly, it is assumed that he or she had free decisional control and that his or her behavior was not determined by uncontrollable causes.

– Furthermore, justifying reasons for the action (or the nonaction) are recognized and accepted.

Being outraged motivates a person to reproach and to demand changes in the behavior of the perpetrator. If that person in turn does not comply with these demands, a conflict becomes manifest. In this case, outrage often motivates the enforcement of demands and normative expectations with aggressive means. Furthermore, outrage motivates punishment of wrong-doing and retaliation, also often with aggressive means. If the perpetrator now becomes outraged about this response, the conflict is likely to escalate.

However, the perception of a person's illegitimate actions does not necessarily lead to conflict, to aggressive responses, or to retaliation. This is the case when:

– Justifying reasons are brought forward or thought of.

- The validity of the supposedly violated norm or normative expectations are qualified – this can be achieved, for instance, by normative discourse (Montada, 2006).
- The responsibility of the agent is questioned with good reasons (Bernhardt, 2000).

Furthermore, admitting one's guilt and blameworthiness, the credible expression of regret such as begging for forgiveness can satisfy the outraged person, as mentioned above. Consequently, outrage and subsequent aggression-related motives activated by this emotion can be eliminated entirely (Goffmann, 1971; Montada & Kirchhoff, 2000).

All these possibilities can decrease the distance between the normative evaluations held by each of the parties in conflict. When the perpetrator honestly asks for forgiveness, he acknowledges the norm or entitlement as valid. Responsibility for the norm violation is not denied. No justifications are brought forward. Thus, blameworthiness is admitted. If compensation is offered, the outrage-evoking incident is neutralized and the conflict is reconciled. Discourse about conflicting normative convictions, searching for justifications, qualifying attributed responsibility, and qualifying the significance of the norm violation are further means to reduce outrage (for a detailed review see Montada & Kals, 2007, Chapters 4, 5, and 9).

Shame and Humiliation

Shame is evoked when a subject believes he has lost esteem and honor in the eyes of significant others or in public. Reasons for expecting or experiencing a decrease in esteem are manifold (cf. Montada & Kals, 2007, Chapter 6):

- Failure in achievement situations.
- Slanderous defeat in a competition.
- Dishonorable behavior.
- Inappropriate clothing.
- Depreciatory, humiliating comments by others which one does not appropriately respond to.
- Being ignored and excluded by others.
- Work assignments beneath one's level of qualification, etc.

Shame can have external or internal reasons depending on whether responsibility is attributed to oneself or to others. An external explanation entails that others are held responsible for a violation of one's honor or reputation: Here, the notion of humiliation is more adequate. In this case, outrage is paired with shame.

One can also be ashamed or feel humiliated when close persons whom one identifies with – one's own group or community – have acted dishonorably or are humiliated by others.

Shame can motivate the person to hide from the public. It can motivate to terminate a relationship or to move into another social context in order to avoid a loss in status. Shame can also motivate a person to regain his reputation and honor. Depending on the particular case, this can be achieved in different ways. An embarrassing defeat can be explained "externally" (e.g., with illness), but also by downsizing the opponent (e.g., claiming that the winner in a sports game was doped, had bribed the referee, or violated other rules).

In the case of moral failure, denial of responsibility or justifications can be used in order to regain self-esteem. For instance, if one fails to support a colleague who is bullied by his or her supervisor, one could argue that the colleague should have reported this case to the management, or that he or she deserved it. Both conclusions can also be false and are, thus, antisocial.

Shame can also motivate a person to strive for high achievements or to commit heroic deeds in order to restore his honor. If violent actions are considered a means to restore one's honor, this can be an option as well. For example, duels once used to be normatively expected in cases of humiliation. Preventive defense of self-esteem is also possible: Adolescents and adults with fragile self-esteem tend to react aggressively toward alleged attacks. Adolescent delinquency can be partly understood as a means for compensating decreases in self-esteem (Streng, 1995). Humiliation in particular motivates a person to commit violent acts of revenge. Even homicides, serial killings, and cases in which people are running amok can be conceived of vengeful acts (Holmes & Burger, 1988).

Public reports of honorable achievements of the ashamed person might be offered as alternatives to alleviate or overcome shame. Another option might be that the ashamed person courageously steps forward and admits to the dishonorable mistakes. It might help when significant others report on their own experiences of shame. A person's humiliation can also be attenuated if the mortifying agents are depreciated or if their behavior is condemned by the own group. In this regard, again, moving to another group may be an option.

Envy

The model of envy contains the following components that are empirically well established (Hildebrandt, 1990; Hupka & Otto, 2000; Tesser, 1991; Wahner, 1998). Envy develops in competitive relationships, namely when a rival is perceived as superior in a personally important aspect. For instance, a rival can be perceived as more talented, as more successful with respect to achievements or career, as more attractive, or more popular. Envy is called "black" if the envious subjects believe themselves to be unable to catch up to the rival or to overtake him or her.

Only rivals are seen with envy. Persons with whom one identifies do not elicit envy if they have similar success or advantages. These persons are admired; one might be tempted to bask in their glory. For example, think of a professor who is delighted at the success of his or her students. Cases in which a target is defeated or devalued are only satisfactory if the target is actually a rival.

"Black envy" makes the envier doubt the rightfulness of his rivals' success. It motivates him to derogate the rival, to engage in intrigues, to socially exclude him, if that is possible. It can even provoke conflicts and violent offenses.

According to this conceptualization, possible interventions can be derived to attenuate envy and any aggressive motives evoked by it. Envy is reduced when the perceived superiority of the envied person is decreased, e.g.,

- When that person is defeated.
- When he or she is devaluated by third parties.
- When the success of the envied person is criticized as cheating.
- When the envious subject experiences success of his own.
- When the envious person becomes aware of his or her own talents, achievements, or when he or she is praised by others.

Envy can be dissolved when the social relationship changes and the competitive relationship is terminated. The relationship could turn into a cooperative one; the envious person could experience appreciation by the envied person; or the envious person could terminate any social contact with the envied person and move into a different social context. Finally, the envied goods, talents, and successes can be reappraised. This can be supported in a social group that holds different values and preferences. For relevant empirical findings see Hildebrandt (1990).

Jealousy

Corresponding with the literature (e.g., Salovey, 1991; Haslam & Bornstein, 1996; Hupka & Otto, 2000), jealousy can be conceptualized with five components:
1. The jealous person is believed to be exceptionally or exclusively appreciated by another person P.
2. P's appreciation is of high importance for the self-esteem of the jealous subject.
3. The jealous subject fears losing the exceptional or exclusive appreciation by P because P now seems to appreciate a third person R to an equal or even higher amount.
4. The subject perceives R as a rival.
5. The subject's self-esteem is threatened by this change in relationship with P.

Jealousy is a specific fear of loss. It not only occurs in close relationships, but in all kinds of social relations including work contexts. One can think of a doctor who is jealous when a patient prefers seeing another doctor, or an employee who is jealous when his supervisor assigns a difficult job to a colleague.

Jealousy can motivate aggression against the rival such as derogation, bullying, or even physical violence. A goal of such jealousy-based aggression can be to deter the rival or to retaliate against his "illegitimate" competitive behavior.

However, deterring the rival does not remove doubts about whether P's appreciation of one's own attractiveness might have diminished and whether P's appreciation of R might persist. Therefore, alternative forms of coping should be considered.

Possibly the subject's appraisal of the incident is erroneous and no reason for jealousy exists at all. P's behavior might have different motives than suspected. For example, P's politeness toward R could have been merely normatively appropriate, or motivated by reciprocity. Taking the supervisor example, it might be that he simply wanted to spare the employee too much more work, thus assigning the difficult job to his colleague.

If the relationship with P is a central source of the jealous subject's self-esteem, jealousy can be reduced when alternative sources for self-esteem are found (e.g., by becoming aware of past achievements or by receiving social recognition or being loved by others). New achievements are helpful, too, as well as affiliating with a new reference group in which one's talents and performances are valued. The correlation of jealousy with low self-esteem is empirically corroborated (Schmitt, Falkenau, & Montada, 1995).

However, many cases of aggression in such triangular constellations that are characteristic for jealousy are not motivated by jealousy in the defined sense. Aggressions toward P are mostly motivated by outrage because of P's alleged lack of loyalty, infidelity, or because of feelings of humiliation. Aggression against R can be motivated by outrage about the perceived violation of unwritten norms that request respect for existing social relationships.

Hostility and Hate

In a common sense, aggression often means a hostile attitude against other persons, social groups, or categories, combined with the desire to impair or degrade them. However, on the behavioral level, aggression is possible without any motivation to impair another person: Aggressive behavior may be a rational choice for pursuing one's self interest, e.g., to enrich oneself, to win a competition, to save one's life when fleeing a burning house, to satisfy sexual needs, or to make someone compliant, etc. The motive to hurt someone, in contrast, implies that the impairment of the other person is explicitly desired, and that aggressive behavior is not merely a means to reach further goals but a goal in itself. In situations involving hate and hostility, this is exactly the case.

Hostility is the emotional evaluation of enemies. Who is perceived as an enemy? We react with hate or hostility when we consider other people to be threatening. We believe that they are able to hurt or impair us. We believe that they are malicious or hostile. At the very least we see them as inconsiderate, exploitative, or scrounging. Additionally, we believe that we are not able to avoid or to master the threats coming from these persons. Hate often results from the experience of being helpless against the aggression of the enemy, of impairment, or of humiliation (Fürntratt, 1974). The power of the enemy is seen as superior. This power may have various sources: physical superiority, higher power, superior rhetoric, influential social networks, unscrupulous choice of means, disrespecting normative orders, information suitable for blackmailing, existential or emotional dependence of the victim, etc.

In two studies, these components of hate and hostility were empirically tested in the context of hierarchically structured organizations – businesses, administrations, and the army (cf., Montada & Boll, 1988; Hilgeforth, 1998). In sum, we found strong evidence for the model of hostility. Hostility resulted from various experiences of workplace bullying, mostly committed by superiors. The bullying incidents were perceived as unjustified and intentional. The strongest predictor for hostility and for aggressive responses was the perception of one's own powerlessness against the perpetrator (Hilgeforth, 1998), which is typical for victims of bullying (Leymann, 1993).

The literature on bullying suggests empowerment of the victims against the experience of helplessness as adequate intervention strategies. Empowerment can be increased by different means and on different levels: Training in martial arts, solidarity among colleagues, information about one's own legal rights, institutional strategies to prevent bullying (e.g., through implementation of rules for good communication and leadership), training in constructive conflict resolution, and conflict mediation.

Victims perceive the injuring party as hostile. In many cases, this is true. Nonetheless, it is important to understand their hostility in turn. The identification of victims and perpetrators is an "interpunction" (Watzlawick, Beavin, & Jackson, 2000) that may be questioned. The perpetrator's hostility may result from conflicts with the victim (Neugebauer, 1999). In such cases, conflict resolution strategies are called for. In order to avoid a "winner–loser" outcome, the settlement of the conflict by mediation might be a good option for preventing further aggression (Montada, 2007).

Targets of hostility may not only be individual persons but also social groups (e.g., families or ethnic groups), social categories (e.g., men, the young, the rich, immigrants), or legal persons (such as political parties, religious communities, states, etc.) and their representatives. In these cases, too, it makes sense to seek understanding of the hostility in order to attenuate or even dissolve it. Note that understanding does not imply approval, least of all approval of the actions that are motivated by hostility.

Xenophobia, more specifically, hostility toward a single category of immigrants, has to be understood in order to recognize potentials for intervention and attenuation. One needs to understand why immigrants are perceived as outraging and threatening (Möller, 1995; Wagner & Zick, 1998; Willems, Würtz, & Eckert, 1993) and why the conflict arises: Because of a competition for scarce resources like jobs, social security, or social housing? Because of increasing adolescent delinquency and terrorist activities of specific groups (and the loss of personal security connected with it)? Because of outrage over entitlements that are claimed and granted? Because of the perception that claims for political asylum might be fraudulent? Does the native population claim the right to define cultural and legal norms? Are native adolescents trying to achieve social status and approval by behaving violently against immigrants? Are they trying to gain a positive social identity by identifying with an ethnocentric group and its ideology?

Again, options to change hostility and hate, e.g., clarifying misunderstandings, starting normative discourses in the mass media, or changing immigration and integration policies, measures against the abuse of social welfare systems, etc., cannot be generated without knowledge of their motivation. For instance, measures are possible through educational policies or through employment policies that enhance integration of immigrants and of those people who have poor chances on the labor market and, therefore, feel threatened by immigrants lowering their chances even further.

Regulation and Self-Regulation of Emotions With a Human-Psychological Approach

In a human-psychological understanding, homo sapiens is conceived:
- As a living being striving for explanations, for sense, and for understanding, forming beliefs and theories as a basis for appraisals, for emotions, and for behavior.
- As a subject having goals and meaningful orientations, not just as an object determined by internal and external forces.

– As a living being that forms a self-concept and reflects on his or her identity.
– As a creator of cultures and normative rule systems (not just as their creature).
– As a subject able to make choices and decisions, good or bad ones, consequently as a subject to be held responsible for his actions.

This has to be considered when emotions and emotion-based actions are analyzed. Emotions presuppose specific subjective beliefs about an incident. If these beliefs and the resulting appraisals of an incident are known, they provide many options for the psychological regulation of emotions and action motives.

Emotions may be subjectively experienced as externally caused by a specific incident. However, as soon as a subject becomes aware of his own beliefs, interpretations, and evaluations involved in the actual emotion, and of her own role in bringing about the incident, he is appraising emotionally, and self-regulation becomes possible. Education, psychological therapies, counseling, conflict mediation, and other forms of interventions have one goal in common: They all aim at expanding the individual horizon for (self-) regulation, (self-)control and decision making, and they aim at diminishing the domain of "determinants" and uncontrollable "conditionals". In sum, they aim at increasing the potential for self-formation and self-control.

All appraisals of an emotionalizing incident may be questioned. This will be illustrated once more using outrage as an example:
– Is it true that the target person of one's outrage has violated a valid norm or entitlement?
– Is the claim of validity well justified?
– Is the person really responsible for his or her behavior? Did he make a choice? Could he foresee the outcome?
– Did he have good reasons or justifications for his action?
– Are the consequences of the action as bad as assumed? Or does the subject dramatize the consequences, and if so, for what reasons?

By means of such questions, the subjective certainty of one's own appraisals, which is characteristic for outrage, may be reduced. The subject's cognitions are turned into questions or hypotheses. Their certainty is qualified and this can decrease or even eliminate the intensity of outrage (Bernhardt, 2000). A person who is aware of this fact can regulate his emotions. Of course, a person can also refrain from doing so. In any case, however, the subject is responsible for his decision.

In the psychology of emotion, a core question of human psychology is at stake: Does homo sapiens have freedom of choice? Or is homo sapiens determined by natural laws? In the psychology of emotion, deterministic models are still predominant. In recent years, doubts about freedom of will in human beings have been raised again by neuroscientists. The debate is conducted on an ontological level (cf. Berlin-Brandenburgische Akademie der Wissenschaften, 2006).

As in any other science, human psychology generates theoretical hypotheses and models. Whether they have ontic truth or not remains a question of belief. Scientifically, they have to be fruitful as theoretically based hypotheses. The hypothesis of freedom of choice is a very fruitful one. A considerable part of the contents of psychological research – the empirically assessable subjective experiencing, judging, appraising, behaving, etc. – cannot be understood without the hypothesis that homo sapiens believes in freedom of choice. Concerning the matter of this chapter, these are, for example, attributions of responsibility. Is it possible to imagine social life without the assumption of freedom of choice? It is hard to think of a society without the concept of actors who have responsibility for their actions and decisions.

Even when criminal offenses are explained (and excused) by developmental "determinants," it is impossible to avoid assumptions of responsibilities: Although the delinquent is not seen as responsible, other subjects or society as a whole are considered responsible for the bad course of the delinquent's development. In specific cases, this may be right. However, this does not imply that the defendant is denied freedom of choice in general, e.g., for his or her future life. This would imply considering him mentally immature.

If freedom of choice is negated, what would be the sense of debates over goals, goal-orientated measures, about rules, and shapes of social systems? What would be the worth of thinking about justice and efficacy if there was no actor who had the responsibility and the decisional control to implement such structures?

We cannot think of ourselves without the conviction that we have the ability to make choices. When our decisional control is restricted, we react with anger and efforts to regain freedom of choice. So why should we take a different view of the subjects of our research or clients in our practical professional activities? Instead, actual restrictions of freedom have to be assessed and options have to be generated for (re)establishing decisional control.

The conclusion is: An action-based theoretical analysis of aggression presupposes the agent's freedom of choice. This has important implications for the understanding of aggression as well as for efforts to prevent aggression.

References

Berkowitz, L. (1990). On the formation of anger and aggression: A cognitive-neoassociationistic analysis. *American Psychologist, 45*, 494–503.

Berlin-Brandenburgische Akademie der Wissenschaften (2006). Zur Freiheit des Willens II. [The freedom of will]. Streitgespräch am 2. Juli 2004. *Debatte, 3/2006*. Berlin, Germany: BBAW.

Bernhardt, K. (2000). *Steuerung der Emotion Empörung durch Umwandlung assertorischer Urteile in hypothetische Urteile und Fragen: Ein Trainingsprogramm* [Controlling moral outrage by changing assertoric judgments into hypothetic judgments and questions]. Unpublished doctoral dissertation, Universität Trier, Trier, Germany.

Bierhoff, H. W. (1998). Ärger, Aggression und Gerechtigkeit: Moralische Empörung und antisoziales Verhalten [Anger, aggression, and justice: Moral outrage and antisocial behavior]. In H. W. Bierhoff & U. Wagner (Eds.), *Aggression und Gewalt* (pp. 26–47). Stuttgart, Germany: Kohlhammer.

Dollard, J., Doob, L. W., Miller, N., Mowrer, O. H., & Sears, R. R. (1939). Frustration and aggression. *Journal of Abnormal and Social Psychology, 34*, 289–313.

Farrington, D. P., & West, D. J. (1990). The Cambridge study of delinquent development: A long-term follow-up of 411 London males. In H. J. Kerner & G. Kaiser (Eds.), *Kriminalität: Persönlichkeit, Lebensgeschichte und Verhalten* (pp. 115–138). Berlin, Germany: Springer.

Frijda, N. H. (1987). Emotion, cognitive structure, and action tendency. *Cognition and Emotion, 1*, 115–143.

Fürntratt, E. (1974). *Angst und instrumentelle Aggression* [Fear and instrumental aggression]. Weinheim, Germany: Beltz.

Goffman, E. (1971). *Relations in public: Microstudies of the public order.* New York: Basic Books.

Gollwitzer, M. (2005). *Ist „gerächt" gleich „gerecht"? Eine Analyse von Racheaktionen und rachebezogenen Reaktionen unter gerechtigkeitspsychologischen Aspekten* [Does „avenged" equal „just"? An analysis of vengeful reactions and revenge-related reaction from a psychology of justice perspective]. Berlin, Germany: wvb.

Graumann, C. F. (1984). Bewusstsein und Verhalten [Consciousness and behavior]. In H. Lenk (Ed.), *Handlungstheorien interdisziplinär III*, Vol. 2 (pp. 547–573). München, Germany: Fink.

Greve, W. (1994). *Handlungsklärung. Die psychologische Erklärung menschlicher Handlungen* [Explanation of actions. The psychological explanation of human actions]. Bern, Switzerland: Huber.

Greve, W., & Montada, L. (in press). Delinquenz und Aggression [Delinquency and aggression]. In R. Oerter & L. Montada (Eds.), *Entwicklungspsychologie* (6th ed.) Weinheim, Germany: Beltz.

Haslam, N., & Bornstein, B. H. (1996). Envy and jealousy as discrete emotions: A taxometric analysis. *Motivation and Emotion, 20*, 255–272.

Hildebrandt, M. (1990). *Neid: Von wem wird er in welchen Situationen erlebt?* [Envy: Who experiences it in which situations?]. Unpublished diploma thesis: Universität Trier, Trier, Germany.

Hilgefort, G. (1998). *Feindseligkeit in hierarchisch strukturierten Organisationen* [Animosity in hierarchically structured organizations]. Hamburg, Germany: Kovacs.

Holmes, R. M., & Burger, J. D. (1988*). Serial murder*. Newbury Park, CA: Sage.

Hupka, R. B., & Otto, J. H. (2000). Neid und Eifersucht [Envy and jealousy] In J. H. Otto, H. A. Euler, & H. Mandl (Eds.), *Emotionspsychologie. Ein Handbuch.* (pp. 272–283). Weinheim, Germany: Beltz.

Jones, E. E., & Nisbett, R. E. (1972). The actor and the observer: Divergent perceptions of the causes of behavior. In E. E. Jones, D. Kanouse, H. H. Kelley, R. E. Nisbett, S. Valins, & B. Weiner. (Eds), *Attribution: Perceiving the causes of behaviour* (pp. 79–94). Morristown, NJ: General Learning Press.

Jüttemann, G. (1978). Eine Prädikationsanalyse des Aggressionsbegriffs [A predicamental analysis of aggression]. *Zeitschrift für Sozialpsychologie, 9*, 299–312.

Jüttemann, G. (2004). *Psychologie als Humanwissenschaft. Ein Handbuch* [Psychology as a human science. A handbook]. Göttingen, Germany: Vandenhoeck & Ruprecht.

Lazarus, R. S. (2001). Relational meaning and discrete emotions. In K. R. Scherer, A. Schorr, & T. Johnstone (Eds.), *Appraisal processes in emotion* (pp. 37–67). New York: Oxford University Press.

Lenk, H. (1987). Motive als Interpretationskonstrukte [Motives as constructs of interpretation]. In H. Lenk (Ed.), *Zwischen Sozialpsychologie und Sozialphilosophie* (pp. 183–206). Frankfurt, Germany: Suhrkamp.

Leymann, H. (1993). *Mobbing.* Reinbek, Germany: Rowohlt.

Möller, K. (1995). Fremdenfeindliche Gewalt: Zwischen „Ausländer raus!" und „Nazis raus" [Xenophobic violence]. In K. Hurrelmann, W. Wilken, & C. Palentien (Eds.), *Anti-Gewalt-Report* (pp. 181–210). Weinheim, Germany: Beltz.

Montada, L. (1989). Bildung der Gefühle [Formation of emotions]? *Zeitschrift für Pädagogik, 35*, 293–311.

Montada, L. (1992). Eine pädagogische Psychologie der Gefühle. Kognitionen und die Steuerung erlebter Emotionen [A pedagogical psychology of emotions. Cognitions and the control of experienced emotions] In H. Mandl, M. Dreher, & H.-J. Kornadt (Eds.), *Entwicklung und Denken im kulturellen Kontext* (pp. 229–249). Göttingen, Germany: Hogrefe.

Montada, L. (2004). Mediation – ein Weg zur Kultivierung sozialen Lebens [Mediation – a way of cultivating social life]. In G. Jüttemann (Ed.), *Psychologie als Humanwissenschaft. Ein Handbuch* (pp. 361–361). Göttingen, Germany: Vandenhoek & Ruprecht.

Montada, L. (2006). Gerechtigkeit in der Mediation [Justice in mediation]. *Perspektive Mediation, 4/2006.*

Montada, L. (2007). Mediation in Fällen von Gewalt, Aggression und Mobbing in der Schule [Mediation in cases of violence, aggression, and mobbing at school]. In M. Gollwitzer, J. Pfetsch, V. Schneider, A. Schulz, T. Steffke, & C. Ulrich (Eds.), *Gewaltprävention bei Kindern und Jugendlichen* (pp. 58–74). Göttingen, Germany: Hogrefe.

Montada, L., & Boll, T. (1988). Auslösung und Dämpfung von Feindseligkeit [Triggering and diminishing factors of hostility]. *Untersuchungen des psychologischen Dienstes der Bundeswehr, 23*, 43–144.

Montada, L., & Kals, E. (2007). *Mediation. Ein Lehrbuch auf psychologischer Grundlage* [Mediation. A psychological textbook]. Weinheim, Germany: Beltz.

Montada, L., & Kirchhoff, S. (2000). *Bitte um Verzeihung, Rechtfertigungen und Ausreden: Ihre Wirkungen auf soziale Beziehungen* [Request for forgiveness, justifications and excuses: Their effects on social relations]. (Berichte aus der Arbeitsgruppe „Verantwortung, Gerechtigkeit, Moral" No. 130). Trier, Germany: Universität Trier, Fachbereich I – Psychologie.

Neugebauer, O. (1999). *Mobbing: Übel mitspielen in Organisationen* [Mobbing. Playing pranks in organizations]. München, Germany: Rainer Hampp Verlag.

Pastore, N. (1952).The role of arbitrariness in the frustration-aggression hypothesis. *Journal of Abnormal and Social Psychology, 47*, 728–731.

Reisenzein, R., Meyer, W.-U., & Schützwohl, A. (2003*). Einführung in die Emotionspsychologie. Band III. Kognitive Emotionstheorie* [Introduction to the psychology of emotion. Volume III. Cognitive theory of emotion]. Bern, Switzerland: Hans Huber.

Salovey, P. (Ed.). (1991). *The psychology of jealousy and envy.* New York: The Guilford Press.

Schmitt, M., Falkenau, K., & Montada, L. (1995). Zur Messung von Eifersucht über stellvertretende Emotionsbegriffe und zur Bereichsspezifität der Eifersuchtsneigung [The measurement of jealousy via vicarious emotions and the domain specificity of jealousy]. *Diagnostica, 41*, 131–149.

Schmitt, M., Neumann, R., & Montada, L. (1995) Sensitivity to befallen injustice. *Social Justice Research, 8*, 385–407.

Straub, J., & Werbik, H. (Eds.). (1999). *Handlungstheorie. Begriff und Erklärung des Handelns im interdisziplinären Diskurs* [Theory of action. Concept and explanation of action in interdisciplinary discourse]. Frankfurt, Germany: Campus.

Streng, F. (1995). Fremdenfeindliche Gewaltkriminalität als Herausforderung für kriminologische Erklärungsansätze [Xenophobic delinquency as a challenge for criminological approaches]. *Jura, 17*, 182–191.

Tedeschi, J. T., & Felson, R. B. (1994). *Violence, aggression, and coercive actions.* Washington, DC: American Psychological Association.

Tesser, A. (1991). Emotion in social comparison and reflection processes. In J. Suls & T. A.Wills (Eds.), *Social comparison: Contemporary theory and research* (pp.115–145). Hillsdale, NJ: Lawrence Erlbaum.

Wagner, U., & Zick, A. (1998). Ausländerfeindlichkeit, Vorurteile und diskriminierendes Verhalten [Xenophobia, prejudice, and discriminating behavior]. In H. W. Bierhoff & U. Wagner (Ed.), *Aggression und Gewalt* (pp.145–164). Stuttgart, Germany: Kohlhammer.

Wahner, U. (1998). Neid: Wie wichtig sind Selbstwertbedrohung und Ungerechtigkeitserleben? [Envy: How important are threats to self-esteem and experiences of injustice?]. In B. Reichle & M. Schmitt (Eds.), *Verantwortung, Gerechtigkeit und Moral* (pp.149–162). Weinheim, Germany: Juventa.

Watzlawick, P., Beavin, J. H., & Jackson, D. D. (2000). *Menschliche Kommunikation* [Human communication]. Bern, Switzerland: Huber.

Willems, H., Würtz, S., & Eckert, R. (1993). *Fremdenfeindliche Gewalt: Eine Analyse von Täterstrukturen und Eskalationsprozessen.* [Xenophobic violence: An analysis of offender structures and escalation processes] Bonn, Germany: Bundesministerium für Frauen und Jugend.

3 Implicit and Explicit Measures for Analyzing the Aggression of Computer Gamers

Matthias Bluemke and Joerg Zumbach

Introduction

The effects of playing computer games on children has become an important issue in psychological research in the last couple of years. The question of whether playing computer games leads to increased aggression, particularly among those playing violent games excessively, has stimulated numerous studies. Currently, the meta-analytic findings seem to imply that being exposed to violent games increases aggressive behavior, aggressive cognition, aggressive affect, and physiological arousal as well as it decreases helping behavior on average (Anderson, 2004; Anderson & Bushman, 2001; Anderson & Dill, 2000). Nevertheless, from a meta-analytical point of view, each effect size is subject to errors of unknown magnitude, and these errors can only be overcome by aggregation of similar studies, yielding more reliable estimates of effect sizes.

It is not surprising that some researchers question that violent video games have detrimental effects in real life contexts – either on the basis of single-study results or on the grounds of legitimate arguments (Scott, 1995). For example, some studies that found null results after substantial exposure to violence warn against neglecting the social context in which the playing takes place (Durkin & Barber, 2002; Williams & Skoric, 2005). In this chapter, we emphasize another important issue when encountering weak or null effects in aggression-related studies: the methods used when assessing aggressiveness and aggressive behaviors. Many null findings could be rooted in some vulnerability of the measures being applied; thus, the negative effects of playing violent video games might accordingly be underestimated. More precisely, it is a well-known problem that self-reports on socially sensitive topics (such as aggressive thoughts, aggressive feelings, and aggressive behavior) can be biased and, thus, lead to inconsistent results. Although some of the findings that enter aggression-related meta-analyses are obtained by unobtrusive methods such as observation and physiological data, many of the studies are based on self-report measures. This is often the case when affective and cognitive dispositions are analyzed (e.g., trait/state questionnaires). Within this contribution we argue that these self-reported variables, i.e., *explicit* measures, might meaningfully be complemented by newly developed methods, so-called *implicit* measures, that aim at assessing automatic affect and cognition.

Implicit measures rely on *spontaneous* reactions toward stimuli that elicit *automatic* cognitive, affective, and behavioral tendencies. Typically, one concludes that there exists some kind of cognitive structure or affective correlate by means of associations which themselves are inferred via response latencies in reaction time tasks. The most prominent measures are the affective priming paradigm (Fazio, Jackson, Dunton, & Williams, 1995) and the Implicit Association Test (IAT, Greenwald, McGhee, & Schwartz,

1998). Implicit measures like these have been used to explore implicit attitudes toward social categories such as Black and White Americans or East and West Germans (Greenwald et al., 1998; Bluemke & Friese, 2006), automatic affect toward phobia-related and fear-arousing objects (Teachman, Gregg, & Woody, 2001), automatic self-concept (Greenwald & Farnham, 2000), attitudes toward important behavioral concepts such as smoking (Sherman, Rose, Koch, Presson, & Chassin, 2003), as well as spontaneous decision-making processes when subjects are confronted with brands and products (Friese, Wänke, & Plessner, 2006).

Although there are still many methodological problems to overcome (Fiedler, Messner, & Bluemke, 2006), implicit measures have already added to our knowledge of pre-activation of emotional and cognitive content in social encounters. In the following, we will (a) highlight advantages of implicit measures, (b) suggest that aggression research might profit from measuring (automatic) affective reactions and predicting (spontaneous) behaviors, (c) describe the general procedure of aggression-related Implicit Association Tests (IATs), (d) and show how these automatic cognitive-affective processes can be integrated into current models of aggressive emotions and aggressive reactions. Finally, we will report our own findings that used implicit measures to explore the consequences of playing violent computer games with regard to the automatic self-concept and attitudes toward aggressive behavior among young adults and school children.

Advantages of Implicit Measures

Social psychology has been concerned with overcoming the limitations of socially desirable responding behavior for many years. In aggression research for instance, a participant might either be unwilling to report on negative emotional consequences of aggressive game playing or might even lack the capacity for introspection to determine such side-effects or suffer from blind spots. Blind spots are likely to occur if a person follows the purpose of keeping up a positive self-concept that is more in line with social demands. One advantage of implicit measures is their potential to bypass the adjustment process that accompanies the deliberate answering of questionnaires. In addition, implicit measures have the advantage of relying on spontaneous affective reactions. Many studies have demonstrated that attitudes and other cognitive content can be activated and processed automatically (unintentionally), even unconsciously (Fazio, 2001; Bargh, 2006) and "it appears that nearly everything is preconsciously classified as good or bad" (Bargh, 1994, p. 19). There is some support to the notion that implicit measures are capable of tapping into automatic affective reactions triggered within the range of milliseconds. Thus, via implicit measures we can disentangle rather uncontrolled factors that guide behavior from rather controlled processes leading to actions. Current dual-process models in psychology distinguish between these two facets: the reflective-impulsive model (RIM; Strack & Deutsch, 2004; cf. Epstein, 1994) suggests the existence of an impulsive system that functions on an associative basis. Activation is spreading within a semantic network in which cognitive and affective aspects are intertwined via links between conceptual nodes. Moreover, the RIM postulates that people have a reflective system that works in parallel and enables reasoning, decision making, and intentionality. Although the systems partly overlap, people's deliberate beliefs and evaluations of objects, behaviors, and actions can be much more complex and multi-faceted than stored associations such as simple object-valence links. Also, spontaneous and reflective affects toward the same object can either coincide or be obverse (Wilson, Lindsey, & Schooler, 2000). For instance, one could consciously object to discrimination against a member of an outgroup, yet at the same time one could nevertheless have negative automatic associations toward the same member. This is just like people reasoning that eating sugar can damage one's health and still feel tempted to consume it and impulsively behave accordingly.

Thus, one of the supposed advantages of implicit measures is to assess primary affective and cognitive reactions that occur quite automatically, are difficult to control, and are valuable for predicting impulsive, less-controlled, or automatic behaviors. For example, Asendorpf, Banse, and Mücke (2002) were able to uniquely predict spontaneous shy behavior (facial and body adaptors, tense body posture) in opposite-sex interaction by means of a shyness-self-concept IAT, whereas explicit self-ratings of trait shyness could only predict controlled behaviors (speech duration and illustrators). Also, the extent of control resources available in situations can moderate the predictability of behaviors. Hofmann, Gschwendner, Castelli, and Schmitt (2006) were able to show that an implicit measure of racial attitudes predicted behavior related to prejudice such as visual contact, speech illustrators, and body adaptors in interracial interaction, particularly when participants' control resources were experimentally reduced. Conversely, an explicit measure of racial attitudes predicted body adaptors only when control resources were fully available. In general, it seems possible to predict behavior by assessing automatic cognitive-affective components. In line with the unintentional nature of these automatic components, our actions often precede our understanding of why we behave in particular ways (Bargh & Chartrand, 1999).

Linking Aggression to Automatic Affective Processes

Applied to the current domain, implicit measures should be particularly useful for (a) avoiding social desirability concerns in self-reports of aggressive traits and states, (b) predicting impulsive aggressive behavior, and (c) predicting aggression that occurs in situations where cognitive control resources are low. Moreover, if implicit measures can be linked to aggressive behavior, it should be possible to (d) demonstrate the detrimental impact of playing violent video games on automatic cognitive-affective tendencies as a precursor to aggressive tendencies if this relationship really exists.

There is initial evidence that these assumptions are correct and that the use of implicit measures spreads in the domain of aggression research. For instance, Uhlmann and Swanson (2004) had an experimental group play a violent computer game. In comparison to a control group that solved a simple puzzle, participants demonstrated a significantly stronger automatic association between themselves and aggression stimuli as evident in the IAT results. In contrast, aggressiveness questionnaires did not reveal any differences between the groups. Explicit measures were thus incapable of demonstrating the effectiveness of the treatment which obviously altered the cognitive system at least in the short-term. Also, both the explicit and the implicit measures explained a unique proportion of variance in the amount of playing outside the lab, thus indicating that the IAT proved sensitive enough to assess long-term changes in the cognitive structure of participants. Furthermore, the IAT captured what participants did not deliberately tell about themselves. Another contribution here comes from Banse and colleagues (Banse, Clarbour, & Fischer, 2005; Banse & Fischer, 2002) who demonstrated that the aggressive behavior of ice-hockey players (as evidenced in peer observation and time-out penalties) could not be predicted by self-reported aggressiveness questionnaires, but by automatic tendencies as assessed by the IAT. In sum, associating oneself more strongly with aggressiveness, as compared to other participants in a reaction-time task, reliably relates to the degree of impulsive aggressiveness and correctly mirrors the extent to which one has been exposed to violent computer games.

Procedure of Implicit Association Tests

The IAT is a double categorization task that can flexibly be applied to various topics. Quite a number of stimuli are presented in a random sequence on a computer screen and have to be sorted into one of four categories by pressing an appropriate response key on the keyboard. Some of the stimuli refer to aggressive behavior (e.g., attack, threat), some of the stimuli describe peaceful or rather calm behavior (compromise, get along), some stimuli are self-related (I, me), and some are related to others (you, yours). There are only two response keys, and the participant has to use the same keys for two categories each. Depending on the instructions of the task, the participant either responds to *self* + *peaceful* stimuli with one key (and *other* + *aggressive* with the other key) or encounters identical stimuli and has to press one key for self-relevant + aggressive items (while using the other key for other-relevant + peaceful items). If a participant was faster in the first than in the second task, one would infer that his or her self-concept is linked more strongly to peaceful than to aggressive items. The difference in reaction times between the two tasks indicates the position of the self-concept on an aggressive-peaceful dimension (IAT effect).

The main focus here is not that many other factors could potentially account for the outcome (researchers typically control many of the extraneous variables affecting the latencies; see Greenwald & Nosek, 2001), but that this so-called IAT effect can potentially be used to differentiate participants' self-concepts in terms of aggressiveness without asking them explicitly (Bosson, Swann, & Pennebaker, 2000; Greenwald & Farnham, 2000). Therefore, one hypothesis could be that playing violent games has short-term consequences by temporarily increasing the cognitive availability of self-related aggression. Repeated playing in turn could chronically activate these self-related aggression associations and eventually alter the self-concept in the long run, thus raising the likelihood of applying aggressive behavioral scripts that are in line with one's altered self-concept.

Interindividual differences between players and nonplayers of violent computer games could also exist in automatic evaluations of aggressive and peaceful behavior, as the game environment requires from a player to appreciate and use aggressive means to reach the goals of the game. Thus, coupling the two categories (*aggressive* and *peaceful*) with a positive and a negative category (*pleasant* and *unpleasant*) in an IAT should indicate the degree of favorableness of aggressive behavior. Even if all participants are skilled in sorting *aggressive* + *negative* (*peaceful* + *positive*) together and find it rather hard to associate *aggressive* + *positive* (*peaceful* + *negative*), participants could differ in the extent to which they do so. Some might have a strict automatic evaluation of aggression; others might hold lenient evaluations as indicated in smaller IAT effects. A reaction time difference in evaluative IATs would thus provide some evidence for the automatic affect regarding aggressive content. The idea is that automatic evaluations of aggressive behavior might control the selection of a behavioral strategy in a fast and frugal manner. This could be important information when hypothesizing about the primary appraisal of one's own behavioral tendencies: Reinforcing aggressive behavior by playing violent video games strengthens the association of aggressive behavior with positive valence. In turn, the likelihood of displaying aggressive behavior rises. Whether changing the cognitive structures in these respects is a relevant mediator for aggressive tendencies in real life is a question that researchers have only recently begun to address.

Models Related to Aggressive Affect, Cognition, and Behavior

Now that we have discussed advantages of implicit measures and their potential usefulness in aggression research, we will focus on underlying automatic cognitive-affective processes and implicit measures and how they fit into current models of aggressive reactions. Advantages of assessment related to automatic processes will also be addressed. The discussion about affective aspects does not preclude the role of cognition during the emergence of appraisals, and vice versa. Rather, cognitive and affective aspects interact in a complex manner. This interaction is evident in emotional-affective states which can provide cognitive information as well as they can induce different modes of information processing (Bless & Fiedler, 1995; Clore, Schwarz, & Conway, 1994).

Lazarus' (1991) well-known cognitive-motivational-relational theory, for example, emphasizes the cognitive interpretation of internal or external stimuli (appraisal) before a flexible emotional reaction occurs, which, in turn, enables a flexible adaptation to the situation. Lazarus distinguishes primary and secondary appraisals of complex stimuli and situations. The primary appraisal enables a quick distinction between goal-relevant and irrelevant situations to determine the strength of an emotional response. It checks whether the situation is congruent with an individual's goals, resulting in positive or negative affect, and it determines the kind of identity relevance in order to subsequently respond with one of various potential emotional reactions. The secondary appraisal addresses causal attributions, an individual's potential to cope with the situation at hand, and future expectations of the development of the situation, all of which can modify and differentiate the initial response. It is noteworthy that the primary appraisal affords a rather undifferentiated view of the situation (pleasant/unpleasant) and elicits a general behavioral tendency (approach/avoidance), before the filtering and narrowing of the emotional response takes place. Comparing the aforementioned aspects of automatic affect and cognition to Lazarus' model, it seems quite evident that the automatic cognitive-affective aspects as assessed by implicit measures lead to similar initial approach/avoidance tendencies that correspond to the behavior elicited by emotions. Thus, automatic evaluations of a target object and the automatic activation of stereotypes (along with attributions and other inferences) could trigger negative affect, influence the emergence of hostile feelings or anger, and lead to the expression of negative affect in an aggressive way. This effect can be more drastic when cognitive control resources are low, as the adequate secondary appraisal of a situation might fail and a maladjusted emotional reaction might emerge. When cognitive resources are abundant, Hogarth (2002, p. 11) states: "Clearly, we can all become angry for a variety of reasons. But this does not mean that we 'must' act in accordance with the angry thoughts that suddenly appear in our consciousness."

Another model is the general aggression model (GAM; Anderson & Bushman, 2002; Anderson & Carnagey, 2004; Lindsay & Anderson, 2000), which describes the route to aggression in a single episode. The GAM assumes a complex interplay of cognition, affect, and arousal which themselves depend on personal and situational variables. Note that the appraisal and decision processes bring about either thoughtful action or impulsive action as outcomes, yet the model does not specify how to predict the outcomes (Figure 1).

We propose that it is automatic appraisals that determine the way toward impulsive action (rather: impulsive *behavior*), and that it is deliberate and resource-consuming decision making processes that result in controllable thoughtful *action*. Whereas the

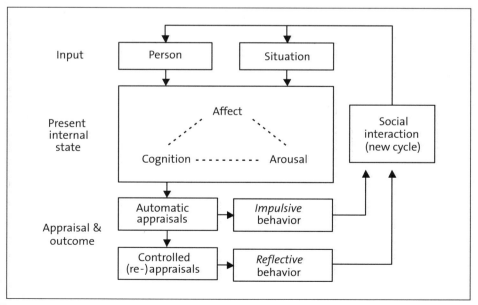

Figure 1. The general aggression model of single episodes (figure adapted from Anderson & Dill, 2000).

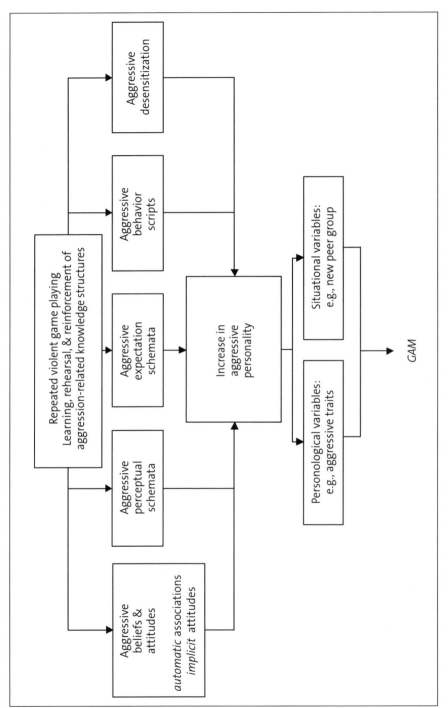

Figure 2. Long-term effects of repeated playing of violent video games as postulated by the GAM (figure adapted from Anderson & Dill, 2000).

former route can be predicted by implicit measures, explicit measures should be particularly appropriate for predicting the reflective pathway, but not necessarily vice versa (Fazio, 1986; Wilson et al., 2000). Also, to the degree that cognitive resources are missing in a given situation, people's behaviors will be influenced by automatic cognitive-affective variables to a stronger degree than by variables assessed in a deliberative mode. We do not posit that reflective and impulsive tendencies are mutually exclusive. They rather pose the prototypical ends of a behavioral continuum that spans from automatic behaviors to deliberate actions.

With regard to long-term effects which involve learning processes, the GAM suggests that various behavioral determinants can potentially be affected by repeated violent game playing (Figure 2).

The first component is a well-established finding stating that attitudes and beliefs are comprised of automatic and reflective components. Therefore, it is likely that attitudes toward aggressive behaviors can also be represented in a reflective and an automatic associative system as well. Measuring one's attitude toward aggression and aggressive ways of conflict resolution is likely to parallel trait aggressiveness via explicit questionnaires. Yet, at the same time a person could hold a different (e.g., positive) implicit attitude that determines behavior in less controlled moments. The interesting implication of such a dissociation of implicit and explicit attitudes is that researchers should take into account automatic cognitive-affective components as dispositions when making predictions about aggressive behavior and particularly spontaneous behavior. Moreover, we assume that almost all of the factors related to aggressive personality can be subdivided in a similar manner in order to reflect the distinction between an impulsive and a reflective system.

Overview of the Current Study

Following these assumptions, it seems worthwhile to take a closer look at some newly developed implicit measures and apply them to aggression research. In the following study we investigated the relationship between automatic cognitive-affective variables, explicit personality questionnaires, and use of aggressive computer games. First-person shooters (FPS) can be considered a subgenre of shooter games where the player has full control over a character and interacts directly with the environment from the character's point of view, for instance, by directing weapons at enemies and fighting them. FPS require enormous amounts of violent actions and have raised teachers' and parents' concerns because FPS have been associated with school shootings like in Littleton or Erfurt. As it is difficult to unequivocally establish an influence of first-person shooting on aggressiveness either on the basis of anecdotal evidence or on the grounds of self-reported personality, it could be that implicit measures are suited to tap into the negative side effects of the repeated playing of violent video games and that variability in violent game consumption results in systematic differences between groups. With regard to explicit measures, we hypothesized that agreeableness and aggression-related traits should differ depending on the amount of violent game playing. Specifically, FPS players should deviate even more strongly from a computer control group than players of other computer games. The same hypothesis should hold for implicit measures, though implicit measures should show even stronger effect sizes, because of the social desirability concerns that are likely to bias the explicit outcome variables.

Method

Participants and Recruitment

We recruited participants via Internet forums reserved for "communities of practice" (FPS: first-person-shooter players) and compared them to other computer game players (PLAY: simulations, racing games, sports games etc.) and personal computer users without extensive game consumption (PC: office applications, World Wide Web, etc.). We carefully concealed aggressiveness as a topic of the study; rather, we described the study as being related to computer use and personality in a general sense. As a means of gratification, we supplied participants with feedback about personality characteristics inferred from response latencies, which should raise curiosity among computer users in general. We did not supply any monetary incentives in order to avoid multiple participation (we also eliminated multiple participation cases by means of a control question). Only during the course of the study could participants have become aware of aggressiveness-related questions, but even this should not have aroused suspicion, because the instructions also allowed for the interpretation that randomly chosen personality characteristics were under investigation.

As personality characteristics are a sensitive topic, we assured participants of anonymity and did not store Internet protocol addresses, however we supplied different hyperlinks to the study hosted at the web lab of the Psychological Institute at Heidelberg University. Thus, we were able to infer the origin of a participant and his or her belonging to one of the three quasi-experimental groups. To ensure the quality of the classification we additionally filtered for the following criteria after study completion: FPS players had to use a personal computer on a regular basis for playing games and they had to have played FPS for at least one hour in the week before. PLAY members had to usually play games different from FPS and they had to have played for at least one hour in the week before. PC users had to report PC usage on a regular basis, but not for playing games. FPS and PLAY did not differ with regard to the amount of playing ($M = 15.6$ vs. 15.0 hrs in the week before, $t < 1$). Deviating from the PLAY group, the FPS group had spent 9.2 hrs. playing FPS.

Whereas 673 participants clicked on the study hyperlinks during one month of recruitment, 238 completed the study. After filtering multiple participation cases, low self-reported quality of data, insufficient language abilities, missing informed consent, and too many errors in the Implicit Association Tests (max. 20% per block, Greenwald et al., 1998), 196 participants were left. Applying the conservative criteria to enter the experimental groups, the final sample consisted of $N = 37$, 49, and 23 participants in the FPS, PLAY, and PC groups, respectively ($M_{age} = 28.00$ yrs., $SD = 10.24$; 80.7% males; nonstudents 32.1%).

Procedure and Material

We used HTML for Web pages and additionally PHP for dynamic parts such as personal feedback. Stimulus presentation and reaction time measurement in the implicit tasks were accomplished by a JAVA applet that renders a platform-independent and operating-system-independent assessment possible. All incoming data were stored in a MySQL database hosted on the Web server and analyzed using SPSS.

After the initial instructions, participants reported sociodemographic variables, computer usage, and the amount of playing. As a first explicit measure we provided a questionnaire assessing the Big Five personality factors. Then two implicit measures followed, a Single-Target IAT assessing the automatic aggressive self-concept and an IAT assessing the automatic evaluation of aggressive behaviors. Only after participants had completed both implicit measures we administered an explicit aggressiveness questionnaire. After the study participants received full information on the nature and the purpose of the study. The final web page provided individual feedback about the outcomes of the implicit measures.

Explicit Measures: For assessment of the Big Five traits, we used the IPIP40, a German 40-item questionnaire based on the International Personality Item Pool (Buchanan, Johnson, & Goldberg, 2005; Hartig, Jude, & Rauch, 2003). The factor "Agreeableness" was the main dependent variable from this questionnaire. The IPIP40 can be used without copyright restrictions in the Internet (Goldberg, 2001) and has already been validated for Internet applications. As a specific measure of aggressiveness, we chose to apply a wide-spread aggressiveness questionnaire (BPAQ; Buss & Perry, 1992; German version by Amelang & Bartussek, 1997). The BPAQ is a 29-item questionnaire that has been validated for German applications (Herzberg, 2003; von Collani & Werner, 2005). The internal consistencies of the subscales within our sample lay in the range typically reported for these measures (Cronbach's α = .61–.82 and .70–.89 for BPAQ and IPIP40, respectively).

Implicit measures: Implicit associations were measured with the Implicit Association Test (IAT; Greenwald et al., 1998) and its descendant, the Single-Target IAT (ST-IAT; cf. Karpinski & Steinman, 2006; Wigboldus, Holland, & van Knippenberg, 2004). The IAT assessed the automatic evaluation of aggressive vs. peaceful behaviors. The ST-IAT tapped into the automatic self-concept in a nonrelative way, that is, we dropped the category "other" which is typically used as a counter category for the target category "self" in an IAT (Karpinski, 2004), hence the name *Single-Target IAT*.

As described in Table 1, the IAT started with a block of trials that asks test-takers to correctly classify attribute stimuli that appear sequentially on a screen as either negative or positive, for instance PAIN, JOY, by pressing a left or a right response key as indicated by the category on the left or right side of the top of the screen (response-key assignment was counterbalanced across participants). We used the same attribute stimuli that were successfully applied in prior studies (Bluemke & Friese, 2006). In a next step, participants exercised the discrimination of aggressive vs. peaceful stimuli, for example BEAT, RECONCILE, which were adopted from Banse et al. (2005). The third block combined all four categories in a double discrimination task, yet only two response keys could be used, one for categories on the left, another one for categories on the right side. Categories either formed a compatible combination, *aggressive + negative* and *peace-*

Table 1a. Structure of an Implicit Association Test Assessing the Automatic Evaluation of Aggressive Behaviors

Sequence	Block 1	Block 2	Block 3	Block 4	Block 5
Task	Attribute discrimination	Target-concept discrimination	Initial combined task (here: compatible)	Reversed attribute discrimination	Reversed combined task (here: incompatible)
Task instructions	• NEGATIVE • POSITIVE	• aggressive • peaceful	• NEGATIVE • aggressive • POSITIVE • peaceful	• NEGATIVE • POSITIVE	• NEGATIVE • aggressive • POSITIVE • peaceful
Stimuli	JOY STINK NICE AVARICIOUS POISON LAUGHTER ILL PAIN HONEST DECEITFUL LOVE DISEASE HAPPY PRESENT UNLOYAL ACCIDENT HOPE MEAN HEALTH GIFTED	compromise fight agree blow (with a fist) reconciliation give in hurt revenge hit make peace	PAIN hit HONEST fight reconciliation LOVE hurt DECEITFUL give in DISEASE ...	ACCIDENT HOPE MEAN HEALTH GIFTED LAUGHTER ILL PAIN HONEST DECEITFUL ...	make peace LOVE blow (with a fist) DISEASE fight HAPPY compromise PRESENT revenge UNLOYAL ...
Number of trials	10 negative 10 positive	2 x 5 = 10 aggressive 2 x 5 = 10 peaceful	10 negative 10 positive 10 aggressive 10 peaceful	10 negative 10 positive	10 negative 10 positive 10 aggressive 10 peaceful

Note: Within the task instructions, spatial position of the categories corresponds to the left or right response key. Target and attribute stimuli alternated in combined blocks (here: depiction of an arbitrary sequence of stimuli). Attribute stimuli and categories were printed in capital letters in order to avoid confusion with the target dimension (lower case letters).

Table 1b. Structure of the Single-Target IAT Assessing the Automatic Aggressive Self-Concept

Sequence	Block 1		Block 2		Block 3	
Task	Attribute discrimination		Compatible block		Incompatible block	
Task instructions	• aggressive peaceful	*	• aggressive peaceful SELF	* *	• aggressive peaceful • SELF	*
Stimuli	compromise • fight agree • blow (with a fist) reconciliation give in • hurt • revenge • hit make peace	* * * * *	ME • hit I • fight reconciliation MYSELF • hurt MINE give in ME ...	* * * * * *	make peace • ME • revenge MINE • fight • MYSELF agree • I • give in ME ...	* * * *
Number of trials	2 x 5 = 10 aggressive 2 x 5 = 10 peaceful		15 aggressive 10 peaceful 2 x 5 = 10 self-related		10 aggressive 15 peaceful 2 x 5 = 10 self-related	

Note: The uneven category number in the combined blocks can result in two confounds:
If the number of key strokes on the right and left side is kept constant, twice as many stimuli belonging to the uncoupled evaluative category have to be presented.
If on the other hand the number of stimuli per category is kept constant, twice as many key strokes for the coupled categories result.
In order to reduce these inversely related problems, we presented coupled and uncoupled stimuli in a ratio of 4:3, thus reducing the ratio of evaluative stimuli to 3:2.

ful + *positive,* thus enabling quick responses, or they posed an incompatible combination, *aggressive* + *positive* and *peaceful* + *negative,* thus inducing slower responses. Afterwards the response-key assignments of the attribute categories were reversed, and participants had to train themselves to use the inverted attribute discrimination. The fifth block combined the attribute and target categories anew, yet the categories were coupled in the alternative way: If participants had encountered the compatible task in the third block first, they solved the incompatible task in the fifth block, and vice versa. The ST-IAT proceeded in a similar, yet simpler way (cf. Table 1). It provided only one block of training trials for the attribute discrimination (aggressive vs. peaceful) and two blocks in which self-related stimuli, for instance ME, MINE, had to be sorted together with aggressive or peaceful stimuli. We counterbalanced the order of the two combined blocks for each implicit measure between participants.

The degree of association between the categories is typically inferred from the difference of the mean response latencies between the two combined blocks (IAT effect). In the IAT, faster reactions in the *aggressive* + *negative* and *peaceful* + *positive* block than in the *aggressive* + *positive* and *peaceful* + *negative* indicate a negative automatic evaluation of aggressive behaviors. In the ST-IAT, any stronger association between the self and peaceful association will be evidenced in shorter latencies in the *self* + *peaceful* block than in the *self* + *aggressive* block, thus yielding an indicator for the automatic self-concept in terms of aggressiveness. The reaction time analysis requires a specific algorithm. In line with typical recommendations in the IAT literature, only correct trials entered the analyses (wrong key strokes yielded missing data) and response latencies were trimmed to 300 ms at minimum and 3000 ms at maximum. In order to control for method variance due to interindividual differences in means and standard deviations of response latencies, reactions times were *intra*individually standardized (cf. Cai, Sriram, Greenwald, & McFarland, 2004; Greenwald, Nosek, & Banaji, 2003). Although we used these z-like scores for the statistical tests, we report the dependent variables in units of milliseconds throughout the text in order to be as clear as possible. Due to the relatively few trials applied per block, the internal consistencies of the implicit measures were modest (r = .53 and .58, split-half reliability according to the odd-even method, Spearman-Brown corrected for scale length).

Results

Table 2 reports means and standard deviations of all the dependent variables.

Table 2. Analysis of Big Five-Specific and Aggression-Specific Questionnaires and Implicit Measures Assessing Aggression

	$\alpha_{N=196}$	$M_{Overall}$ (SD)	M_{FPS} (SD)	M_{PLAY} (SD)	M_{PC} (SD)
IPIP40					
Neuroticism	.89	2.32 (.78)	2.25 (.65)	2.37 (.83)	2.32 (.90)
Extraversion	.84	3.00 (.79)	3.15 (.70)	2.83 (.85)	3.10 (.77)
Openness	.76	3.53 (.63)	3.50 (.72)	3.48 (.57)	3.70 (.62)
Agreeableness	.70	3.54 (.58)	3.69 (.52)	3.33 (.62)	3.72 (.47)
Conscientiousness	.86	3.26 (.75)	3.10 (.77)	3.18 (.74)	3.66 (.63)
BPAQ					
Overall	.88	2.43 (.56)	2.47 (.51)	2.57 (.59)	2.08 (.40)
Physical Aggression	.82	1.87 (.71)	2.05 (.61)	1.93 (.83)	1.46 (.30)
Verbal Aggression	.61	2.99 (.59)	2.94 (.58)	3.18 (.57)	2.66 (.48)
Anger	.79	2.46 (.81)	2.47 (.77)	2.57 (.86)	2.18 (.72)
Hostility	.77	2.62 (.65)	2.58 (.56)	2.83 (.56)	2.26 (.64)
Implicit Measures					
IAT	.53	.99 (.36)	.98 (.36)	.90 (.40)	1.13 (.29)
ST-IAT	.58	.24 (.31)	.30 (.27)	.18 (.33)	.29 (.32)

Note: Analysis of Big Five-specific (IPIP40) and aggression-specific (BPAQ) questionnaires plus implicit measures assessing the automatic evaluation of aggressive behaviors (IAT) and the automatic aggressive self-concept (ST-IAT), N = 109, split for players of First-Person-Shooters (FPS), nonviolent games (PLAY), and a control group of users of personal computers (PC).

IPIP40 – Agreeableness: Testing the hypothesis that self-reported repeated computer playing is associated with lower agreeableness, an ANOVA revealed significant differences among the three groups, $F(2, 106) = 5.98$, $p = .003$, $\eta^2 = .10$. Mean values show that the PLAY group deviated from the PC control group, whereas FPS and PC were comparable.

BPAQ: More differentiated results are obtained by the analysis of aggression-specific traits. Overall, the BPAQ exhibited significant differences of aggressiveness among participants, $F(2, 106) = 6.93$, $p = .001$, $\eta^2 = .12$. On a conventional level of significance, only the BPAQ subscale *anger* failed to demonstrate reliable differences among the groups, $F(2, 106) = 4.66$, $p = .16$, $\eta^2 = .03$. By contrast, all other subscales displayed significantly lower scores for the PC control group: *physical aggression*, $F(2, 106) = 5.73$, $p = .004$, $\eta^2 = .10$, *verbal aggression*, $F(2, 106) = 6.86$, $p = .001$, $\eta^2 = .12$, and *hostility*, $F(2, 106) = 6.92$, $p = .001$, $\eta^2 = .12$. Posthoc analyses confirmed that FPS and PLAY did not differ significantly from each other, although PLAY descriptively received higher scores than FPS. Taken together, both groups of computer players differed from a PC control group.

Aggression Evaluation IAT: Before analyzing the implicit measures, we checked whether the groups differed from each other in terms of overall response speed which could indicate a potential bias due to differential experience with regard to PC use or responding quickly in PC games. This was not the case, $M = 987$ ms, $SD = 186$, $F(2, 106) = 1.00$, *ns*. As expected, the IAT effects of all three groups indicated that participants were quick to associate aggressive with negative (and peaceful with positive) but slow to associate the incompatible category arrangement (mean IAT effect = 446 ms). However, the PC control group was 522 ms faster in the compatible than in the incompatible block, whereas FPS and PLAY had smaller latency differences between the critical blocks (436 and 425 ms). Thus, the player groups associated aggressive with negative rather than with positive, too, but the negative association was not as strong as for PC control participants. This finding could be either due to *less negative* aggression-related associations or due to *more positive* aggression-related associations. Given the attenuated reliability of the implicit tasks, the omnibus F test in a 3 (target group: FPS, PLAY, PC) × 2 (order of blocks: compatible or incompatible block first) ANOVA failed to reliably discriminate between all three groups, $F(2, 103) = 2.20$, $p = .12$, $\eta^2 = .04$, yet contrasting both FPS and PLAY at once against PC confirmed the trend, $t(106) = 2.07$, $p = .04$. Order of blocks did not qualify the results in any way (F values < 1.40).

Aggressiveness Self-Concept ST-IAT. As expected, overall, participants associated themselves more easily with peaceful than with aggressive stimuli (mean ST-IAT effect = 117 ms). Conducting an analogous ANOVA on ST-IAT effects revealed a significant influence of order of blocks, such that participants had higher scores when starting with the *peaceful + self* block (181 vs. 53 ms). This influence probably reflects a methodological artifact, because the ST-IAT is a relatively simple sorting task with only three categories. However, the relative ease of the task is magnified as soon as one starts with the easier of the two blocks, whereas the relative difficulty increases when participants work through the block that is incompatible with their self-concept as a second step, thus giving rise to augmented ST-IAT effects in the compatible first condition. This effect does not occur in the incompatible first condition, when participants heighten their response criterion for correctly classifying stimuli from the very beginning of both blocks.

Comparing all three groups, PC showed the highest ST-IAT effect, that is, the strongest association of self and peaceful (140 ms), whereas PLAY had significantly lower scores (71 ms), $F(2, 103) = 3.18$, $p = .046$, $\eta^2 = .06$. However, FPS did not deviate from the PC control group (139 ms). If we interpret a lower ST-IAT effect as a stronger association of self and aggressive, then players of computer games that did not play FPS regularly tended to have a less peaceful automatic self-concept than FPS players.

Correlations: Across the whole sample, ST-IAT and IAT did not correlate, $r = .09$ ($p = .19$), lending support to the notion that automatic aggressive self-concept and automatic evaluation of aggressiveness are distinct concepts and that shared method variance did not affect the outcomes. Whereas the IAT did not correlate with BPAQ, $r = -.09$ ($p = .20$), the ST-IAT did show a weak negative relationship with self-reported aggressiveness, $r = -.17$ ($p = .021$). Thus, the less peaceful the automatic self-concept (lower ST-IAT effects), the higher trait aggressiveness.

Discussion

In general, the IAT and ST-IAT displayed reaction-time differences between the critical blocks that were in line with the hypothesized direction of automatic evaluation and self-concept. Moreover, they proved sensitive enough to detect differences among different groups of computer users. Nevertheless, we failed to find evidence for the hypothesis that the automatic evaluation of aggression and the automatic self-concept is most strongly affected by playing violent FPS. If we take the explicit measures as a comparison standard, then the implicit measures reflect the same trend that the PC control group was more agreeable and held less aggressive dispositions than the computer game players. Both explicit and implicit measures converge regarding the unexpected finding that players of FPS shooters were *less* affected than players of other games.

We can only speculate about why we found results that tended to support the opposite of our expectations regarding FPS and PLAY. Maybe the recruiting process suffered from self-selection despite the fact that we tried to conceal the true purpose of the study. There has been some discussion about FPS and their side-effects in the aftermath of school shootings in Germany and other countries worldwide. Perhaps some players of FPS tried to "prove" that they are harmless people, or some participants who observed negative side-effects of playing FPS voluntarily dropped out from the study. Both behaviors could be motivated by the goal not to endanger one's (positive) self-concept or to disconfirm existing (negative) stereotypes about the in-group. Another explanation could be that PLAY indeed was a group with higher aggressiveness, but we are unable to prove so as we did not control for the amount of violence exposure in non-FPS games. We used categories that allowed separation by the type of game, but we had better assessed the amount of playing and the amount of violence entailed in games so as to get an impression of each participant's amount of violence exposure. Note that playing modern racing games can result in violence exposure, too, just like playing modern sports games can require the use of aggressive tactics and performing virtual violence in order to succeed.

We also found no support for the notion that implicit measures are more sensitive than explicit measures in detecting side effects of computer playing. If this hypothesis was correct, there should be stronger effect sizes of ST-IAT and IAT in comparison to the effect sizes of questionnaires. Obviously, this was not the case. Whether this simply reflects the fact that reliability of implicit measures is not yet optimal or whether the hypothesis really does not hold cannot be judged by the current data. Another idea could be that assessing automatic self-concept works better if relying on a *relative* implicit measure despite our initial reasoning that the "other" category might introduce unwanted error variance (Pinter & Greenwald, 2005). Thus, Uhlmann and Swanson (2004) as well as Banse and colleagues (2005) might have confirmed their hypotheses, because they used an IAT that requested a *necessary* or at least very *helpful* social comparison by making use of the opposite category "other."

Supplementary Data: We sought additional evidence in a more controlled setting, because in Internet studies a researcher simply has to assume that (potentially more) disturbances and (potentially lower) commitment do not affect the outcomes. We furthermore wanted to preclude self-selection and instead recruit a quite homogeneous sample in terms of socio-demographic variables. Although this step decreases external validity and generalizability, it should be potentially useful in reducing error variance, thus raising the power of the statistical analyses. Therefore, we drew a sample of student classes at school (9th grade; age ~ 15 yrs.), as playing PC games has become quite common among students and adolescents and because these groups might contain the most vulnerable subgroup of gamers (Gentile & Anderson, 2003). We also asked for the specific games each individual had played and the amount of playing a week before. We thus estimated an individuals' violence exposure by summing the hours of playing a game weighted by the violence rating of a game (Krahé & Möller, 2004). Finally, we replaced the evaluative IAT by a Self–Other IAT that addressed the self-concept in a relative manner and that had been successfully applied by two groups of researchers in the past. As we wanted to compare the usefulness of ST-IAT and IAT tapping into the aggressive self-concept, we also employed the nonrelative ST-IAT. To prevent priming of the "other" category and stimulation of social comparison processes in the ST-IAT, we always administered the ST-IAT ahead of the IAT.

Overall, the procedure and measures of the additional study conceptually mirrored the first one. However, for practical reasons, we administered the questionnaire assessing socio-demographic variables and game consumption as well as the IPIP40 in the classroom in a first wave one week prior to the administration of implicit tasks and the BPAQ, which in turn were administered in small groups of up to four students in a separate room at school (second wave). After having obtained consent from school headmasters, teachers, and parents, 86 participants (M_{age} = 14.79 yrs., SD = .95) from two schools (three high school classes and three secondary school classes) completed the study in both phases. Males dominated less (62%) than in the previous study. About a quarter of the students had a non-German ethnic background. After examination of the implicit measures, 16 participants had to be excluded because of more than 20% errors per critical block.

The controlled situation provided the means for answering students' questions and ensuring that the implicit procedures were understood and carried out appropriately.

Having solved the self-selection problem of the previous study, we were interested if the more homogeneous sample would reveal that implicit measures are indeed sensitive to the amount of violence exposure in computer games. Therefore, we used a dummy coding for type of school and sex of participant. Violence exposure was a continuous variable. However, violence exposure did not account for variance in any of the explicit and implicit indicators. The only significant relationship existed between type of school and ST-IAT such that participants from secondary school had lower ST-IAT effects (25 ms) than those from high school (114 ms), $\beta = -.272, p = .02$. Although this finding could be interpreted in line with stereotypical perceptions of aggression of students from different school types, we do not accept this interpretation because of many other differences that exist between the groups as explained below.

In light of these disappointing findings, one could doubt the use of implicit measures. But instead of abandoning the use of IATs, some problems that have to be overcome have to be addressed. There were some major obstacles in our additional study. Though the 9th grade is the maximum level of Germans' minimal education, many students had difficulties in understanding the meaning of questions in the standard questionnaires IPIP40 and BPAQ. The same problem occurred with the stimuli employed in the (ST-)IATs which were held constant with Study 1. Participants' interruptions and the experimenter's explanations of the semantic meaning of certain stimuli imply that there were many problems with spontaneity during the categorization tasks, rendering the interpretation of the latencies as indexes for spontaneous or automatic associations at least equivocal. Thus, we cannot expect these measures to have acceptable psychometric qualities in terms of reliability (Cronbach's α for ST-IAT and IAT .55, IPIP40 .49 – .78; BPAQ .60 – .68; cf. Study 1) and, more importantly, validity. Similar problems will always occur whenever the participants' language abilities are insufficient to deal with the stimulus materials, thus questioning the application of unaltered implicit measures to students and children in particular. We did not expect such problems with 9th graders, but experience convinced us to do so in future studies. When examining such participant groups, a solution to this problem could be the use of pictures as stimuli, the disposal of age-inappropriate semantic content, and simpler task procedures (Mienert, Scheer, & Frey, 2005).

In conclusion, we suggest that optimizing the stimulus materials and the reliability of the implicit measures seems to be the next major step in aggression research. Following the difficulties in our additional study, this optimization also addresses explicit questionnaires that should be suitable for the examination of juveniles. Unless these methodological changes are made, we cannot expect to find consistent and substantive evidence confirming or disconfirming any relationship between aggressive dispositions and violence exposure in young computer gamers. In the beginning of this chapter, we addressed the topic that explicit measures suffer from specific limitations. We have to admit here that implicit measures also have their weaknesses. Nevertheless, implicit measures provide an interesting methodology that should be used more frequently in aggression research. The mere possibility to predict spontaneous aggressive behaviors by utilizing implicit tools should inspire researchers to examine the relationships between violence exposure, automatic affective processes, and actual aggression by taking a still uncommon, yet promising methodological approach.

References

Amelang, M., & Bartussek, D. (1997). *Differentielle Psychologie und Persönlichkeitsforschung* [Differential Psychology and Personality Research]. Stuttgart, Germany: Kohlhammer.

Anderson, C. A. (2004). An update on the effects of playing violent video games. *Journal of Adolescence, 27*, 113–122.

Anderson, C. A., & Bushman, J. B. (2001). Effects of violent video games on aggressive behavior, aggressive cognition, aggressive affect, physiological arousal, and prosocial behavior: A meta-analytic review of the scientific literature. *Psychological Science, 12*, 353–359.

Anderson, C. A., & Bushman, B. J. (2002). Human aggression. *Annual Review of Psychology, 53*, 27–51.

Anderson, C. A., & Carnagey, N. L. (2004). Violent evil and the general aggression model. In A. Miller (Ed.), *The social psychology of good and evil* (pp. 168–192). New York: Guilford Publications.

Anderson, C. A., & Dill, K. E. (2000). Video game and aggressive thoughts, feelings, and behavior in the laboratory and in life. *Journal of Personality and Social Psychology, 78*, 772–790.

Asendorpf, J. B., Banse, R., & Mücke, D. (2002). Double dissociation between implicit and explicit personality self-concept: The case of shy behavior. *Journal of Personality and Social Psychology, 83*, 380–393.

Banse, R., Clarbour, J., & Fischer, I. (2005). *Implicit and explicit aggressiveness, social desirability, and the prediction of aggressive behaviour.* Manuscript in preparation.

Banse, R., & Fischer, I. (2002, July). *Implicit and explicit aggressiveness and the prediction of aggressive behavior.* Poster presented at the 11th European Conference on Personality of the European Society for Personality Psychology, Jena, Germany.

Bargh, J. A. (1994). The four horsemen of automaticity: Awareness, intention, efficiency, and control in social cognition. In: R. S. Wyer & T. Srull (Eds), *Handbook of Social Cognition*: Vol. 1. Basic Processes (2nd ed., pp. 1–41). Hillsdale, NJ: Erlbaum.

Bargh, J. A. (2006). What have we been priming all these years? On the development, mechanisms, and ecology of nonconscious social behavior. *European Journal of Social Psychology, 36*, 147–168.

Bargh, J., & Chartrand, T. (1999). The unbearable automaticity of being. *American Psychologist, 54*, 462–479.

Bless, H., & Fiedler, K. (1995). Affective states and the influence of activated general knowledge. *Personality and Social Psychology Bulletin, 21*, 766–778.

Bluemke, M. & Friese, M. (2006). Do features of stimuli influence IAT effects? *Journal of Experimental Social Psychology, 42*, 163–176.

Bosson, J. K., Swann, Jr., W. B., & Pennebaker, J. W. (2000). Stalking the perfect measure of implicit self-esteem: The blind men and the elephant revisited? *Journal of Personality and Social Psychology, 79*, 631–643.

Buchanan, T., Johnson, J. A., & Goldberg, L. R. (2005). Implementing a five-factor personality inventory for use on the Internet. *European Journal of Psychological Assessment, 21*, 115–127.

Buss, A. H., & Perry, M. (1992). The aggression questionnaire. *Journal of Personality and Social Psychology, 63*, 452–459.

Cai, H., Sriram, N., Greenwald, A. G., & McFarland, S. G. (2004). The Implicit Association Test's *D* measure can minimize a cognitive skill confound: Comment on McFarland and Crouch (2002). *Social Cognition, 22*, 673–684.

Clore, G. L., Schwarz, N., & Conway, M. (1994). Cognitive causes and consequences of emotions. In R. S. Wyer & T. K. Srull (Eds.), *Handbook of social cognition* (2nd ed., Vol. 1, pp. 323–417). Hillsdale, NJ: Erlbaum.

Durkin, K., & Barber, D. E. (2002). Not so doomed: Computer game play and positive adolescent development. *Applied Developmental Psychology, 23*, 373–392.

Epstein, S. (1994). Integration of the cognitive and the psychodynamic unconscious. *American Psychologist, 49*, 709–724.

Fazio, R. H. (1986). How do attitudes guide behavior? In R. M. Sorrentino and E. T. Higgins (Eds.), *Handbook of motivation and cognition: Foundations of social behavior* (pp. 204–243). New York: The Guilford Press.

Fazio, R. H. (2001). On the automatic activation of associated evaluations: An overview. *Cognition and Emotion, 15*, 115–141.

Fazio, R. H., Jackson, J. R., Dunton, B. C., & Williams, C. J. (1995). Variability in automatic activation as an unobtrusive measure of racial attitudes: A bona fide pipeline? *Journal of Personality and Social Psychology, 69*, 1013–1027.

Fiedler, K., Messner, C., & Bluemke, M. (2006). Unresolved problems with the "I", the "A" and the "T": Logical and psychometric critique of the Implicit Association Test (IAT). *European Review of Social Psychology, 17*, 74–147.

Friese, M., Wänke, M., & Plessner, H. (2006). Implicit consumer preferences and their influence on product choice. *Psychology and Marketing, 23,* 727–740.

Gentile, D. A., & Anderson, C. A. (2003). Violent video games: The newest media violence hazard. In D. Gentile (Ed.), *Media violence and children* (pp. 131–152). Westport, CT: Praeger.

Goldberg, L. R. (2001). *International Personality Item Pool. A scientific collaboratory for the development of advanced measures of personality traits and other individual differences.* Retrieved April 28, 2005 from http://ipip.ori.org.

Greenwald, A. G., & Farnham, S. D. (2000). Using the Implicit Association Test to measure self-esteem and self-concept. *Journal of Personality and Social Psychology, 79*, 1022–1038.

Greenwald, A. G., McGhee, D. E., & Schwartz, J. K. L. (1998). Measuring individual differences in implicit cognition: The Implicit Association Test. *Journal of Personality and Social Psychology, 74*, 1464–1480.

Greenwald, A. G., & Nosek, B. A. (2001). Health of the Implicit Association Test at age 3. *Experimental Psychology, 48*, 85–93.

Greenwald, A. G., Nosek, B. A., & Banaji, M. R. (2003). Understanding and using the Implicit Association Test: I. An improved scoring algorithm. *Journal of Personality and Social Psychology, 85*, 197–216.

Hartig, J., Jude, N., & Rauch, W. (2003). *Entwicklung und Erprobung eines deutschen Big-Five-Fragebogens auf Basis des International Personality Item Pools (IPIP40)* [Development and testing of a German Big Five questionnaire based on the International Personality Item Pools (IPIP40)]. (Arbeiten aus dem Institut für Psychologie der Johann Wolfgang Goethe-Universität, Heft 1, 2003). Frankfurt, Germany: Johann Wolfgang Goethe-Universität, Institut für Psychologie.

Herzberg, P. Y. (2003). Faktorstruktur, Gütekriterien und Konstruktvalidität der deutschen Übersetzung des Aggressionsfragebogens von Buss und Perry [Factor structure, psychometric properties, and construct validity of the German aggression questionnaire by Buss and Perry]. *Zeitschrift für Differentielle und Diagnostische Psychologie, 24*, 311–323.

Hofmann, W., Gschwendner, T., Castelli, L., & Schmitt, M. (2006). *Implicit and explicit attitudes and interracial interaction: The moderating role of situationally available control resources.* Unpublished manuscript.

Hogarth, R. (2002, October). *Deciding analytically or trusting your intuition? The advantages and disadvantages of analytic and intuitive thought.* UPF Economics and Business Working Paper No. 654. Retrieved June 18, 2006 from http://www.recercat.net/bitstream/2072/799/1/654.pdf.

Karpinski, A. (2004). Measuring self-esteem using the Implicit Association Test: The role of the other. *Personality and Social Psychology Bulletin, 30*, 22–34.

Karpinski, A., & Steinman, R. B. (2006). The Single Category Implicit Association Test as a measure of implicit social cognition. *Journal of Personality and Social Psychology, 91*, 16–32.

Krahé, B., & Möller, I. (2004). Playing violent electronic games, hostile attribution bias, and aggression-related norms in German adolescents. *Journal of Adolescence, 27*, 53–69.

Lazarus, R. S. (1991). *Emotion and adaptation.* New York: Oxford University Press.

Lindsay, L. L., & Anderson, C. A. (2000). From antecedent conditions to violent actions: A general affective aggression model. *Personality and Social Psychology Bulletin, 26*, 533–547.

Mienert, M., Scheer, B., & Frey, A. (2005, November). *Implicit and explicit measures of aggressive behavioral tendencies of adolescents – results of an intervention study.* Paper presented at the X. Workshop Aggression, Universität Luxembourg, Luxembourg.

Pinter, B., & Greenwald, A. G. (2005). Clarifying the role of the "other" category in the self-esteem IAT. *Experimental Psychology, 52*, 74–79.

Scott, D. (1995). The effect of video games on feelings of aggression. *The Journal of Psychology, 129*, 121–132.

Sherman, S. J., Rose, J. S., Koch, K., Presson, C. C., & Chassin, L. (2003). Implicit and explicit attitudes toward cigarette smoking: The effects of context and motivation. *Journal of Social and Clinical Psychology, 22*, 13–39.

Strack, F., & Deutsch, R. (2004). Reflective and impulsive determinants of social behavior. *Personality and Social Psychology Review, 8*, 220–247.

Teachman, B. A., Gregg, A. P., & Woody, S. R. (2001). Implicit associations for fear-relevant stimuli among individuals with snake and spider fears. *Journal of Abnormal Psychology, 110*, 226–235.

Uhlmann, E., & Swanson, J. (2004). Exposure to violent video games increases automatic aggressiveness. *Journal of Adolescence, 27*, 41–52.

von Collani, G., & Werner, R. (2005). Self-related and motivational constructs as determinants of aggression: An analysis and validation of a German version of the Buss-Perry aggression questionnaire. *Personality and Individual Differences, 38*, 1631–1643.

Wigboldus, D. H. J., Holland, R. W., & van Knippenberg, A. (2004). *Single target implicit associations.* Unpublished manuscript.

Williams, D., & Skoric, M. (2005). Internet fantasy violence: A test of aggression in an online game. *Communication Monographs, 72*, 217–233.

Wilson, T. D., Lindsey, S., & Schooler, T. Y. (2000). A model of dual attitudes. *Psychological Review, 107*, 101–126.

Part 3

Anger and Aggression

Angry Emotions and Aggressive Behaviors

Roy F. Baumeister and Brad J. Bushman

Everybody gets angry, but angry feelings do not always lead to aggression and violence. Consider two people who appeared in the news for how they responded to receiving junk e-mail or spam. The first person is Charles Booher, a 44-year-old computer programmer (Tanner, 2003). Booher was arrested for threatening to torture and kill employees of the company who bombarded his computer with spam ads. According to prosecutors, Booher threatened to mail a "package full of Anthrax spores" to the company, to "disable" an employee with a bullet and torture him with a power drill and ice pick; and to hunt down and castrate the employees unless they removed him from their e-mail list. Booher used intimidating return e-mail addresses such as Satan@hell.org. Booher said he used the threats because the company had rendered his computer almost unusable for about two months by a flood of pop-up advertising and e-mail messages. Booher was arrested and later released on $75,000 bond.

The second person is Brad Turcotte, a 26-year-old musician (Whyte, 2003). Turcotte was also flooded with spam ads. He said, "I was just staring at my inbox one day and looking at all these ridiculous subject lines" – such as "Feel Better Now," "Look and Feel Years Younger," and "Do You Measure Up," to name but a few – "and I started thinking that some of these were pretty surreal and bizarre. And at the same time, I had been having trouble coming up with titles for some of my songs, so I started thinking that maybe there was something here." He recruited other musicians through the Internet, and together they compiled a CD (called "Outside The Inbox") that contains 14 songs with spam titles. Although everybody hates getting spam, Booher and Turcotte responded very differently to it.

We define *emotion* as a subjective state, often accompanied by a bodily reaction (e.g., increased heart rate) and an evaluative response, to some event. Some emotions (such as anger, frustration, shame and humiliation) increase aggression, whereas other emotions (such as guilt) decrease aggression.

We define *aggression* as any behavior that is intended to harm another person who is motivated to avoid the harm (Baron & Richardson, 1994). Thus, whereas emotion is a feeling state, aggression is a behavior.

Although no one denies that emotions can play an important role in causing aggression, the debates have been frequent and fierce as to what role emotions play. In this chapter we discuss theoretical perspectives on emotion and aggression. We also review the research on the role of specific emotions on aggression.

Theoretical Perspectives

Frustration-Aggression Hypothesis

In their 1939 book *Frustration and Aggression*, Yale researchers Dollard, Doob, Miller, Mowrer, and Sears proposed the frustration-aggression hypothesis. The two main points of their hypothesis were: (a) "the occurrence of aggressive behavior always presupposes the existence of frustration" (p. 1), and (b) "the existence of frustration always leads to some form of aggression" (p. 1). They defined frustration as "an interference with the occurrence of an instigated goal response at its proper time in the behavior sequence" (p. 7). In other words, an event is frustrating if it blocks with one's ability to achieve a goal.

The early writings of Sigmund Freud (1917) formed the basis of the frustration-aggression hypothesis. Freud argued that people are motivated to seek pleasure and avoid pain, and when these motives are blocked people become frustrated. Freud regarded aggression as the "primordial reaction" to frustration. Later, Freud revised his opinions and began to propose that some aggression derives from an innate drive or instinct (e.g., Freud, 1920, 1930). The view that aggression is innate and instinctual was controversial then, and still is now. By insisting that frustration always preceded aggression, Dollard and his colleagues offered a formula that dispensed with any need to postulate an aggressive instinct. The widespread reality of aggression could be understood in terms of frustration.

Over the years it became obvious that Dollard and his colleagues had substantially overstated the role of frustration in causing aggression. Hence, Miller (1941), one of the original authors of *Frustration and Aggression*, revised the second statement that frustration always leads to aggression. He recommended that the statement be changed to: "Frustration produces instigations to a number of different types of response, one of which is an instigation to some form of aggression" (p. 338). Miller believed that the first statement of the hypothesis was true (i.e., aggression is *always* preceded by frustration).

Revised Frustration-Aggression Hypothesis

Fifty years after the frustration aggression hypothesis was proposed, Berkowitz (1989) proposed a reformulation. Recognizing that many acts of aggression do not follow from any apparent frustration, Berkowitz proposed that all unpleasant events – instead of only frustration – deserve to be recognized as causes of aggression. Aversive events can be either nonsocial (e.g., physical pain, extreme temperatures, loud noises, unpleasant odors, smoke) or social (e.g., interpersonal frustration and provocation). Berkowitz also proposed that negative affect, an unpleasant emotional state, is the mediator between aversive events and aggression. That is, aversive events cause these states of negative affect to arise. Negative affect, in turn, causes aggression. Berkowitz's theory is thus the broadest statement about the link between emotions and aggressiveness. From Berkowitz's perspective, any sort of bad feeling is likely to increase aggressive tendencies.

Critics, however, suggest that it may be too broad to say that all negative affect increases aggression. There is a broad range of bad moods and unpleasant emotional states, and many of them have not been shown to cause aggression. Berkowitz extrapolated from a limited range of findings to propose the generalization that all negative affect increases aggression, but this must be recognized as an extrapolation rather than a proven fact. In any case, the next generation of research can build on Berkowitz's theory to determine more precisely what negative emotional states cause aggression and under what circumstances they do so.

Catharsis Theory

One of the most influential theories about the links between aggression and emotion is catharsis theory. The first recorded usage of the term catharsis was in Aristotle's *Poetics*, in which he proposed that the audience of a play experiences an emotional purging as a result of the drama they witness. The term catharsis literally means cleansing or purging.

The central point of the catharsis theory of aggression is that negative emotions such as anger build up over time but can be released or vented by participating in aggressive acts, or even by watching others behave aggressively (such as in violent films). In this view, hostile feelings are either kept inside or let out through aggressive activity. Two important consequences of aggression are central to the catharsis theory. First, getting rid of the bad feelings (even by means of aggression) is good for you, whereas holding them inside is bad for you. Second, aggressive tendencies are reduced by means of aggressive acts, because the negative emotions and impulses that are released by aggressive action are removed from the self, and so the subsequent urge to aggress is diminished.

Catharsis is an especially important concept in relation to theories that regard aggression as innate or instinctual behavior. Such theories assume that aggressive tendencies will build up over time regardless of what happens in one's surroundings, because aggression derives from natural and innate drives. By refusing to aggress, the person will keep these impulses inside, where they may be harmful. Finding ways to express them is natural and healthy.

In psychology, the most influential statement of the catharsis theory was by Freud. In one of his earliest writings, he and Breuer proposed that the treatment of hysteria required the discharge of the emotional state that was previously associated with the trauma (Breuer & Freud, 1955). They claimed that for interpersonal traumas, such as insults and threats to the ego, emotional expression could be obtained through direct aggression: "The reaction of an injured person to a trauma has really only a 'cathartic' effect if it is expressed in an adequate reaction like revenge." Breuer and Freud believed that expressing anger was much better than bottling it up inside. They also considered substitute targets as effective for catharsis.

Other psychologists have agreed with Freud's position. In their book *Frustration and Aggression*, Dollard and his colleagues (1939) asserted that, "The expression of any act of aggression is a catharsis that reduces the instigation to all other acts of aggression" (p. 53). Even today, popular psychologists like to assert that expressing aggression (preferably by seemingly innocuous means such as hitting a pillow) will reduce aggressive tendencies (e.g., Lee, 1993). In some therapies, couples are encouraged to hit each other with foam bats that do not cause injury. An important extension of catharsis theory has proposed that viewing violence can provide release, and so it is supposedly healthy and socially beneficial to watch violent movies or play violent video games, which are predicted to lead to reductions in actual aggressive actions.

Unfortunately the facts and findings do not support catharsis theory. Venting anger tends to make people more aggressive afterward (Geen & Quanty, 1977). Venting anger is also linked to higher risk of heart disease (Lewis & Bucher, 1992). Even among people who believe in the value of venting and catharsis, and even when people enjoy their venting and feel some satisfaction from it, they are more likely to become aggressive after venting (Bushman, Baumeister, & Stack, 1999). Likewise, viewing violence and playing violent video games make people more aggressive, rather than less aggressive (Anderson & Bushman, 2001, 2002).

Affect Regulation Theory

Another very important link between emotion and aggression involves self-control. Possibly the most sweeping and influential statement of that link is described in the book *A General Theory of Crime* (Gottfredson & Hirschi, 1990). The criminologists who wrote this book concluded that low self-control is the single most important factor for understanding criminal and violent behavior. They provided plenty of data to back up their theory. For one thing, criminals seem to be impulsive individuals who simply don't show much respect for rules in general. In the movies, criminals often specialize in one specific kind of crime, almost like any other job. But in reality, most criminals are arrested multiple times – for different crimes. If self-control is a general capacity for bringing one's behavior into line with rules and standards, criminals lack this capacity. Another sign is that the lives of criminals show low self-control even in behaviors that are not against the law (e.g., smoking cigarettes, unplanned pregnancies, failure to show up for work or school regularly).

A similar conclusion was reached from different evidence by Baumeister (1997), who acknowledged the wide assortment of factors that have been shown to cause violence and concluded that the traditional question of "Why does violence occur?" should be at least partly supplanted by the question "Why isn't there more violence than there is?" After all, who hasn't experienced numerous factors that increase aggression, such as frustration, anger, insult, alcohol, media violence, or hot weather in the past year? Yet most people do not hurt or kill anyone. These factors may give rise to violent impulses, but mostly people have learned to control these impulses.

Emotional distress is generally recognized as a powerful impediment to effective self-control (Baumeister, Heatherton, & Tice, 1994). When people are upset, they lose or abandon their ordinary ability to control their behavior. Several effects of emotional distress appear to contribute to these breakdowns in self-control, which can then allow aggressive behavior to emerge. One way that emotional distress contributes to aggression is by curtailing decision-making, leading people to engage in high-risk, high-payoff behaviors. In a series of studies (Leith & Baumeister, 1996), research participants chose between several options that varied in their level of risk. The choice was specifically structured so that choosing the low-risk option was objectively the better decision. Most participants seem to have recognized this and chose the low-risk option, but participants who were experiencing emotional distress showed a strong preference for the high-risk, high-payoff option. These shifts in choice patterns were mediated by a tendency to not think through all the possible outcomes and contingencies. Instead, people who were distressed simply jumped at the chance to do something that seemed appealing. Although this series of studies did not specifically include measures of aggression, it seems clear that aggression is often a high-risk option in many situations, because attacking someone carries the risk that one may be injured or killed (or may incur other costs, such as arrest). Angry or upset people may therefore give in to violent impulses without pausing to consider the potential negative consequences of their risky behavior.

Another way that emotional distress contributes to aggression is based on the self-control of emotion. Sometimes people give priority to their feelings and the prospect of feeling better, as opposed to doing what might be best in the long run. In a conflict situation, for example, people may feel like using aggression or force to get their way, but in recognition of the potential dangers and drawbacks of aggression they may hold back. Emotionally upset people may however believe that attacking their opponent would make them feel better, and so they may aggress as a means of regulating their emotions (i.e., bringing about an improvement in mood). In essence, they decide to regulate their feelings rather than regulate their aggressive impulses and behavior.

Support for the affect regulation theory of aggression was found in a series of laboratory studies by Bushman, Baumeister, and Phillips (2001). Participants were angered by means of having a confederate criticize an essay they had written. In one study, half the participants were led to believe that aggressing would make them feel better, such as by causing a catharsis that would purge their unpleasant, angry feelings. In another study, participants' own naturally occurring beliefs in the benefits of expressing one's anger were assessed. One finding was that people showed higher aggression when they believed that aggression would make them feel better.

The crucial manipulation, however, involved telling some participants that their emotional states were "frozen" and thus not subject to change. This was accomplished by giving them a pill and telling them (falsely) that the pill (actually vitamin B6) had been shown to have a side effect – it would freeze their mood for about an hour. This manipulation effectively makes affect regulation impossible: Nothing you do will make you feel better. This manipulation eliminated the aggressive responses to the insult. Even people who believed that aggression normally makes a person feel better refrained from aggression when they had been told that their moods were frozen.

Taken together, these findings indicate that people sometimes aggress as a way of improving their mood. Some people believe that expressing their anger, even by means of aggressive behavior, will help them purge their angry feelings and end up in a more pleasant state. These people are normally prone to deal with their feelings of anger by aggressing against the person whom they hold responsible. But if they believe that their moods have been artificially frozen and cannot be changed, they cease to aggress. When affect regulation is supposedly impossible, aggression is diminished.

In the next section we discuss the role of specific emotions on aggression. Some of these emotions (i.e., anger, shame and humiliation, sadistic pleasure) increase aggression, whereas other emotions (i.e., guilt) decrease aggression.

Role of Specific Emotions on Aggression

Anger

Anger is an emotional response to a real or imagined threat or provocation. Anger can range in intensity from mild irritation to uncontrollable rage. Anger is associated with

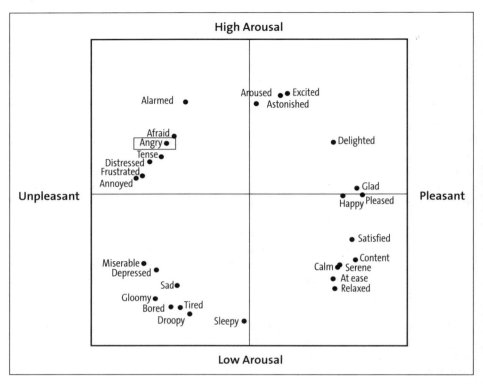

Figure 1. Emotions can be sorted into four categories, defined by crossing the pleasant versus unpleasant dimension with the high versus low arousal dimension (Russell, 1980). Anger is in the unpleasant, high arousal category.

aggression in popular beliefs, and in this case the popular beliefs are correct: Anger does indeed increase aggression. Aggression researchers have found that many other variables only produce aggression in combination with anger. For example, nonangry people who drink alcohol do not typically become more aggressive, but when alcohol combines with anger people do become more aggressive (Bushman, 1997; Bushman & Cooper, 1990). Likewise, media violence alone often fails to increase in aggression, but media violence combined with anger can produce an increase in aggression (Berkowitz & Geen, 1966; Geen & Berkowitz, 1967). In other words, alcohol and media violence only cause aggression in combination with anger. Researchers who are interested in the effects of alcohol or media violence therefore induce anger in their research participants even though the researchers are not specifically interested in the effects of anger.

As with frustration, the link between anger and aggression should not be overstated. People often become angry without behaving aggressively, and some aggression occurs in the absence of anger. Thus, anger is neither necessary nor sufficient to cause aggression (see Averill, 1982; Tavris, 1989). Still, anger is an important and powerful cause of aggression.

Current research sorts emotions into four categories, defined by crossing unpleasant versus pleasant feelings with high versus low arousal (see Figure 1). Anger falls in the unpleasant, high arousal category. Anger therefore both feels bad and arouses or energizes the person. Angry people are thus highly motivated to take action, because the unpleasant feeling makes people want to do something to bring about a change, and the high arousal contributes to initiative.

The tendency to take action does not mean that effective or desirable actions are taken. In fact, angry people often act foolishly. Research shows that angry people are especially likely to take high-risk, high-payoff courses of action that often backfire and produce disastrous consequences (Leith & Baumeister, 1996). Anger makes people downplay risks and overlook dangers (Lerner, Gonzalez, Small, & Fischhoff, 2003; Lerner & Keltner, 2001).). Angry people also become more optimistic that their actions will be effective (Lerner et al., 2003).

Guilt

Guilt is a negative emotional feeling that is usually associated with some implicit reproach that one has acted badly or wrongly. By and large, everyone occasionally does something wrong, and so the difference between people lies in whether one feels bad about it or not. Guilt is especially associated with acts that could damage a relationship about which one cares.

It is useful to distinguish guilt from shame (Tangney & Dearing, 2002). The difference lies in how widely the bad feeling is generalized. Guilt focuses narrowly on the action, whereas shame spreads to the whole person. Guilt says, "I did a bad thing." Shame says, "I am a bad person." In this section we discuss the role of guilt on aggression, and we discuss the role of shame on aggression in the next section.

Guilt is an important cause of prosocial behavior and an important potential restraint on aggression. Although a misreading of psychodynamic theories caused many people in the past to regard guilt as an antisocial, pathological feeling that caused neurosis while accomplishing little of value, the weight of expert opinion has shifted substantially toward a more favorable view of guilt in light of studies that attested to its positive effects.

Guilt appears to be strongly linked to empathy and to the desire to maintain good interpersonal relationships (Hoffman, 1982; Tangney, 1991). The prototype cause of guilt is causing harm or suffering to somebody one cares about (Baumeister, Stillwell, & Heatherton, 1994). Thus, because aggression is often a central means of causing such suffering, guilt may be an important mechanism for punishing and preventing aggression. To the extent that people wish to avoid guilt, they should refrain from aggressing and causing harm to other people.

Assorted evidence confirms the value of guilt for reducing aggression. Research has shown that guilt tendencies are associated with lower levels of anger, hostility, resentment, and even lower self-reports of assaultive behavior toward others, even after one corrects for shame tendencies (Tangney, Wagner, Fletcher, & Gramzow, 1992). Even more dramatic evidence comes from studies of people who seem to lack any sense of guilt. These people, typically known as psychopaths, are notoriously prone to criminal and violent behavior. Although psychopaths make up less than 1% of the population, they account for 50% of serious crimes (Hare, 1993). Psychopaths are not mentally ill in the usual sense, because they can function effectively in society and are well aware of its norms, rules, and expectations. Psychopaths know the difference between right and wrong, but they simply do not care all that much about it. In a sense, they are ruthless pragmatists who are willing to victimize others for the sake of their own self-interest. Lacking a sense of guilt, they do not feel any distress or inner turmoil over bringing suffering to others (even those who are close to them). Guilt is an important emotion that causes people to respect the welfare of others and feel bad whenever they cause others to suffer.

Guilt appears to arise most strongly in the context of close relationships, and indeed some studies suggest that guilt is more strongly linked than other emotions to close relationship contexts (Baumeister, Reis, & Delespaul, 1995). For example, people may feel fear or irritation toward strangers, but guilt is mostly reserved for partners in relationships. Hence guilt will be most effective at discouraging aggression between people who know each other.

In practice, the power of guilt for restraining and discouraging aggression entails that aggressors must often find a way to deal with their guilt. Psychopaths may be able to inflict harm without feeling guilty, but psychopaths only constitute 1% of the population. Most people are prone to feel moderate to acute guilt when they hurt someone. Baumeister (1997) surveyed an assortment of techniques that aggressors use to minimize their feelings of guilt. Some aggressors seek to distance themselves from their victims by regarding them as thoroughly unrelated and dissimilar to the self, even to the extent of speaking of victims as less than human. Others downplay the amount that the victim suffered and regard their aggressive acts as trivial or ephemeral matters. Others rely on complex rationalizations that justify their actions or depict the aggression as having benefited the victim. Others deny their responsibility by insisting they had no choice. Many others use alcohol to escape from full awareness of what they were doing.

Shame

An important set of emotional causes of violence and aggression consists of the feelings that arise when one's pride, reputation, or self-esteem is impugned or threatened by others. Threats to self-esteem set off feelings of anger, shame, and humiliation. Shame involves a global condemnation of the self ("I am a bad person"), coming usually after some misdeed. Shame may also become acute when some other person calls attention to possible or alleged shortcomings in the self.

Shame evokes a variety of responses, only some of which are aggressive. Shame is often experienced as an unsolvable problem – after all, if the whole self is bad, there is not much that can be easily done. In this respect, shame contrasts sharply with guilt, because guilt focuses narrowly on a specific action, and its ill effects can often be addressed. Guilt therefore motivates people to apologize, make amends, resolve to change their future behavior, or in other ways repair any interpersonal damage that may have been done (see Baumeister, Stillwell, & Heatherton, 1994). Shame, in contrast, creates a sense of helplessness, and so the person may withdraw and hide from social contact. Alternatively, shame may cause the person to lash out aggressively.

Research has shown that shame-prone people reported higher levels of anger arousal, suspiciousness toward others, resentment, and irritability (Tangney et al., 1992). Shame-prone people were more likely than others to shift the blame for problems onto other people, away from themselves. Shame-prone people showed a pronounced tendency to engage in indirect hostility toward others. Shame was also linked with many measures of trait anger and angry dispositions. The authors favored the interpretation that shame leads to anger and aggression. In their view, shame is highly aversive and is experienced as unfair, in part because it condemns the whole self as bad, which strikes the person as an excessive response to an individual misdeed. The shamed person may therefore regard other people as the source of unfair treatment and become indignant and angry toward them. Thus, the shamed person feels acutely bad and refuses to accept that bad feeling, blames his or her own distress on others, and becomes angry and potentially aggressive toward them (see also Retzinger, 1991).

The link between shame and aggression had contributed to the view, once widespread and still popular in some quarters, that low self-esteem was a significant cause of aggression. The belief was that people with low self-esteem were especially prone to experience bad feelings about the self and therefore would be most likely to exhibit aggressive, violent tendencies. The link is more apparent than real; after all, the key for aggression is that the person is unwilling to feel shame, and people with high rather than low self-esteem may be more unwilling to feel shame. Although precious little data and no major theoretical statement can be found in the literature to articulate the view that low self-esteem causes aggression, the assumption was widely cited and repeated (e.g., Horney, 1950).

However, a literature review by Baumeister, Smart, and Boden (1996) found no evidence for the view that low self-esteem causes aggression. These authors found that the self-images of aggressive, violent people were typically quite favorable, contrary to the assumption that low self-esteem would be widespread among them. Where groups differed in their average self-esteem, the more aggressive group was typically the one with higher self-esteem. Violent groups and violent individuals often expressed strong views of their superiority over others.

Baumeister and his colleagues (1996) concluded that threatened egotism was the most important link between self-appraisal and aggression. That is, violent and aggressive behavior was most likely when people hold a favorable opinion of themselves and then encounter someone else who disputes that favorable opinion, such as by delivering an insult or showing disrespect. The insulted person may therefore attack the source of the insult, as a way of rejecting the threat to his or her self-esteem and avoiding any loss of self-esteem.

The threatened egotism hypothesis received support in laboratory work by Bushman and Baumeister (1998). In two studies, participants were randomly praised or insulted and then had an opportunity to aggress against the source of evaluation or against another person. The researchers also assessed people's self-appraisals with measures of self-esteem and narcissism. Narcissism is a newly popular trait construct that refers to feelings of personal superiority, an inflated sense of entitlement, and self-admiration. The term comes from the mythical Greek character Narcissus who fell in love with his own image reflected in the water. The view that low self-esteem would cause aggression received no support whatsoever, and in fact different measures of self-esteem in different studies consistently yielded no significant results. In contrast, people who scored high on narcissism responded to insults with exceptionally high levels of aggression (but only toward the person who had insulted them, not toward innocent third parties). More recent analyses have shown that high narcissism in combination with high self-esteem leads to the highest levels of aggression.

The threatened egotism view, as well as the important mediation by emotional responses such as shame, was further attested in questionnaire studies by Kernis, Granneman, and Barclay (1989). These authors not only measured participants' level of self-esteem but also assessed the stability of self-esteem, defined in terms of how much a person's self-esteem score fluctuated from one occasion to another. They found people with high self-esteem scored at both extremes on an inventory of hostility. Specifically, people with high but unstable self-esteem exhibited the highest levels of hostility. In contrast, people with stable high self-esteem were the least hostile and aggressive. The implication of Kernis et al.'s work is thus that unstable high self-esteem is an important predisposition to aggression. By definition, these people have favorable opinions of themselves, but these favorable opinions are vulnerable to events that might raise or lower them, and so criticism or disrespect holds the potential to cause a loss in self-esteem. Losses of self-esteem typically evoke negative emotional responses such as shame, and so these people become aggressive as a way of warding off these very unpleasant feelings. The findings of Kernis et al. overlap with the conclusions of Bushman and Baumeister (1998), because other work has confirmed that narcissists tend to fall in the category of having high, unstable self-esteem (Rhodewalt, Madrian, & Cheney, 1998) – precisely the category of people who are most hostile and aggressive. In summary, experiences that reflect badly on the self evoke very negative emotions such as shame and anger. An increase in aggressive tendencies is a common result.

Sadistic Pleasure

The notion of sadism points toward a link between aggression and emotion that is quite different from the emotions we have considered thus far. *Sadism* implies that the perpetrator actually enjoys inflicting harm and gets pleasure from the victim's suffering. Thus, the quest for positive, pleasant emotional states may cause sadists to behave aggressively. This stands in sharp contrast to the pattern we noted with guilt. Guilt is an impediment to aggression, and so avoiding guilt often motivates an attempt to ignore or minimize the victim's suffering. The sadist however is precisely motivated to maximize the victim's suffering and derive pleasure by focusing on it.

Sadism is an important theme in many victims' accounts. They often emphasize that the persons who were harming them were doing so because they enjoyed it. Laughter or other apparent signs of pleasure are very salient to victims. Still, these accounts cannot be fully trusted, because victims tend to assimilate their tormentors' actions to the culturally dominant images of evil, which often include sadistic pleasure (Baumeister, 1997; Dower, 1986).

Perpetrators' accounts generally offer far less evidence of sadism. Still, there is some evidence, and it seems sufficiently widespread to conclude that some degree of sadism exists. Several observations suggest that a small minority of perpetrators actually do get pleasure from causing their victims to suffer. For example, about 5% of rapists fall into the sadistic category (Groth, 1979). Toch's (1993/1969) classic study of violent men concluded that about 6% fell in the sadistic category. Toch explained that most bullies would be aggressive until the victim would give in and show signs of weakness and suffering, whereupon the attackers would stop. The sadistic minority, however, would increase their tormenting behaviors instead of stopping at that point.

The idea that perpetrators enjoy inflicting suffering supports popular mythology of evil (such as reflected in movies and cartoons), but it seems contradicted by evidence that perpetrators typically experience considerable distress over hurting others. Browning's (1992) account of German reserve policemen assigned to kill Jews in Poland, for example, reports that the initial assignments produced extremely negative reactions, including anxiety attacks, nightmares, and gastrointestinal disturbances. Later, however, the men appeared to become desensitized to the killing duties. There was not much evidence, however, that the men came to actually enjoy the killing duties.

One possible explanation for the emergence of sadism would be based on opponent-process theory (Solomon & Corbit, 1974; Solomon, 1980). This theory is based on human homeostatic mechanisms, and so any departure from the normal state sets off an opposite process designed to restore the original status quo. If the experience is repeated many times, the second (opponent) process becomes stronger and the initial reaction becomes weaker. For example, when an out-of-shape person runs up a flight of stairs, the body responds by making the person breathe faster and by pumping more blood. Then, when running ceases, the opponent processes gradually slow the breathing and pulse to their normal, resting levels. If the person runs every day, the speed-up in breathing and pulse become less pronounced, and the restoration becomes quicker and more efficient. This theory helps explain how people can learn to enjoy such paradoxical experiences as falling (e.g., in bungee jumping or skydiving), which evoke some of the most natural and deeply rooted fears in the human psyche. The terror of falling evokes a pleasant, even euphoric reaction to restore the ordinary state, and after repeated jumps the person may experience euphoria rather than terror.

Applied to violence, opponent-process theory would suggest that the initial feelings of nausea, revulsion, and other distress are initially very salient and powerful, whereas the more positive feelings the body needs to offset those feelings start off being slow and inefficient. Through repeated participation in violent acts, however, the person is likely to find that the initial, negative state becomes weaker whereas the compensatory (and pleasant) process becomes stronger. Ultimately the person may begin to find that inflicting harm on others becomes positively appealing because of the rising predominance of the positive, pleasant feelings. To be sure, most people would still be restrained by guilt and would probably not permit themselves to acknowledge that they enjoyed inflicting harm. But people with a relatively weak sense of guilt might be susceptible to recognizing that they have learned to enjoy harming others, and these individuals could develop into full-blown sadists (Baumeister, 1997).

Excitement

Sadistic pleasure through enjoyment of a victim's suffering is not the only possible mechanism by which positive affective states can be gotten from aggressive action. Another important category involves excitement and thrills (see Baumeister & Campbell, 1999). Committing violent acts is often very exciting. Such excitement may appeal especially to people who find life boring, because the thrills of crime and violence may constitute a powerful antidote to boredom.

A memorable analysis of the quest for "sneaky thrills" was provided by Katz (1988) in his book *Seductions of Crime*. Even minor crimes such as shoplifting may appeal to people more because the episode is emotionally exciting than because of the cash value of the stolen item. Katz found that shoplifters often did not value the items they stole and either discarded them or put them away and forgot about them after the event, but they retained vivid memories of the suspense and excitement that accompanied the theft itself. Their accounts emphasized the exciting process of planning the theft, the fear of getting caught while attempting to leave the store, and the euphoric sense of victory that came upon the success of their mission. Apter (1992) and other writers have similarly emphasized how the quest for excitement can lead people to court danger, including through criminal and violent activity.

Viewing aggression as a potential source of emotional gratification that provides thrills and excitement and banishes boredom can help predict what kinds of individuals are more likely to engage in it. People with sensation-seeking or thrill-seeking temperaments would be prominent candidates, as would people whose ordinary lives lack alternative sources of excitement. Some observers have noted that adolescents are likely to qualify on both counts, insofar as they regard school and adult-supervised activities as boring (e.g., Larkin, 1979) but are in a developmental phase where the desire for affectively intense experiences is unusually powerful (e.g., Baldwin, 1985). The relatively high rates of criminal and aggressive behavior (especially of the exuberant, thrill-seeking type) among adolescents provides some support for that hypothesis, as does the frequent combination of aggressive, antisocial behavior with alcohol or drug abuse.

Conclusion

Emotion has multiple links to aggressive behavior. Two major theories have dominated the twentieth century, namely frustration-aggression and catharsis. The catharsis theory has been proven wrong, whereas the frustration theory has evolved into broader formulations about how various states of negative emotion instigate aggression. However, new evidence points to other theoretical contributions. Emotional distress impairs self-control, and loss of self-control is a widespread proximal cause of aggression.

Anger and shame have been particularly linked to aggression. Angry people feel better when they aggress, and some people appear to engage in aggression because they are seeking this emotional benefit. Some people seem to learn to gain sadistic pleasure from aggression, although the emotional processes that produce such pleasures remain at the stage of mere theory. Last, it is important to recognize that not all emotions contribute to increasing aggression. Guilt, at least, appears to have some power to restrain and prevent aggression.

References

Anderson, C. A., & Bushman, B. J. (2001). Effects of violent video games on aggressive behavior, aggressive cognition, aggressive affect, physiological arousal, and prosocial behavior: A meta-analytic review of the scientific literature. *Psychological Science, 12*, 353–359.

Anderson, C. A., & Bushman, B. J. (2002). Media violence and societal violence. *Science, 295*, 2377–2378.

Apter, M. J. (1992). *The dangerous edge: The psychology of excitement*. New York: The Free Press.

Aristotle (1970). *Poetics*. Ann Arbor: University of Michigan Press.

Averill, J. (1982). *Anger and aggression: An essay on emotion*. New York: Springer-Verlag.

Baldwin, J. D. (1985). Thrill and adventure seeking and the age distribution of crime: Comment on Hirschi and Gottfredson. *American Journal of Sociology, 90*, 1326–1330.

Baron, R. A., & Richardson, D. R. (1994). *Human aggression* (2nd ed.). New York: Plenum.

Baumeister, R. F. (1997). *Evil: Inside human violence and cruelty*. New York: W. H. Freeman.

Baumeister, R. F., & Campbell, W. K. (1999). The intrinsic appeal of evil: Sadism, sensational thrills, and threatened egotism. *Personality and Social Psychology Review, 3*, 210–221.

Baumeister, R. F., Heatherton, T. F., & Tice, D. M. (1994). *Losing control: How and why people fail at self-regulation*. San Diego, CA: Academic Press.

Baumeister, R. F., Reis, H. T., & Delespaul, P. A. E. G. (1995). Subjective and experiential correlates of guilt in everyday life. *Personality and Social Psychology Bulletin, 21*, 1256–1268.

Baumeister, R. F., Smart, L., & Boden, J. M. (1996). Relation of threatened egotism to violence and aggression: The dark side of high self-esteem. *Psychological Review, 103*, 5–33.

Baumeister, R. F., Stillwell, A. M., & Heatherton, T. F. (1994). Guilt: An interpersonal approach. *Psychological Bulletin, 115*, 243–267.

Berkowitz, L. (1983). Aversively stimulated aggression: Some parallels and differences in research with animals and humans. *American Psychologist, 38*, 1135–1144.

Berkowitz, L. (1989). Frustration-aggression hypothesis: Examination and reformulation. *Psychological Bulletin, 106*, 59–73.

Berkowitz, L. (1990). On the formation and regulation of anger and aggression: A cognitive-neo-associationistic analysis. *American Psychologist, 45*, 494–503.

Berkowitz, L. (1993). *Aggression: Its causes, consequences, and control*. New York: McGraw-Hill.

Berkowitz, L., & Geen, R. G. (1966). Film violence and the cue properties of available targets. *Journal of Personality and Social Psychology, 3*, 525–530.

Breuer, J., & Freud, S (1955). Studies on hysteria. In J. Strachey (Ed. & Trans.) *The standard edition of the complete psychological works of Sigmund Freud* (Vol. 2). London: Hogarth. (Original work published 1893–1895).

Browning, C. R. (1992). *Ordinary men: Reserve police battalion 101 and the final solution in Poland*. New York: Harper Collins.

Bushman, B. J. (1997). Effects of alcohol on human aggression: Validity of proposed explanations. In D. Fuller, R. Dietrich, & E. Gottheil (Eds.), *Recent developments in alcoholism: Alcohol and violence* (Vol. 13, pp. 227–243). New York: Plenum.

Bushman, B. J., & Baumeister, R. F. (1998). Threatened egotism, narcissism, self-esteem, and direct and displaced aggression: Does self-love or self-hate lead to violence? *Journal of Personality and Social Psychology, 75*, 219–229.

Bushman, B. J., Baumeister, R. F., & Phillips, C. M. (2001). Do people aggress to improve their mood? Catharsis beliefs, affect regulation opportunity, and aggressive responding. *Journal of Personality and Social Psychology, 81*, 17–32.

Bushman, B. J., Baumeister, R. F., & Stack, A. D. (1999). Catharsis, aggression, and persuasive influence: Self-fulfilling or self-defeating prophecies? *Journal of Personality and Social Psychology, 76*, 367–376.

Bushman, B. J., & Cooper, H. M. (1990). Effects of alcohol on human aggression: An integrative research review. *Psychological Bulletin, 107*, 341–354.

Dollard, J., Doob, L., Miller, N., Mowrer, O., & Sears, R. (1939). *Frustration and aggression.* New Haven, CT: Yale University Press.

Dower, J.W. (1986). *War without mercy: Race and power in the Pacific war.* New York: Pantheon.

Ekman, P., & Friesen, W. V. (1975). *Unmasking the face.* Englewood Cliffs, NJ: Prentice-Hall.

Ekman P., Friesen, W. V., O'Sullivan, M., Chan, A., Diacoyanni-Tarlatzis, I., Heider, K., et al. (1987). Universals and cultural differences in the judgments of facial expressions of emotion. *Journal of Personality and Social Psychology, 53*, 712–717.

Freud, S. (1930). *Civilization and its discontents.* London: Hogarth Press.

Freud, S. (1959). *Mourning and melancholia.* In E. Jones (Ed.), *Collected papers* (Vol. 4). London: Hogarth Press. (Original work published 1917).

Freud, S. (1961). *Beyond the pleasure principle.* London: Norton. (Original work published 1920)

Geen, R. G., & Berkowitz, L. (1967). Some conditions facilitating the occurrence of aggression after the observation of violence. *Journal of Personality, 35*, 666–676.

Geen, R. G., & Quanty M. B. (1977). The catharsis of aggression: An evaluation of a hypothesis. In L. Berkowitz (Ed.), *Advances in experimental social psychology* (Vol. 10, pp. 1–37). New York: Academic Press.

Gottfredson, M. R., & Hirschi, T. (1990). *A general theory of crime.* Stanford, CA: Stanford University Press.

Groth, A. N. (1979). *Men who rape: The psychology of the offender.* New York: Plenum.

Hare, R. (1993). *Without conscience: The disturbing world of the psychopaths among us.* New York: Simon & Schuster/Pocket.

Hepworth, J. T., & West, S. G. (1988). Lynchings and the economy: A time-series reanalysis of Hovland and Sears (1940). *Journal of Personality and Social Psychology, 55*, 239–247.

Hoffman, M. L. (1982). Development of prosocial motivation: Empathy and guilt. In N. Eisenberg (Ed.), *The development of prosocial behavior* (pp. 281–313). New York: Academic Press.

Hornberger, R. H. (1959). The differential reduction of aggressive responses as a function of interpolated activities. *American Psychologist, 14*, 354.

Horney, K. (1950). *Neurosis and human growth.* New York: Norton.

Hovland, C. I., & Sears, R. (1940). Minor studies of aggression: Correlation of lynchings with economic indices. *Journal of Psychology, 9*, 301–310.

Katz, J. (1988). *Seductions of crime: Moral and sensual attractions in doing evil.* New York: Basic Books.

Kernis, M. H., Grannemann, B. D., & Barclay, L. C. (1989). Stability and level of self-esteem as predictors of anger arousal and hostility. *Journal of Personality and Social Psychology, 56*, 1013–1022.

Larkin, R. W. (1979). *Suburban youth in cultural crisis.* New York: Oxford University Press.

Lee, J. H. (1993). *Facing the fire: Experiencing and expressing anger appropriately.* New York: Bantam.

Leith, K. P., & Baumeister, R. F. (1996). Why do bad moods increase self-defeating behavior? Emotion, risk taking, and self-regulation. *Journal of Personality and Social Psychology, 71*, 1250–1267.

Lerner, J. S., Gonzalez, R. M., Small, D. A., & Fischhoff, B. (2003). Effects of fear and anger on perceived risks of terrorism: A national field experiment. *Psychological Science, 14*, 144–150.

Lerner, J. S., & Keltner, D. (2001). Fear, anger, and risk. *Journal of Personality and Social Psychology, 81*, 146–159.

Lewis, W. A., & Bucher, A. M. (1992). Anger, catharsis, the reformulated frustration-aggression hypothesis, and health consequences. *Psychotherapy, 29*, 385–392.

Miller, N. E. (1941). The frustration-aggression hypothesis. *Psychological Review, 48*, 337–342.

Retzinger, S. M. (1991). *Violent emotions*. Newbury Park, CA: Sage.

Rhodewalt, F., Madrian, J. C., & Cheney, S. (1998). Narcissism, self-knowledge organization, and emotional reactivity: The effects of daily experiences on self-esteem and affect. *Personality and Social Psychology Bulletin, 24*, 75–86.

Russell, J. A. (1980). A circumplex model of affect. *Journal of Personality and Social Psychology, 39*, 1161–1178.

Sears, R. R., & Sears, P. S. (1940). Minor studies of aggression: V. Strength of frustration-reaction as a function of strength of drive. *Journal of Psychology, 9*, 297–300.

Solomon, R. L. (1980). The opponent-process theory of acquired motivations: The costs of pleasure and the benefits of pain. *American Psychologist, 35*, 691–712.

Solomon, R. L., & Corbit, J. D. (1974). An opponent-process theory of motivation: I. Temporal dynamics of affect. *Psychological Review, 81*, 119–145.

Tangney, J. P. (1991). Moral affect: The good, the bad, and the ugly. *Journal of Personality and Social Psychology, 61*, 598–607.

Tangney, J. P (1995). Shame and guilt in interpersonal relationships. In J. P. Tangney & K. Fischer (Eds.), *The self-conscious emotions* (pp. 114–139). New York: Guilford.

Tangney, J. P., & Dearing, R. L. (2002). *Shame and guilt*. New York: Guilford.

Tangney, J. P., Wagner, P. E., Fletcher, C., & Gramzow, R. (1992). Shamed into anger? The relation of shame and guilt to anger and self-reported aggression. *Journal of Personality and Social Psychology, 62*, 669–675.

Tanner, A. (2003, November 21). *Spam rage: Man arrested for threats to company*. Retrieved October 13, 2006, from Reuters News Service http://www.globalaffairs.org/forum/archive/index.php/t-17696.

Tavris, C. (1989). *Anger: The misunderstood emotion*. New York: Simon & Shuster (Touchstone).

Toch, H. (1993). *Violent men: An inquiry into the psychology of violence*. Washington, DC: American Psychological Association. (Original work published 1969)

Whyte, M. (2003, November 10) *Put your spam to music: Musician culls unwanted e-mail for song titles compilation CD made, distributed via the internet. Toronto Star.* Retrieved August 5, 2004, from http://www.thestar.com/NASApp/cs/ContentServer?pagename=thestar/Layout/Article_Type1&c=Article&cid=1068419407812&call_pageid=991479973472&col=991929131147.

5 The Functional Neuroanatomy of Anger and Aggression

Sylvia Richter, Kirsten Jordan, and Torsten Wüstenberg

Within the last few decades there has been an increase in the number of publications on the topic of aggression in emotion literature. In much of this literature, however, the emotion of anger and its possible role as a moderator or trigger of aggressive behavior have been neglected. Anger belongs to the so-called basic emotions, associated with a specific, universal (i.e., cross-cultural) facial expression and physiological components like cardiologic and vegetative responses. Averill (1982) concluded that "most people report becoming mildly to moderately angry anywhere from several times a day to several times a week" (p. 1146). Therefore, anger obviously is socially a very important emotion that should be explored by a wide range of methods and analyses (Berkowitz & Harmon-Jones, 2004).

After a long period of neglect, the neurosciences have now also embraced emotions as a topic of research, thereby creating new possibilities for investigating the physiological basis of anger and aggression. In the following chapter we present a beginners-level introduction to the fascinating topic of neuroscience and one of its major methods, functional imaging. Afterwards we give an overview of the state of the art research on the *neurophysiological* basis of anger and aggressive behavior.

Neuroscience and Functional Imaging

The neurosciences represent an integrated, multidisciplinary, and multilevel approach to understanding how the brain and nervous system acquire and process information, including the higher mental functions of humans. Triggered by the ground-breaking development of noninvasive methods of measurement by the end of the twentieth century, the neurosciences have undergone an almost explosive growth within the last thirty years. Thus, more has been learned about the workings of the brain in this period than in all of history before (Gazzaniga, Ivry, & Mangun, 2002).

Before presenting a short introduction into methods of neuroimaging, we will give an overview of some basic terminology concerning the neuroanatomy of the brain, e.g., the *cerebrum*. We will present only neuroanatomical terms which are strongly needed for the understanding of our further remarks. At the very beginning one has to consider helpful topographic terms. Because the brain is a rather complex, three-dimensional object with a great number of structures and pathways that are hard to visualize from two-dimensional pictures, it is important to use conventions for describing the relationships between regions. In Figure 1 you can see anatomical terms for describing various views of the anatomy and sections of the brain.

The cerebrum is divided into two *hemispheres* that are connected by several *commissures*. The most important of the latter is the *corpus callosum,* a horizontal joist in

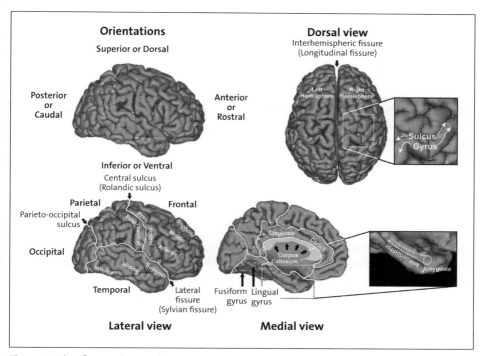

Figure 1. The figure shows the most prominent neuroanatomical structures and corresponding topographic terms.

the middle of the brain. Each hemisphere is divided into four *lobes*, the frontal, parietal, temporal, and occipital lobes, which have different functional properties and can be distinguished from one another by anatomical landmarks.

Among these are the inward grooves, the *sulci* and *fissures,* which alternate with outward bulges, the *gyri.* The central or *Rolandic sulcus* separates the frontal lobe from the parietal lobe, the lateral or *Sylvian fissure* separates the temporal from the frontal and parietal lobes. The occipital lobe is demarcated by the parieto-occipital sulcus and, finally, the left and right hemispheres of the brain are separated by the interhemispheric fissure. The frontal and temporal lobes are additionally divided into a superior, middle and inferior gyrus (these are the anatomical landmarks discussed before).

Up to now, the cognitive neurosciences (i.e., the areas of neuroscience that focus on the study of mental functions) were mostly interested in the *gray matter* or *cortex.* The cortical tissue contains the cell bodies of neurons with their synaptic connections; the so-called glial cells – a very important type of cell which supports the neural metabolism and a close network of vessels. The cortex can further be subdivided into the following parts:

Neocortex and Limbic Cortex
The classification into neo- and limbic cortex is based on the evolution of the central nervous system. Evolutionarily, the youngest part is called the *neocortex* – an ap-

proximately one-centimeter thick, intensely folded layer of gray matter which covers the whole surface of the cerebrum. The largest part of the evolutionarily oldest cortex belongs to the *limbic cortex*. Its most important structures are the *cingulate gyrus*, the *amygdala* and the *hippocampus*.

Cortex and Subcortical Structures
All of the gray matter below the cortex is called *subcortical*. It is concentrated in *nuclei* which are circumscribed regions of high neuron density. Many of these subcortical structures are important for memory processes as well as for emotional perception and experience.

Paralimbic Structures
The term *paralimbic* means that these cortical or subcortical areas are functionally very closely connected to limbic structures.

The various brain structures have a variety of functional roles in neural processing. Major identifiable systems can be localized within a lobe, others involve more than one lobe. In a short overview, this means the following:

The frontal lobe, especially the prefrontal areas, plays a major role in modulating behavior, like the planning and execution of social interactions and inhibition of anger and aggression. For understanding our subsequent remarks, it is important to know that visual information, e.g., color, luminance, and orientation, are processed in the occipital lobe and in the middle and inferior regions of the temporal lobe.

Before starting with the functional neuroanatomy of anger and aggression, a few remarks on the technology that allows researchers to observe the work of the human brain are needed. These so-called imaging techniques allow for the localization of the neuro-functional correlates of cognitive processes.

Functional Magnetic Resonance Imaging (fMRI) of the human brain has been especially well received as a noninvasive method for studying brain function. It has therefore rapidly become one of the most widely used methods for investigating brain function.

In fMRI, the enourmous field of a superconductive magnet leads to almost all cores of hydrogen atoms of the human body being aligned parallel to that field. Radio waves emitted by the machine evoke a resonant oscillation of these nuclei, and a detector measures local energy fields that are emitted when the nuclei return to the orientation of the external magnetic field. This process is extremely sensitive to the magnetic properties of the imaged tissue.

FMRI thus does not directly measure neural events. It rather measures local blood flow effects caused by metabolic changes that are correlated with neural activity. Neurons, like all other body cells, require energy to perform their specialized functions. The brain is metabolically an extremely demanding organ. Although it accounts for only 2% of our body weight, it requires 20% of the total oxygen consumption of our bodies (Gazzaniga et al., 2002). When a brain area is active, more oxygen and glucose are made available by locally increased blood flow. FMRI exploits the fact that the magnetic properties of oxygenated (HbO_2) and deoxygenated (HbR) hemoglobin are different.

Whereas HbO_2 has no influence on local magnetic properties, HbR interacts with the oscillating atomic nuclei.

FMRI detectors measure the small absolute amount of this endogenous contrast agent. The effect of neuro-metabolically induced changes in HbR-concentration is re-

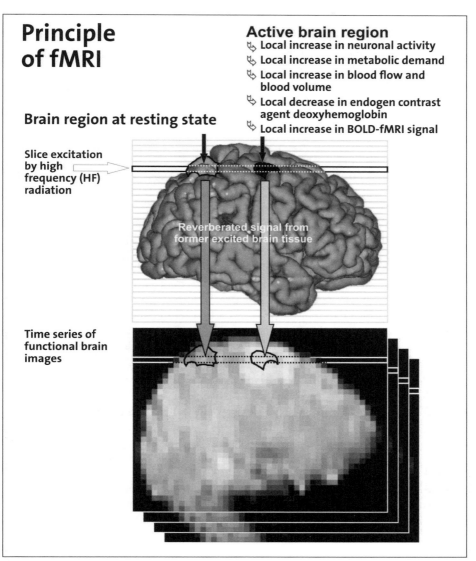

Figure 2. Principle of functional magnetic resonance imaging: Neuronal activated areas show higher local cerebral blood flow (rCBF) and less total amount of the endogeneous contrast agent HbR. Thus, the signal reremitted from these areas is higher, and active areas appear brighter in functional images. Statistical analyses use this effect to localize, in vivo, neural function in the brain.

ferred to as the *blood-oxygenation-level dependent effect* [BOLD-effect] (Ogawa, Lee, Kay, & Tank, 1990). The BOLD effect is time-locked to specific events which allow for graphing the time course of neural activity (see Figure 2).

In view of these excellent possibilities, however, the limitations of fMRI also need to be kept in mind. Despite intensive research, the exact principles of neuro-vascular coupling in the human cerebrum still remain unclear. Thus, we measure a neuro-metabolically induced, vascular effect in a particular area correlated with an experimental variation. The interpretation of these data regarding functional contribution should be performed carefully, however, because correlation does not imply causation.

Independent of these limitations, neuroimaging studies have begun to explore the functional neuroanatomy of emotion. These studies report emotion-related increases in the cerebral blood flow in limbic, paralimbic and neocortical regions. One obvious idea was that specific brain regions have specialized functions for emotional operations. Indeed, there are some brain structures which seem to be *more* important for one emotion than for others (Phan, Wager, Taylor, & Liberzon, 2002). But though there seems to be general agreement about the existence of specialized "emotion regions," highly conflicting findings are presented and discussed in the current literature. Many of these are produced by using different experimental designs and imaging techniques (Phan et al., 2002). Moreover, divergent results concerning the topic *anger and aggressive behavior* may be caused by a confusingly different use of the terms anger, aggression, and hostility.

In 1997, Hodapp et al. stated that this confusion is a fundamental problem in the progressive investigation of the relationship between anger and psychiatric disorders (Hodapp, Sicker, Wick, & Winkelstrater, 1997). Due to insufficient definitions these different concepts were often used mixed or alternatively. This problem also occurred in neuroimaging studies and – even almost 10 years later – one can find synonymous use of the terms anger and aggression in some papers. It therefore seems necessary to differentiate the terms once more.

Investigating Anger and Aggression – Why There Is a Difference

Anger is a specific *emotion*, one of the so called basic emotions (happiness, fear, anger, disgust, sadness, [surprise, contempt]). *Aggression*, on the other hand, is an *action* with the goal of causing damage (Hodapp et al., 1997). That means that one can understand anger as one emotional motive of aggressive behavior (Berkowitz, 1962). Beyond that, one needs to distinguish between *offensive aggression*, associated with *anger*, and *defensive aggression*, associated with *fear* (Harmon-Jones, 2004). Additionally, there is another, at least historically important difference: The offensive and defensive types of aggression are both emotionally motivated (hot aggression). There also exists a so-called *instrumental or cold aggression* (Bandura, 1973), which is mainly driven by nonemotional motives and with a goal other than harming the victim. Anderson and Bushman (2002) rightly emphasize that the differentiation between hostile aggression (also called hot, reactive, or impulsive) and instrumental aggression was very helpful in recent decades of aggression research since it pointed to the complexity of the concept

(Anderson & Bushman, 2002). That differentiation emerged as inadequate, however, for satisfying all types and motives of aggressive behavior. Anderson and Bushman thus argued for distinguishing between different types of aggression only at the level of the ultimate goal. In their opinion, acts of aggression always include the intention to cause harm, at least as a proximate goal. Aggression differs, however, in ultimate goals like being profit-orientated or primarily harm-based, and mixed motives also need to be kept in mind (Anderson & Bushman, 2002; Bushman & Anderson, 2001). The concept of *hostility* reflects a cognitive-affective *orientation* of a person (Buss, 1961; Izard, 1981). The emotional and behavioral reactions of hostile persons reflect anger, rage, suspicion, and/or hate against others (Hodapp et al., 1997). Anger and hostile feelings can be worked off outwardly or can be suppressed. Aggressive behavior can be directed against other persons or against oneself as well. These different kinds of anger expression will be of further interest in a later part of this chapter. A clear differentiation between the terms anger, aggression, and hostility is very important in order to avoid confusing data and to reach a progressive understanding of the neuronal basis that underlies these concepts.

The Functional Neuroanatomy of Anger

Besides modern neuroscientific techniques, which have been briefly described above, clinical data can provide information about specific functions of neuroanatomic structures. In the beginning of the 19th century, the observations of damage-caused neuropsychological phenomena were the only possibility for drawing conclusions on the functional neuroanatomy of the living brain. Well-established and often cited within the neurosciences is the now classic, tragic story of Phineas Gage.

In the summer of 1848, Phineas Gage was foreman of a construction crew who built the extension of the Rutland and Burlington Railroad. His task was the setting of dynamite charges. While setting such a charge and waiting for his assistant to pour in sand, to ensure that the explosion would impact the rock itself, he was distracted and failed to check whether the powder was covered. He thrust down his tamping iron bar – the iron set off a spark and the explosion ripped out through the worksite (Gazzaniga et al., 2002). The approximately two meter long iron had careened through Gage's skull and brain. Within a few minutes, Gage, who was still conscious, sat up and spoke to his men. Fortunately, Phineas Gage was treated by an excellent physician – Dr. John Harlow. Two months after the accident, he was declared cured. The cure was only superficial, however. Before his accident, he had been described as a hard working, energetic, gentle, and excellent citizen. Afterwards, he was impatient and rude, with outbursts of anger and rage. His physician, John Harlow, observed the life of his former patient again and reported these observations in the first worldwide article about the neural basis of personality traits (Harlow, 1999). Hanna Damasio and colleagues (1994) at the University of Iowa used the preserved skull of Phineas Gage to reconstruct his lesion (Damasio, Grabowski, Frank, Galaburda, & Damasio, 1994). They found that the iron had destroyed the ventromedial aspects of the most anterior portions of the frontal cortex in both hemispheres which means that the orbitofrontal cortex was destroyed (see Figure 3).

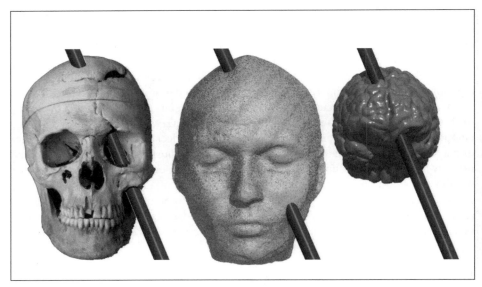

Figure 3. Reconstruction of the neuronal consequences of Phineas Gage's accident. As you can see here, the iron bar penetrated the head below the left cheekbone and exited the skull after having destroyed both the right and left prefrontal areas.

Case studies like the one of Phineas Gage caused the orbitofrontal cortex (OFC) to move (among other structures) into the focus of interest with regard to angry, aggressive, and antisocial behaviors. Gage's misbehavior supplied a hint that the frontal cortex and in particular the OFC could be involved in the control (inhibition) of anger. Moreover, case studies and clinical observations led to hypotheses regarding the functions of specific brains structures. Modern neuroscientific methods allow for exploration into the working mechanisms of the healthy brain to test the existing hypotheses and, based on the data, to approve, correct, or abolish them.

In the following paragraphs, we briefly report the current findings on the functional neuroanatomy of anger from this neuroscientific viewpoint. In 1993, Cloninger et al. stated that the emotion *anger* is primitive and ancient from an evolutionary perspective (Cloninger, Svrakic, & Przybeck, 1993). It is therefore thought to be based on ancient, limbic regions. In contrast, evolutionarily younger cortical regions, like the prefrontal cortex, should have a more modulatory role. Phineas Gage's destiny may serve as evidence for this hypothesis. Based on the shift in his personality, neuroscientists argued that the OFC might inhibit anger-caused misbehavior. A number of studies using fMRI support this hypothesis by finding increased activation in the orbitofrontal and anterior cingulate cortex (ACC) when subjects view facial expressions of anger, but not of sadness, for example (Adolphs, Baron-Cohen, & Tranel, 2002; Phan et al., 2002). In addition, the superior frontal gyrus (SFG) was also observed to be activated while perceiving angry faces (Kesler-West et al., 2001). Several studies also reported activation of the medial prefrontal cortex (MPFC), the insula, and the temporal pole (Figure 4). Specifically the MPFC is thought to be a key structure for perceiving and experiencing

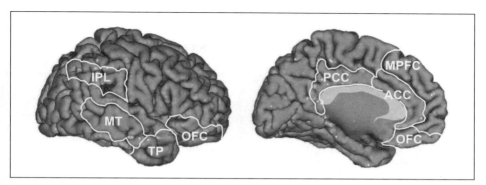

Figure 4. Overview of the neuroanatomical structures that seem most relevant in the perception and experience of anger. OFC = orbitofrontal cortex, TP = temporal pole, MT = middle temporal cortex, IPL = inferior parietal lobe, MPFC = medial prefrontal cortex, ACC = anterior cingulate cortex, PCC = posterior cingulate cortex.

emotion in general. With respect to the perception of anger, this prefrontal structure may also play an important role.

The anterior temporal region contains paralimbic structures. As discussed before, we identified those structures as being closely connected to the limbic system and therefore responsible for emotional processes. Up to now it has not been clear which function the insula might have within this context. The close anatomical connections between the insula and limbic and paralimbic structures may provide a hint for the involvement of insular regions in emotion processing.

Currently, one of the most interesting structures regarding anger recognition is the nucleus accumbens. This nucleus is part of the ventral striatum (see Figure 5), another paralimbic region. Several studies have shown that this small structure enables individuals to identify anger in another's facial expression (Calder, Keane, Lawrence, & Manes, 2004; Lawrence, Calder, McGowan, & Grasby, 2002; Strauss et al., 2005). If this structure is lesioned (e.g., by a stroke) or is temporarily impaired by psychopharmacological treatment, we cannot recognize the emotion anger, whereas other emotions are not affected. That means that the nucleus accumbens is a key structure regarding the processing of anger.

While these new results are highly promising, we are just at the very beginning of understanding the neural mechanisms of anger. One very important critical point can be elucidated here. Please note that emotion – similar to cognition – is not a fixed parameter of personality, but rather changes with aging. Albeit, most studies investigate young healthy people. However, it is still unclear to what extent these findings can be generalized across the adult life span. The influence of aging on neural activation is of growing interest. For example, the group of Hakan Fischer and Lars Bäckman (2005) compared the neuronal activation patterns of younger (ages ranged from 20 to 30 years) and older persons (ages ranged from 70 to 80 years) while perceiving angry faces (Fischer et al., 2005). Their data indicated that aging is associated with decreased activity in the limbic areas and increased activity in the insula while processing angry faces. Whether older persons actually process emotional information differently from young adults will have to be shown in further research. Independent from this lack of knowledge, it is notewor-

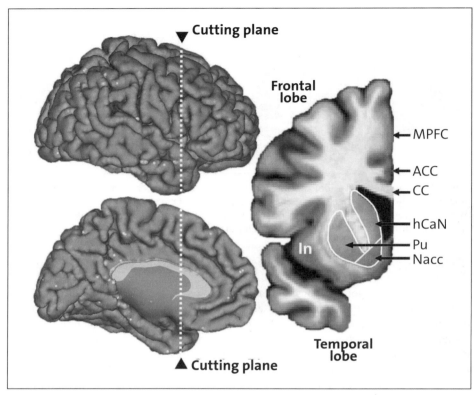

Figure 5. Anatomical relations within the ventral striatum. MPFC = medial prefrontal cortex, ACC = anterior cingulated cortex, CC = corpus callosum, hCaN = head of caudate nucleus, Pu = putamen, Nacc = nucleus accumbens, In = insula.

thy that changes in neuronal activity may be caused by possible age-related changes in neurovascular reactivity as well. Taking this into account, possible age-related changes in neuronal activity should be cautiously included in amplified models concerning neuronal networks of anger and aggression.

As you might have seen in the paragraphs above, there is one very often used method for investigating the perception of emotion. Most research groups use faces with an emotional expression. Face perception is thought to be one of the best trained perceptual tasks in humans because the ability to decode emotional information on the face is critical to communication (Kesler-West et al., 2001).

The Functional Neuroanatomy of Aggression

Because aggression has a much more active characteristic, the implementation of an experimental psychological setting concerning this matter is more difficult. Thus, morphologic and lesion studies play a more important role in this research area. The largest number of cortical dysfunctions in subjects and patients with abnormal aggressive behavior were found in the prefrontal cortical regions and the temporal lobes. Raine and coworkers investigated violent offenders or persons with an antisocial personality to search for anatomical deviations from the normal population (Raine, Lencz, Bihrle, LaCasse, & Colletti, 2000; Scarpa & Raine, 2000). The authors reported prefrontal gray matter that was reduced by at least 11%. Other investigators found a loss in hippocampal brain volume in violent offenders (Bassarath, 2001; remember that the hippocampus belongs to the limbic system).

Clinical lesion studies support the reported findings. Patients with frontal lobe damage show a typical pattern of personality changes including impulsivity, lack of concern for consequences of behavior, emotional lability, and violence (Scarpa & Raine, 2000). In addition, there is evidence that patients with temporal lobe epilepsy show increased aggressive behavior. It is not quite clear whether a nonseizure temporal dysfunction also increases violence (Scarpa & Raine, 2000).

The aforementioned group of Adrian Raine compared the prefrontal glucose metabolism of murderers whose acts were planned, instrumental, and predatory, with the metabolism of those whose attacks were impulsive and emotionally reactive. Their results indicate that emotionally reactive murderers were characterized by a significant prefrontal dysfunction, whereas predatory murderers show, within the prefrontal cortex, a metabolism similar to control subjects (Scarpa & Raine, 2000). Intuitively, one would expect this outcome because the prefrontal cortex is involved in the planning and execution of social behavior. Based on that background information, predatory murderers should have an intact prefrontal cortex, whereas the lack of behavioral control in emotionally reactive murderers may be caused by a prefrontal hypometabolism. These findings support the assumption that a prefrontal dysfunction is related to an impulsive-emotional aggression.

It is important to note that most of these studies have used only rather small sample sizes and heterogeneous samples of patients or volunteers. Because of these deficiencies, many results lack replicability. There is a large number of patients and offenders who do not show these abnormalities in MRI (Bassarath, 2001). The aforementioned results should thus be interpreted with great caution as long as the precise pathways and neurobiological mechanisms are not clear.

Besides patient studies and studies investigating violent offenders there are studies on the neuro-functional correlates of aggression in healthy young subjects. In these, subjects are typically asked to view violent pictures or scenes, and the resulting brain activation is compared to activation patterns while perceiving neutral scenes. Another method was used by Pietrini et al. (2000). The subjects imagined scenarios with emotionally neutral or aggressive behaviors. While imagining an aggressive as compared to a neutral behavior, reduced orbito-frontal activity was found (Pietrini, Guazzelli, Basso, Jaffe, & Grafman, 2000). This is an important difference for the results regarding the perception of angry faces discussed above. The neuronal correlates of anger and aggression are thus similar but not identical, and differ in this respect.

We already discussed the increased orbitofrontal activity while perceiving angry faces. This *increase* is also found when one imagines anger situations (Pietrini et al., 2000). The orbitofrontal cortex thus gets more active, the more a possible aggressive

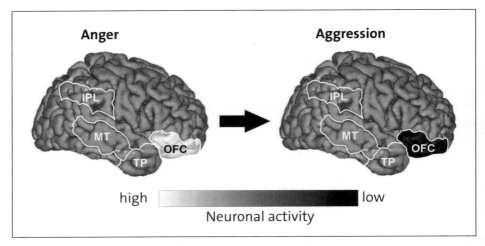

Figure 6. Visualization of the activity changes in the orbitofrontal region when changing from being angry to becoming aggressive. Which inhibitory or exhibitory influences on the OFC causes the changes in activation is not quite clear. OFC = orbitofrontal cortex, IPL = Inferior parietal lobule, MT = middle temporal gyrus, TP = temporal pole.

reaction needs to be inhibited in a situation that provokes anger. Orbitofrontal activation *decreases* when aggressive behavior is actually shown or at least imagined. Abnormal aggressive behavior may be accompanied by a functional "shut down" of the OFC (see Figure 6).

The Way In-Between: Investigating the Neurophysiology of the Anger Trait

As already said, one widely accepted approach within the affective neurosciences is the use of emotional faces for investigating emotional processes. We used this procedure too, but in combination with an established approach for different anger expression styles.

Theoretical background

Apart from functional neuroimaging, there are also many investigations that aim to explain the construct of *anger* on a behavioral and peripheral-physiological level. For example, there is a dissociation of distinct *anger dispositions* and *anger expression styles*. Persons who get significantly angry faster than average and tend to turn their anger against themselves are called anger-in persons (AI). Anger-out persons (AO) also get significantly angry faster than average, but tend to direct their anger primarily against other people or objects (Averill, 1982; Tavris, 1982). Thus, there are two independent dimensions for determining anger expression and anger experience. This concept has been found to be beneficial in describing clinical populations (Jorgensen, Johnson, Kolodziej, & Schreer, 1996; Linden & Lamensdorf, 1990; Martin, Wan, David, Wegner, Olson, & Watson, 1999). Funkenstein and colleagues (Funkenstein, King, & Drolette, 1954) already assumed that the so-called anger expression style could be linked to physiological components. They demonstrated that there was a threefold increase in heartbeat in anger-in persons in comparison to anger-out persons during anger situations (Funkenstein et al., 1954). These concepts are understudied in the context of the affective neurosciences, and the neural underpinnings of anger and AI/AO are not well understood. The understanding of anger expression styles in healthy, normal subjects may be fundamental for understanding borderline or even pathological anger expressions in psychiatric or neurological patients. Considering the reported differences in behavior and physiology, as shown within the behavioral-experimental and peripheral-physiological research on anger, we suggest that differences between the two aforementioned groups could be detectable on the neuronal level as well. Interactions of brain function and behavior suggest different styles of neuronal processing of identical emotional stimuli.

Therefore, it would be interesting to know whether the state AI or AO is related to trait-specific neural networks involving cortical as well as subcortical regions. In our study we used fMRI to examine how AI and AO subjects differ with regard to neural structures involved in the processing of facial anger images, which have previously been shown to evoke differential physiological and facial responses in the two subject groups (Jäncke, 1996).

Based on this knowledge we had the following research questions and hypotheses:

1. Are differences in activation of the previously reported brain structures between AO and AI subjects detectable while they perceive or recall angry faces? We hypothesize that AO subjects should show stronger activations to angry faces in neural networks known to process angry faces (the limbic and paralimbic systems, and the temporal and the frontal cortex including the anterior cingulum and the orbitofrontal cortex).

2. Is there a corresponding effect on subjects' behavior? Based on the findings of Jäncke (1996), we hypothesize that AO persons will show better recognition performance regarding angry faces.

Subjects and Methods

Twenty healthy male volunteers (ten AI, ten AO) took part in our study. For the selection of adequate subsamples we used the State-Trait-Anger-Expression Inventory (STAXI) (Schwenkmezger, Hodapp, & Spielberger, 1992). The choice of our subjects was based on the stanine scores which were obtained on the different scales of the STAXI. That means that all subjects showed a score of 8 or 9 (the highest obtainable scores) on either the Anger Out Scale or on the Anger In Scale. The scores on the other scales were about a stanine of 5, but not higher than 6. That enabled us to ascribe only one pronounced anger-expression style to each subject.

To select our subjects, 145 subjects were screened and two subgroups of 10 volunteers each were defined (all male and right-handed, mean age = 24.2 years; SD = 4.1 years).

During the imaging experiment our participants viewed happy and angry faces while performing fMRI measurements. For these purposes, seventy grayscale pictures of human faces (35 female, 35 male, Karolinska series [http://www.ki.se/cns/news/AKDEF-e.html]), matched in an elliptic outer shape, were used in two experimental periods. After an initial baseline of 10 seconds, every 12 seconds a picture was presented for 6 seconds. The order of presentation was randomized for all periods separately. During the first period, subjects had to learn a random selection of 32 faces (16 female, 16 male) showing the already mentioned emotional expressions. In the second period, all 70 faces were presented with a neutral expression. By pressing a response button, the subjects declared whether or not they could remember the presented faces.

The detailed task instruction was:

Before the first experimental period: "In the following task you will see faces. Please memorize them as well as possible. In a second part of this task we will present you those faces mixed with novel faces. You will have to recognize the learned faces then."

Before the second experimental period: "Now you will see the faces again, but mixed up with novel faces. Your task is to recognize the learned faces and to press the response button then."

The volunteers were not informed about the emotional category of the presented stimuli at any time. The intention was to put an emphasis on the *implicit* perception of the emotional stimulus contents. After the fMRI experiment, a German aggression questionnaire was completed (Fragebogen zur Erfassung von Aggressivitäts-Faktoren; Hampel & Selg, 1975). Furthermore, to avoid confounds caused by other cognitive components such as sympathy, dominance and arousal, subjects were requested to rate the faces they had seen on the basis of the self assessment manikin (SAM; Bradley & Lang, 1994). This provided a control for any neuronal activity that might not be induced by paradigm-related emotional stimulation.

Results

To examine learning success, we calculated d' ("d-prime"), a measure from signal detection theory (Macmillian, 1991) which represents the recognition performance for each subject independent of subjective response biases. More precisely d' is a measure of sensitivity for stimulus detection. It can be calculated by subtracting the z score of false positive answers from the z score of all correct answers. We found no significant differences in recognition performance between the two experimental groups. The d-prime scores within the AI-group ranged from $-.79$ to $.87$ ($M = 0$; $SD = .63$) and the scores of the AO-persons ranged from -2.05 to 1.64 ($M = 0$; $SD = .99$). That means that both groups performed comparatively poorly in the recognition task. The analysis of the stanine-based aggression questionnaire (FAF) showed that none of the participants demonstrated increased aggression tendencies. We did, however, find significantly higher scores for the AO compared to the AI group in the scales "Spontaneous Aggression," $p < 0.05$ (AI: $M = 3.88$, $SD = 0.78$; AO: $M = 5.00$, $SD = 1.33$), "Reactive Aggression," $p < 0.05$ (AI: $M = 3.89$, $SD = 1.26$; AO: $M = 5.60$, $SD = 1.26$), and "Arousal," $p = 0.05$ (AI: $M = 4.33$, $SD = 2.23$; AO: $M = 6.40$, $SD = 1.34$), all three Mann-Whitney Test. No sig-

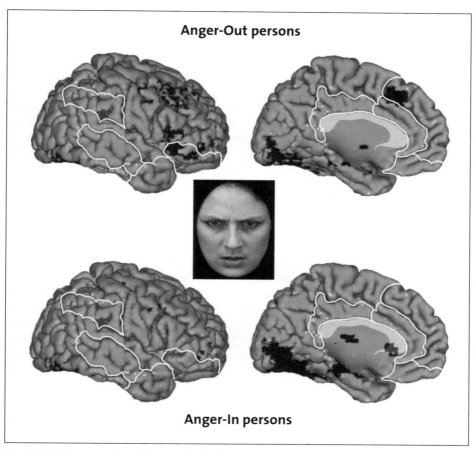

Anger-Out persons

Anger-In persons

Figure 7. Differences in cortical activation between AO and AI persons while perceiving the *same* angry faces. Using the schematic illustration of anger-relevant neuronal structures once again (white lines), one can compare the reported structures with the results found in our study. The upper part of the figure shows the neuronal network involved in the perception of angry faces in AO persons. The lower part of the figure shows the same for the AI persons.

nificant differences between the experimental groups were detected in the SAM ratings, dominance: $p = 1.00$, (AI: $M = 4.47$, $SD = 0.81$; AO: $M = 4.4$, $SD = 1.08$); sympathy: $p = 0.19$, (AI: $M = 5.51$, $SD = 0.30$; AO: $M = 6.405.38$, $SD = 0.73$); arousal: $p > 0.5$ (AI: $M = 3.6$, SD = 1.12; AO: $M = 3.15$, $SD = 1.36$), Mann-Whitney Test. The scores of the SAM rating ranged from 1 to 9 points.

We then analyzed the functional MRI data on the perception of angry faces. Brain activity during the presentation of angry faces was compared with that during the presentation of a fixation cross (baseline or resting activity). This comparison revealed highly interesting results. There are different activation patterns for the two groups while performing the same task under identical conditions.

As seen in Figure 7, the AI group showed stronger activity (bold responses) in occipital areas of the brain. This activation in the middle occipital cortex extends into inferior regions, specifically the lingual gyrus. One area that seems to be particularly important concerning face perception, the so-called fusiform face area, was also found to be activated within the AI group. Only weak frontal and prefrontal activations were found.

Also interesting is the activation pattern of the AO group displayed in Figure 7. In comparison to the AI group, we found weaker activations in the occipital areas of the brain. Interestingly, there are stronger bold responses in frontal brain regions. The frontal activations that we found are located in inferior frontal and middle frontal areas. As mentioned above, the middle and inferior frontal gyri were also found to be activated in other imaging studies concerning anger and aggression. In addition, we found activation of the medial frontal gyrus (MFG).

Discussion

We searched for differences in neuronal activation patterns with respect to different styles of anger expression in the context of implicitly perceiving emotional stimuli. As hypothesized, we found activation of different brain areas in the two groups. The mainly occipital activations of the AI group led us to assume that these volunteers strictly followed the task. They saw the presented faces and tried to memorize them for recognition in the second part of our task. There was no emotion-related activation found for the AI people. In contrast, AO people seem to react emotional as well. The frontal activation found in these subjects may indicate that the AO people indeed processed the anger in the seen faces. Therefore, AO subjects differed from AI subjects with respect to brain activation during the perception of angry faces, even though emotional processing was not explicitly required in our task. These differences demonstrate that anger expression style was accompanied by characteristic neurophysiological activations which may modulate behavior.

In conclusion, AI subjects reacted in a task oriented fashion, whereas AO subjects reacted in a more emotion-oriented manner. Thus, we were able to show in a first study that the personality trait *anger expression* possesses specific neuronal correlates.

It took a long time to progress from peripheral-physiological research questions to neurophysiological ones within the investigation of anger and aggression. In the meantime a growing number of studies have addressed the neuronal basics of anger. Up to now, interindividual neuronal differences in healthy subjects were not considered. To the best of our knowledge we are the first group reporting data in this area. The differentiation between AO and AI is useful and established and we show that the often described behavioral differences indeed possess a neuronal foundation.

Future Directions in the Neuroscience of Anger and Aggression

Currently, there are many more neuroimaging studies on aggression than on anger. Further investigations of the processes underlying anger are clearly needed for a more substantial comprehension of the neuronal basis of normal and abnormal anger.

The concept of investigating anger expression styles is rather promising. The findings are of interest within the affective and social neurosciences, concerning the investigation of the biopsychological basics of personality and clinical psychological forensic research.

Although we were able to show that the personality trait of anger expression possesses neuronal correlates and that the neuronal basics of anger in general are more complex than often expected, there are a lot of remaining questions. Thus, further studies should explore the neuro-functional principles of suppressing (AI) or acting out (AO) anger. In addition, it will be interesting to study groups showing these styles using aggression paradigms. This may enable us to investigate the switch from anger to aggression in general and as related to AO or AI. Common areas as well as differences in the functional neuroanatomy of anger and aggression could thus be studied more systematically. Investigating groups showing significantly different anger-expression styles and comparing them with average controls might help provide an understanding for the range of inconspicuous anger behavior. This knowledge is needed for examining pathological anger behavior and to explain its neuronal mechanisms. Furthermore, it could elucidate the question of whether it is really possible to differentiate between "normal" and "pathological" neuronal activation patterns in a valid approach. It may also help in analyzing anger-motivated aggression and may lead to the development of new preventive concepts to avoid increased aggressive behavior or new clinical treatments for pathological anger and aggression.

Understanding the switch from anger to aggression and possible differences in dependency from anger expression styles also includes questions regarding the impact of transmitter systems like serotonin and dopamine on angry and aggressive behavior.

Taken together, the growing knowledge concerning the neurobiology of anger and aggression may be helpful for developing new therapeutical approaches with respect to developmental sociopathy and acquired sociopathy, for example. Keeping the multidimensionality and complexity of the relationship between anger and aggression in mind, a closer cooperation among all related scientific disciplines is necessary to get to the bottom of biological as well as social and environmental factors of anger and aggression in a more systematic way.

Acknowledgement

The authors would like to thank Hans Strasburger, Andrea Bendel, and Gregor Kilian for critical reading, feedback, and excellent comments on the manuscript and for providing us with their time.

Authors' note

Dedicated to Lutz Jäncke – in memory of the good old times!

References

Adolphs, R., Baron-Cohen, S., & Tranel, D. (2002). Impaired recognition of social emotions following amygdala damage. *Journal of Cognitive Neuroscience, 14*, 1264–1274.

Anderson, C. A., & Bushman, B. J. (2002). Human aggression. *Annual Review of Psychology, 53*, 27–51.

Averill, J. R. (1982). *Anger and aggression. An essay on emotion.* New York: Springer.

Bandura, A. (1973). *Aggression: A social learning analysis.* Englewood Cliffs, NJ: Prentice-Hall.

Bassarath, L. (2001). Neuroimaging studies of antisocial behavior. *Canadian Journal of Psychiatry, 46*, 728–732.

Berkowitz, L. (1962). *Aggression: A social psychological analysis.* New York: McGraw-Hill.

Berkowitz, L., & Harmon-Jones, E. (2004). Toward an understanding of the determinants of anger. *Emotion, 4*, 107–130.

Bradley, M. M., & Lang, P. J. (1994). Measuring emotion: the Self-Assessment Manikin and the semantic differential. *Journal of Behavior Therapy and Experimental Psychiatry, 25*, 49–59.

Bushman, B. J., & Anderson, C. A. (2001). Is it time to pull the plug on the hostile versus instrumental aggression dichotomy? *Psychological Review, 108*, 273–279.

Buss, A. H. (1961). *The psychology of aggression.* New York: Wiley.

Calder, A. J., Keane, J., Lawrence, A. D., & Manes, F. (2004). Impaired recognition of anger following damage to the ventral striatum. *Brain, 127*, 1958–1969.

Cloninger, C. R., Svrakic, D. M., & Przybeck, T. R. (1993). A psychobiological model of temperament and character. *Archives of General Psychiatry, 50*, 975–990.

Damasio, H., Grabowski, T., Frank, R., Galaburda, A. M., & Damasio, A. R. (1994). The return of Phineas Gage: Clues about the brain from the skull of a famous patient. *Science, 264*, 1102–1105.

Fischer, H., Sandblom, J., Gavazzeni, J., Fransson, P., Wright, C. I., & Backman, L. (2005). Age-differential patterns of brain activation during perception of angry faces. *Neuroscience Letters, 386*, 99–104.

Funkenstein, D., King, S., & Drolette, M. (1954). The direction of anger during a laboratory stress-inducing situation. *Psychosomatic Medicine, 16*, 404–413.

Gazzaniga, M., Ivry, R., & Mangun, G. (2002). *Cognitive neuroscience* (2nd ed.). New York: Norton.

Hampel, R., & Selg, H. (1975). *Fragebogen zur Erfassung von Aggressivitätsfaktoren (FAF)* [Questionnaire for the investigation of factors of aggressiveness (FAF)]. Göttingen, Germany: Hogrefe.

Harlow, J. M. (1999). Passage of an iron rod through the head. *Journal of Neuropsychiatry and Clinical Neuroscience, 11*, 281–283.

Harmon-Jones, E. (2004). Contributions from research on anger and cognitive dissonance to understanding the motivational functions of asymmetrical frontal brain activity. *Biological Psychology, 67*, 51–76.

Hodapp, V., Sicker, G., Wick, A. D., & Winkelstrater, R. (1997). Ärger und Suizidrisiko: Untersuchung an älteren psychiatrischen Patienten [Anger and risk of suicide. Study of elderly psychiatric patients]. *Nervenarzt, 68*, 55–61.

Izard, C. E. (1981). *Die Emotionen des Menschen* [The emotions of man]. Weinheim, Germany: Beltz.

Jäncke, L. (1996). Facial EMG in an anger-provoking situation: individual differences in directing anger outwards or inwards. *International Journal of Psychophysiology, 23*, 207–214.

Jorgensen, R. S., Johnson, B. T., Kolodziej, M. E., & Schreer, G. E. (1996). Elevated blood pressure and personality: A meta-analytic review. *Psychological Bulletin, 120*, 293–320.

Kesler-West, M. L., Andersen, A. H., Smith, C. D., Avison, M. J., Davis, C. E., Kryscio, R. J. et al. (2001). Neural substrates of facial emotion processing using fMRI. *Cognitive Brain Research, 11*, 213–226.

Lawrence, A. D., Calder, A. J., McGowan, S. W., & Grasby, P. M. (2002). Selective disruption of the recognition of facial expressions of anger. *Neuroreport, 13*, 881–884.

Linden, W., & Lamensdorf, A. M. L. (1990). Hostile affect and causal blood pressure. *Psychology and Health, 4*, 343–349.

Macmillian, N. A., Creelman, C. (1991). *Detection theory: A user's guide.* Cambridge, MA: Cambridge University Press.

Martin, R., Wan, C. K., David, J. P., Wegner, E. L., Olson, D. B., & Watson, D. (1999). Style of anger expression: Relations to expressivity, personality, and health. *Personality and Social Psychology Bulletin, 2*, 1196–1207.

Ogawa, S., Lee, T. M., Kay, A. R., & Tank, D. W. (1990). Brain magnetic resonance imaging with contrast dependent on blood oxygenation. *Proceedings of the National Academy of Sciences of the United States of America, 87*, 9868–9872.

Phan, K. L., Wager, T., Taylor, S. F., & Liberzon, I. (2002). Functional neuroanatomy of emotion: A meta-analysis of emotion activation studies in PET and fMRI. *Neuroimage, 16*, 331–348.

Pietrini, P., Guazzelli, M., Basso, G., Jaffe, K., & Grafman, J. (2000). Neural correlates of imaginal aggressive behavior assessed by positron emission tomography in healthy subjects. *American Journal of Psychiatry, 157*, 1772–1781.

Raine, A., Lencz, T., Bihrle, S., LaCasse, L., & Colletti, P. (2000). Reduced prefrontal gray matter volume and reduced autonomic activity in antisocial personality disorder. *Archives of General Psychiatry, 57*, 119–127.

Scarpa, A., & Raine, A. (2000). Violence associated with anger and impulsivity. In J. Borod (Ed.), *The neuropsychology of emotion.* New York, Oxford University Press.

Schwenkmezger, P., Hodapp, V., & Spielberger, C. D. (1992). *Das State-Trait-Ärgerausdrucks-Inventar STAXI* [The State-trait-anger-expression-inventory (Staxi)]. Bern, Switzerland: Huber.

Strauss, M. M., Makris, N., Aharon, I., Vangel, M. G., Goodman, J., Kennedy, D. N. et al. (2005). fMRI of sensitization to angry faces. *Neuroimage, 26*, 389–413.

Tavris, C. (1982). *Anger: The misunderstood emotion.* New York: Simon & Schuster.

Does Anger Treatment Reduce Aggressive Behavior?

Georges Steffgen and Jan Pfetsch

Introduction

Anger and aggression are seen as interdependent aspects of human experience, standing in a narrow interrelation. Therefore, one often finds psychological anger intervention programs with the explicit purpose of directly or indirectly changing aggressive behavior (Edmondson & Conger, 1996; Mayne & Ambrose, 1999). Furthermore, there is a multiplicity of trainings for the reduction of aggression in which the intention is to reduce aggression by changing the experience or regulation of anger (Feindler & Scalley, 1998). Some researchers place importance on the proximity and potential overlapping variance of these constructs when expanding theoretical models regarding anger and aggression (Kassinove & Eckhardt, 1995).

On the other hand, some investigators allude to evident differences in the experience and expression of anger and aggression (Weber, 1994, 1999), from which diverse paths to establish changes in these different constructs would be expected.

Therefore, a basic question stemming from these different findings and approaches is whether anger treatment necessarily reduces aggressive behavior.

As a first step towards answering this question, the notions of anger and aggression will be defined and differentiated in this review. Furthermore, the theoretical relationship between these two concepts will be thoroughly investigated. We will subsequently highlight different approaches for modifying anger processes on the one hand and aggressive behavior on the other. With reference to findings of comparative and meta-analytic studies, the specific effectiveness of intervention programs regarding anger is characterized. A summary of specific indication criteria and target groups also is presented. This article will then be concluded with a summary of principles for anger treatments that should be considered for reduction of aggressive behavior.

Definition and Theory of Anger and Aggression

The conceptual confusion over the concepts of anger and aggression will become evident in the following brief definitions (Spielberger, 1988).

Anger is both an emotional state, varying across time, situation, and intensity, as well as a stable personality trait, reflecting a person's tendency to experience anger frequently or intensely (Spielberger, Reheiser, & Sydeman, 1995). Anger is associated with cognitive distortions (e.g., misappraisals and attributions of blame), physiological changes (e.g., hypertension), and behavioral reactions (e.g., fighting; Kassinove & Sukhodolsky, 1995).

In addition to the experience of anger, the expression of anger is seen as an essential part of the anger construct. More than other emotions, anger can be expressed in varying ways. Deffenbacher, Oetting, Lynch, and Morris (1996) have identified 14 different ways to express anger. Aggression here is considered as just one of many different possible forms of anger expression. Some forms of anger expression (e.g., humor reactions) may even prevent aggression (Schwenkmezger, Steffgen, & Dusi, 1999).

Aggression is defined by Buss (1961, p. 1) as "a response that delivers noxious stimuli to another organism." Today a concise definition is proposed by Baron and Richardson (1994, p. 7) characterizing aggression as "any form of behavior directed toward the goal of harming or injuring another living being who is motivated to avoid such treatment" (see Krahé, 2001). Different forms (i.e., physical and relational) and functions (i.e., reactive and proactive) of aggression should be distinguished. Reactive aggression is defined as an angry defensive response to a threat or frustration (hot-blooded). Proactive aggression is a deliberate behavior that is controlled by external reinforcements and is usually a means of reaching a desired goal (e.g., cold-blooded aggression; Connor, Steingard, Cunningham, Anderson, & Meloni, 2004; Little, Henrich, Jones, & Hawley, 2003).

The basic distinction between the two concepts is that anger is defined as an emotion and aggression as a behavior (see also Baumeister & Bushman, this volume). Anger as an emotional state can underlie aggression, and aggression can be considered as a form of anger expression. Therefore, anger can share properties with aggression. The terms are not synonymous, but they do overlap.

One crucial question is: To what extent is the behavioral component an essential part of anger versus the emotional state an essential part of aggression? There are different theoretical positions, for instance, Edmondson and Conger (1996) attribute a behavioral component to anger, whereas Eckhardt and Deffenbacher (1995) do not.

All in all there is no consensus among researchers regarding the definitions of anger and aggression (see Baumeister & Bushman; Juen, Peham, Juen, & Benecke, this volume).

In addition to these different definitions, different theoretical approaches should also be considered. Here, the relationship between anger and aggression is discussed by both sides – in anger theories as well as in aggression theories. In the following, these approaches are examined closer.

Theoretical Approach From an Anger Perspective

Different theories of anger take aggression into consideration to different extents. There are no specific anger theories that claim that anger has no relationship to aggression. The theories and models in this research domain assign inherent reaction tendencies to anger, from which a relationship with aggression is made (Weber, 1994).

Novaco (1994) considers anger as an affective stress reaction which occurs after a provocation. In this view, anger as an emotional state is a consequence of an experienced physiological arousal and its cognitive interpretation. In reference to the transactional stress theory of Lazarus (1966), anger is caused through external events, internal processes like cognitive appraisal and behavior reactions. The external events do not have a direct influence on anger, but they do influence cognitions which are seen as mediators for the anger release. Therefore, the manner in which situations are cognitively reconstructed and assessed is central for the experience of anger. External events receive an anger releasing function if they are assessed as provoking. In feedback processes, experienced anger, behavior reactions, and appraisal can influence and enhance each other. Novaco (1994, p. 53) left regulatory systems unspecified, stating that regarding "the capacity to regulate anger and aggression... much remains to be addressed with regard to psychological deficits in anger control" (see Chemtob, Novaco, Hamada, & Gross, 1997). A substantial factor of aggression as a consequence of anger is, according to Novaco (1986), rumination – the continued revival of anger in thoughts – which finally escalates to aggression.

Averill's (1982) social constructive approach is based on the assumption that anger is a holistic reaction to social situations and a complex syndrome. The regularity with which the syndrome occurs is determined by social norms. Thus, anger serves as a function in social contexts. Anger here is a conflict relevant emotion, which inherits the monitoring of those misbehaviors and violations of norms to which official norm sanctions have no access. Here, two rules come into conflict: On the one hand there is a perceived misbehavior. On the other hand, there exists a social prohibition to aggress intentionally. Because the aggressive reaction occurs in passion and the victim has provoked the aggressor, the behavior of the aggressor – which implies a violation of a social norm – is justified.

In a process orientated framework from Steffgen (1993; see Schwenkmezger et al., 1999), four different phases of the evolution and progression of an anger episode are described: *anger activation, anger appearance, anger regulation,* and *anger stabilization* (see Figure 1). These phases do not evolve like a one-way street, but rather, stand in a transactional relationship (see also the working model of anger from Eckhardt & Deffenbacher, 1995; Kassinove & Eckhardt, 1995).

Anger Activation
Important situational release conditions of anger are the following: action-blocking of unpleasant stimuli, blocking of goal attainment, nonfulfillment of a need, personal attacks and offenses, interruption of concentration-requiring tasks, frustrations, impairment of self value feelings by the words or actions of a person, and provocations or provocative stimuli. The level of person-specific anger is determined through biological vulnerabilities, e.g., characteristics of the autonomic nervous system or the endocrine system, and dispositional constructs. It is difficult to distinguish situational and person-specific parameters from cognitions or subjective evaluations of a situation. Within cognitive approaches this dilemma is solved, as the emergence of anger is explained by relevant emotion-specific evaluation patterns.

Similar to Lazarus (1966), in this model there is a differentiation between primary and secondary evaluations. The process of primary evaluation covers the perception that an action goal is blocked, as well as cognitions of attribution of responsibility concerning the obstruction or handicap of the goal attainment and the attribution of guilt in responding to the question of whether personal standards, requirements or obligations were violated (Averill, 1982). Cognitions concerning the intention and effectiveness of anger coping and competence or helplessness expectations within an anger situation can be regarded as components of the secondary evaluation. The three components of person, situation and evaluation are in direct connection with each other (Steffgen & Schwenkmezger, 1990).

Anger Appearance and Anger Regulation
Anger appearance and anger regulation processes, likewise, can be separated with difficulty. The actual anger state can be differentiated with regard to the components of

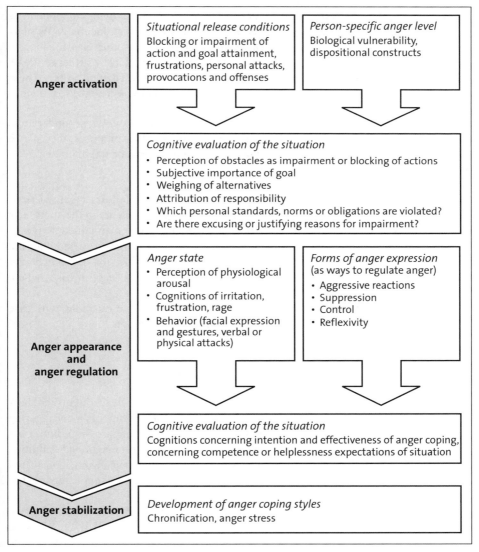

Figure 1. Process orientated framework of anger from Steffgen (1993; cf. Schwenmezger, Steffgen, & Dusi, 1999).

experience into physiological, cognitive, and behavioral forms of the anger phenomenon. Thus, anger is defined as a complex organized state, consisting of cognitive reactions, action impulses (behavior), and the perception of physiological concomitants.
The mutual influence of cognitions and excitation is strengthened through rumination
(Zillmann, 1988). During high excitation, cognitive control is more and more decreased,
and among other factors, this favors the occurrence of aggressive automatisms.

With regard to anger processing, forms of anger regulation can be differentiated.
Anger coping can be aligned as both intra- and interpersonal. Within the domain of
anger research, the distinction of different forms of *expressive coping components* is
seen as particularly important (Spielberger, Johnson, Russell, Crane, Jacobs, & Worden,
1985; Spielberger, 1988; Steffgen & Schwenkmezger, 1990; for other classification of
anger regulation see Deffenbacher et al., 1996; Harburg, Blakelock, & Roeper, 1979;
Kassinove & Eckhardt, 1995; Salisch & Pfeiffer, 1998; Weber & Titzman, 2003). These
different forms of anger regulation indicate that, in addition to aggressive reactions, a
multiplicity of nonaggressive coping reactions can arise with anger.

In the phases of anger appearance and anger regulation can evolve secondary and
tertiary evaluation processes sensu Lazarus (1966). Among other purposes, they play a
substantial role in facilitating the transition to the next phase, anger stabilization.

Anger Stabilization
Depending upon adjustment and frequency of coping success or failure, anger reactions
are either *stabilized* or *destabilized*. Coping forms of anger, which are in the short term
successful and/or socially strengthened, have the tendency to be maintained and to be
used in future anger situations. However, if a behavior arises chronically and does not
yield to other new reaction forms, this leads to a substantial restriction of the behavior
repertoire and, in the long run, to negative social consequences (e.g., in cases where
there are constant situational maladjusted anger outbreaks).

As a consequence of affective excitation, whether aggressive reactions will arise
depends crucially on the (learned) regulation of affective excitation.

Theoretical Approach From an Aggression Perspective

Referring to aggression theories, three forms of aggression are to be distinguished: hostile, expressive, and instrumental aggression (Feshbach, 1964). Anger is a cotriggering
factor for hostile (desire to hurt) and expressive (desire to hit) aggression, but is not
originally merged with instrumental aggression (see also the aforementioned definition
of aggression). This is reflected also in aggression theories, in which anger is considered
to different degrees – from anger-free theories, to theories in which anger is regarded as
a prerequisite of aggression.

Following Weber (1994), other anger-free aggression theories are mentioned in the
ethological approach (Lorenz, 1963), the sociobiological (Wilson, 1978), the classical
psychoanalytic (Freud, 1923), and the social interactional approach (Tedeschi & Felson,
1994). Additionally, the classical frustration–aggression hypothesis of Dollard, Doob,
Miller, Mowrer, and Sears (1939) does not consider anger explicitly. Other theories

discuss aggression as occurring both in and between groups (theory of realistic group conflict, Sherif, Harvey, White, Hood, & Sherif, 1961; theory of relative deprivation, Stouffer, Suchman, DeVinney, Star, & Williams, 1949).

In contrast, aggression theories which consider the presence of anger explicitly are the successors of the frustration–aggression hypothesis (Berkowitz, 1962; Berkowitz, 1989; Kornadt, 1984), the social-cognitive learning theory of Bandura (1973), the attribution conception of Ferguson and Rule (1983), and the excitation transfer theory (Zillmann, 1988). The general affective aggression model (GAAM) from Lindsey and Anderson (2000) as an integrative model is also based on the assumption that individual differences in the preparedness for aggression interact with characteristics of the respective situation to determine the evocation of an affective reaction (in particular anger), which leads through cognitive evaluation processes to the execution of an aggressive action. Anderson and Bushman (2002) subsequently specified that anger plays several causal roles in aggression (see Berkowitz, 2003). Therefore, anger reduces inhibitions against aggressing, allows a person to maintain an aggressive intention over time, is used as an information cue, primes aggressive thoughts, scripts, and associated expressive-motor behaviors and energizes behavior by increasing arousal levels. Given that aggression-related knowledge structures are also primed by anger, aggressive behavior is one likely form of behavior that is energized by anger.

These approaches overlap insofar as they explain aggressive behavior as a reaction to (aversive) affective excitation and its cognitive processing. Hence it follows that aggressive behavior cannot be due to anger alone, but also to other emotions.

Theoretical Relationship Between Anger and Aggression

For most aggression theorists the relationship of anger to aggressive behavior consists of the fact that anger is a significant activator of aggression and is reciprocally influenced by aggression but it is neither necessary nor sufficient for aggression to occur (Chemtob, Novaco, Hamada, & Gross, 1997; Konecni, 1975; Novaco, 1986). Only Berkowitz (1993) pointed out that anger occurs in parallel to aggression. Both are produced by negative affect induced by unpleasant external events. The idea is that it is a bidirectional causality: anger influences the level of aggression and vice versa.

It has not been demonstrated yet, under which conditions anger leads to aggression. Anger can activate aggression, but aggressive behavior is not an automatic consequence of anger because aggression is regulated by inhibitory mechanisms (regulatory control of aggression). Anger can be an important activator of aggressive behavior, particularly under conditions of arousal intensity, which can serve to override inhibitory controls (Novaco, 1994). However, not all anger will lead to aggression and not all aggression is the result of anger (Averill, 1982).

If aggressive behavior is defined as conceptually distinct from anger, do anger and aggression therefore require somewhat different interventions? If anger is neither necessary nor sufficient for aggressive behavior as an antecedent, why treat anger to reduce aggression?

Treatment of Anger and Aggression

Treatment of Anger

The evaluation of the effectiveness of (coping via) anger turns out to be difficult. Here, both – the functions (Novaco, 1976) and the intentions (Weber & Titzman, 2003; assertive, defensive, and self-related goals) of anger and coping behavior – seem relevant. The different functions and intentions of anger clarify the fact that a generally valid evaluation of the (in)effectiveness of an anger coping mechanism is therefore hardly possible. The estimation of the effectiveness of a coping reaction is only possible with regard to the relevant situation, function, and intention.

Edmondson, Conger, and Tescher (2000) propose four dimensions of anger behavioral competence: appropriateness, effectiveness, anger display, and effects on others. Results of their study show that anger-prone individuals reported less appropriate and less effective anger-management strategies (higher amounts of anger displayed and more negative effects on other people). These results suggest that it is important to use interventions that help people with anger problems improve their competence in anger provoking situations.

Anger treatment programs start at three potential change levels of anger experience and expression: the level of psychophysiological processes, the level of cognitive processes, and the level of social interaction processes (behavior, social competences, and social skills). Concerning the change of the psychological processes in question, specific psychological training concepts were developed (Deffenbacher, Oetting, & DiGuiseppe, 2002; Steffgen & Schwenkmezger, 1993). The assignment of a training procedure to a process level of change can be made as a second step on the basis of the priority of the intended change areas (Edmondson & Conger, 1996; Novaco, 1994). The different training procedures are already disscussed elsewhere in detail, so the empirically relevant studies are not specified here (see also Dahlen & Deffenbacher, 2001; Steffgen & Schwenkmezger, 1993):

- *Modification of physiological arousal*: These include systematic desensitization (Hart, 1984) and relaxation treatment that are intended to reduce physiological arousal associated with anger and to prevent unpleasant feelings and unfavorable behavior (for findings, see Dahlen & Deffenbacher, 2001).
- *Modification of cognitive processes*: These are cognitive treatments that are intended to modify cognitive processes such as hostile appraisals and attributions, irrational beliefs, and inflammatory thinking (Ellis, 1977). Alternative cognitions are developed and rehearsed. The experience of anger will be reduced so that anger intensity will remain at a level that allows adaptive behavior and in consequence the expression of anger will also be changed.
- *Modification of behavior (social interaction)*: These social skills trainings are common approaches to anger treatment. In order to arrange interpersonal communication appropriately, the procedures in this area are based on the assumption that some people have social deficits. Anger feelings cannot be expressed in a socially appropriate way, e.g., resistance to provocations or violations of justified requirements without hurting the feelings of others (Moon & Eisler, 1983; Def-

fenbacher, Story, Stark, Hogg, & Brandon, 1987; Deffenbacher, 1988). Social skills training teaches clients appropriate skills for handling anger in social situations.

– *Modification of several psychological processes*: These cognitive-relaxation treatments (Deffenbacher, Story, Brandon, Hogg, & Hazaleus, 1988; Hazaleus & Deffenbacher, 1986; Novaco, 1975, 1977, 1978) combine the effect of cognitive processes and physiological arousal.

In problem solving treatments, social skills trainings are combined with elements of cognitive reorganization (Moon & Eisler, 1983). The purpose of this form of treatment is to find appropriate strategies to resolve anger-provoking situations. The approach is to facilitate adaptive reactions to anger. In problem solving trainings of the working group of Lochman (Lochman, Nelson, & Sims, 1981), aggressive children are instructed by means of an operant reward system to restrain their impulsive behavior, to learn positive self instructions and problem solving competencies and to form their own plans.

Additionally, multicomponent programs are also used, in which changes are intended on every one of the three regulation levels: psychophysiological processes, cognitive processes, and social interaction processes (Schwenkmezger, Steffgen, & Dusi, 1999; Feindler & Ecton, 1986; Nomellini & Katz, 1983).

All in all, a treatment package of anger should include the following components: addressing motivation, cultivating the therapeutic alliance, managing physiological arousal, fostering cognitive change, implementing behavioral change, providing environmental supports for change, teaching relapse-prevention skills, and initiating restitution and reintegration (DiGuiseppe, 1999; Schwenkmezger, Steffgen, & Dusi, 1999).

Treatment of Aggression

More generally, Krahé (2001) differentiates between some universal approaches to prevent and reduce aggression. The cathartic release of aggressive tension (see Baumeister & Bushman, this volume), punishment of aggressive behavior, training of anger management skills, and the provision of nonaggressive role models are listed as approaches targeting the individual aggressor (individual oriented). Legal regulations and community-based interventions are considered as societal responses to reduce aggressive behavior (context oriented).

Furthermore, concerning the *context* level, it is assumed that changing contextual conditions – like changing the learning condition with rewards of prosocial behavior and punishments of aggressive behavior, changing social norms and expectations for behavior in a specific context, changing the organization of social groups to gain from beneficial social contacts – will positively influence aggressive behavior (Gottfredson, 1997).

Concerning the *individual* level, the starting point for a change may begin with social attitudes, beliefs, and knowledge, secondly, with social competences and skills, and thirdly, with social behavior (Gottfredson, 1997). The intention to influence social attitudes, beliefs, and knowledge may be to increase the awareness of aggressive individuals of social influences on misbehavior, or to modify stereotypes and prejudices towards social minorities. Training of social skills is based on the assumption that an improvement of positive social behavior options will heighten the possibility of prosocial behavior and decrease the possibility of antisocial behavior (e.g., aggressive behavior, deliquency). The modification of social behavior is intended through interventions like modeling, rehearsal, feedback, and reinforcement and relies on learning principles.

A popular approach of the aforementioned strategies to prevent aggression is social skills training. Nangle, Erdley, Carpenter, and Newman (2002) regroup various intervention studies in the area of social skills as follows:

- *Social skills training:* Treatments in this category attempt to compensate for a lack of social skills in order to negotiate conflicts more competently or to influence peers in a socially accepted and effective way. Different training procedures are used, including instruction, modeling, behavioral rehearsal, feedback, and discussion. Providing children and adolescents with more social skills, like participation, cooperation, or communication, is assumed to reduce aggressive behavior indirectly through a broader behavioral spectrum.

- *Cognitive-behavioral skills training:* This approach concentrates on modifying thought processes which underlie aggressive behavior rather than on changing overt behavior (see social information-processing model from Crick & Dodge, 1994). The interventions mentioned by Nangle et al. (2002) mostly represent adaptations of the classical social problem-solving skills training by Spivack and Shure (1974), which focuses on problem-solving skills as generating alternative solutions, thinking of consequences of actions, and pairing solutions and consequences.

- *Multicomponent cognitive-behavioral skills training:* Multicomponent interventions combine skills training procedures (e.g., instruction, modeling, rehearsal, or feedback) with cognitive-behavioral training components, like training of anger control techniques, social problem solving, self-instruction, relaxation, perspective taking, and self-regulation (e.g., Coping Power Program, c.f. Lochman & Wells, 2004).

Concerning therapeutical treatments of aggression, it is suggested (Bor, 2004; Greenberg, Domitrovich, & Bumbarger, 2001; Tate, Reppucci, & Mulvey, 1995; Scheithauer & Petermann, 2004) to apply pharmacological interventions as well as psychological treatments like the aforementioned cognitive problem-solving trainings, supporting interventions for parents (e.g., Triple P, c.f. Turner & Sanders, 2006), functional family therapy (Barton & Alexander, 1981; Barton, Alexander, Waldron, Turner, & Warburton, 1985), and multisystemic therapy (Borduin, 1999; Curtis, Ronan, & Borduin, 2004; Henggeler, Schoenwald, Borduin, Rowland, & Cunningham, 1998).

Combined Treatment of Anger and Aggression

Traditional behavioral approaches to aggression management have been criticized for a failure to address the intense emotional arousal that may accompany impulsive and explosive behavior. Although aggression can occur in the absence of anger arousal, anger can act as a determinant of aggressive behavior and can influence the cognitive processes used to mediate one's response to a perceived provocation (Feindler, 1990).

Therefore, in addition to the treatments that are addressed for the prevention or reduction of anger or of aggressive behavior, further approaches can be differentiated, which can be derived from the background of a (postulated or accepted) connection between anger and aggression. Five different positions can be described:

- It is assumed that anger proceeds to aggression. The goal is to regulate negatively experienced anger as an aversive emotional reaction, in order to reduce the probability of aggressive behavior (e.g., Feindler & Scalley, 1998; Adolescent anger management groups for violence reduction).
- It is assumed that anger and aggression arise parallely (as a syndrome). An anger intervention should inevitably change aggressive behavior as well (Berkowitz, 1993).
- It is assumed that anger and aggression show a high proximity of constructs. Based on this assumption, anger-aggression treatments are implemented, in which parallel effects on anger and aggression are to be strived for *directly* (persons at risk for anger and aggression related problems)
- It is assumed that anger and aggression are strongly overlapping. By developing general prosocial behavior (social skills) or conflict resolution competence (problem-solving), anger and aggression are both influenced *indirectly*.
- It is assumed that aggression is a mediator of the emergence of anger. Thus, trait aggressiveness determines, among other things, the quality and intensity of anger reactions. By reduction of aggressiveness, anger reactions are also changed.

On one side, anger treatment is often based primarily on the understanding of anger reactions, and aggression is treated as a secondary phenomenon. Anger management training helps to prevent aggressive behavior by cognitive restructuring. In this manner, principles of anger management work to reduce and prevent anger and sometimes also aggression.

On the other side, in respect to aggression, cognition and physiological processes are seen as preliminary stages of aggression (Anderson & Bushman, 2002). However, they are a substantial component of anger. Cognitive mediators of aggression (e.g., attributional processes, Crick & Dodge, 1994) and social problem-solving skills are therefore often targeted by anger treatments.

In comparing the treatment approaches of anger and aggression aforementioned it is obvious that anger management approaches bear strong resemblance to aggression treatment – especially in multicomponent trainings. Behaviorally-oriented anger treatments integrating social skills and problem-solving trainings coincide strongly with aggression treatment. Therefore, effects on both the emotional (anger) and behavioral (aggression) levels are expected and not surprising.

Comparative and Meta-Analytic Studies Regarding Anger

Apart from studies in which the effectiveness of individual programs was evaluated (for an overview see Schwenkmezger et al., 1999; Steffgen & Dusi, 2006), in other studies, a comparison of the differential effectiveness of different techniques and training procedures for anger reduction and for modification of forms of dealing with anger were also made (see Novaco, 1975; Moon & Eisler, 1983; in particular the working group around Deffenbacher, see, e.g., Deffenbacher, Oetting, & DiGuiseppe, 2002).

An overview of these comparative studies verifies the fact that all groups of procedures – relaxation procedures, cognitive training forms, cognition-relaxation-trainings, social competence trainings, problem solving trainings, and multicomponent trainings – can significantly change the occurrence of different aspects of the emotion of anger.

In particular, meta-analysis on the effectiveness of anger treatments permits a few more far reaching conclusions (Beck & Fernandez, 1998; Edmondson & Conger, 1996; Tafrate, 1995; DiGuiseppe & Tafrate, 2003).

Beck and Fernandez (1998) document the effectiveness of the cognitive-behavioral-therapy approach on the basis of a meta-analysis with 50 empirical studies, in which multicomponent programs incorporating diverse predominantly clinical samples receiving a combination of cognitive and behavioral techniques were used. It was found that cognitive-behavioral therapy produced a grand mean weighted effect size of .70. Thirty-five studies used self-reported anger and fifteen studies referred to anger but reported behavioral ratings of aggression as the dependent variable. The authors' exluded single-modality treatments.

Tafrate (1995) identified 17 published studies and found empirical support for cognitive, relaxation, skills training, and multicomponent interventions. He restricted the analysis to subjective reports of anger intensity and frequency, and to physiological measures. He did not include effect sizes from behavioral outcome measures of aggression. DiGuiseppe and Tafrate (2003) additionally noted, on the basis of a meta-analysis in which 57 evaluation studies were considered, that independently of the orientation of the procedure, the anger interventions generally reduced both anger and aggressive behavior and strengthened adaptive behavior. They found significant differences in effect sizes for different dependent variable categories. Aggression had the highest effect size of any type of dependent measure. However, the study failed to find significant differences between types of treatment for different dependent measures. This is due to many different interventions which have been studied only a few times, contributing to weak statistical power.

Gansle (2005; 20 evaluation studies) mentions a weighted mean effect size of school-based anger interventions post treatment of .31 across outcomes. The largest effects were found for externalizing behaviors and anger, internalizing, and social skills. Dependent variables measuring externalizing behaviors of anger included deviant behavior, disruptive behavior, aggressive behavior, off-task disruptive behavior, conduct problems, state and trait anger expression, general anger, and anger toward specific people. Most anger-related interventions used multicomponent treatment packages, whereas socially focused intervention packages (identifying problems, generating possible responses, making eye contact, communication skills) seem to be more effective than self-focused interventions (recognizing and labeling emotions, relaxation, imagery). The study failed to examine differences between specific types of treatment for specific dependent measures.

In a meta-analysis of 23 studies from Del Vecchio and O'Leary (2004), effect sizes were derived only from anger measures. Consistent with previous reviews, the results support the use of anger treatment for anger problems (as driving anger, anger suppression and anger expression difficulties) with medium and large effects (.61 to .90). In summary, when treating generalized anger, the treatments reviewed (cognitive-behavioral, cognitive, relaxation, and other – miscellaneous treatment category) all produced similar positive results. For anger expression problems (e.g., anger outbursts), cognitive behavioral treatment appears to be the most effective treatment. For anger suppression, cognitive treatment is the most effective form. The findings show that specific anger problems can be treated differentially by various forms of anger treatments. Not all treatment is equally effective for different anger problems.

The meta-analysis of Sukhodolsky, Kassinove, and Gorman (2004), based on 40 studies, found a mean effect size in the the medium range ($d = .67$). A differential effect shows that skills training and multimodal treatments were more effective in reducing measures of aggressive behavior and improving measures of social skills, whereas problem-solving treatments showed greater effects for reducing subjective reports of anger by children and adolescents. The cognitive-behavioral treatment approach shows only moderate effects.

Edmondson and Conger (1996) included a wide range of outcome measures in their meta-analytic review of 18 studies. They found that different types of interventions (relaxation, cognitive, cognitive-relaxation, and social skills) have different effects on different types of treatment outcome variables. Social skills training had a larger effect on treatment variables that assess anger behavior/aggression. However, the small number of studies did not allow for statistical examination of the differences between effect sizes.

A meta-analysis which synthesized research on the effectiveness of school based programs for preventing or reducing aggressive behavior showed some significant variation across different intervention strategies. Behavioral approaches and counseling show the largest effects, social competence with and without cognitive-behavioral components followed close behind and multimodal and peer mediation programs showed the smallest effects (Wilson, Lipsey, & Derzon, 2003).

All in all, the meta-analytic reviews show medium to large effect sizes and the results demonstrate that effective interventions are available for the treatment of anger problems in different populations. Most of the research focuses on cognitive and behavioral interventions. There is emerging empirical support for the effectiveness of several anger-reduction strategies. The use of multicomponent procedures has especially demonstrated promise as an appropriate proceeding for global anger interventions.

However, there is little or no evidence supporting the relative efficacy of one treatment over another. There are too few replicated studies that employ well-defined interventions with specific populations to assess effects by type of anger problem and client group (Deffenbacher, Oetting, & DiGuiseppe, 2002). A clarification of whether the dependent variable is able to differentiate between anger and aggression may enable the careful matching of treatments to specific problems/clients.

Some methodological problems of meta-analysis should also be considered. Del Vecchio and O'Leary (2004) highlight in particular that most of the reviews included measures of assertiveness, hostility, and/or aggression as measures of the anger construct (Beck & Fernandez, 1998; Edmondson & Conger, 1996). Therefore the effect sizes are not indicators of change in anger alone. If anger is to be considered a construct distinct from hostility and aggression, separate analyses are needed.

Furthermore, it is inappropriate to compare effect sizes across interventions and class- es of measures. Such comparisons are often based on a relatively small number of studies of any intervention modality and include different types of measures across studies.This introduces a source of measurement confounding that may inflate or deflate effect sizes when conducting between-intervention comparisons (Deffenbacher et al., 2002).

Indication and Target Groups

Anger can present serious problems when it is intense or expressed in dysfunctional ways. Since there has been no conceptualization of problematic anger until today, there are no disorders where anger is a necessary or defining condition. Therefore, a descrip- tion of diagnostic criteria for anger disorders is needed. Diagnostic criteria would facili- tate intervention decisions by providing agreed-upon criteria for defining and selecting samples (Dahlen & Deffenbacher, 2001; Deffenbacher, Oetting, & DiGuiseppe, 2002; Eckhardt & Deffenbacher, 1995).

As long as these criteria are not specified within the domain of anger research, four indication areas for the modification of anger should be differentiated (Steffgen & Schwenkmezger, 1993; Weber, 1994):

- *Social indication:* It is assumed that anger experience leads to aggression and acts of violence, and primarily damages other persons. Increased aggressive, violent behavior is to be reduced by changing anger experience. Interventions were carried out and evaluated for the following target groups: Offenders (adults and adolescents), violent criminals, couples with aggressive pair relations and/or violent marriage partners, violent parents, aggressive children and adolescents, groups of psychiatric patients, and aggressive road users.
- *Health-related indication:* It is assumed that anger is a risk factor for psychoso- matic diseases and can lead to health damage. Anger can either directly cause health-endangering psychological and physiological changes of the organism, or can have indirect effects through chronic health-endangering behaviors (e.g., smoking, consumption of alcohol), which represent risk factors. Interventions were carried out and evaluated for the following target groups: Patients with es- sential hypertonia, patients with coronary heart diseases or pronounced type-A behavior, chronic pain patients, persons with posttraumatic stress disorders, per- sons with brain damage, persons with mental retardation/cognitive and learning disorders, and drug addicts.
- *Occupational and activity-related indication:* It is assumed that anger reactions impair the action execution of activities, which are to be implemented in respect to work and/or in the execution of the occupational role. Occupations, in which confrontation situations full of conflict arise frequently or represent a main com- ponent of the work content, are to be considered in particular. Thus far, interven- tions have been carried out and evaluated for the following target groups: Police officers, military staff, personal in helping occupations (therapists, social work- ers, probation officers, consultants, nurses), teachers, sportsmen, truck drivers, bus and car drivers, and managers.

- *Subjective well-being-related indication:* It is assumed that anger reactions lead to an impairment of subjective well-being. Target groups are persons who notice increased excitability, frequent aggressive-expressive, extrapunitive anger outbreaks, or also constant anger suppression as ineffective forms of anger coping with negative effects on their well-being. Thus far, interventions have been carried out and evaluated for the following target groups: Students and participants in courses of adult education.

Unlike anger, aggression is a defining condition of different clinical disorders. Especially in childhood and youth, aggressive-antisocial behavior as a clinical problem is distinguished from normal, developmental phenomena (Scheithauer & Petermann, 2000). For a classification concerning aggression-related problems following DSM-IV (American Psychiatric Association, 1994) or ICD-10 (World Health Organization, 1992), the following disorders are especially relevant: conduct disorder, childhood onset type/ adolescent onset type (312.8/F 91.8) and oppositional defiant disorder (313.81/F 91.3). Other relevant psychiatric diagnoses associated with aggressive behavior in children and adolescents are attention deficit hyperactivity disorder (ADHD), psychotic disorders, traumatic brain injury, seizure disorder, mental retardation, pervasive developmental disorders, depression, bipolar disorder, and posttraumatic stress disorder (PTSD; see Connor & Steingard, 1996). For adults, antisocial personality disorder (301.7/F 60.2) is relevant. These disorders represent indications for aggression treatments through consultation or psychotherapy.

Indications for aggression treatment can be structured following the classification of Gordon (1983). Universal, targeted, selective, and indicated prevention levels can be considered:

- *Universal* prevention is dedicated to populations that do not (yet) show aggression disorders or a special risk for developing aggression problems (this category is close to primary prevention). Target groups may include populations like all first grade students in an elementary school or all children of a certain school district.
- *Targeted* prevention on the other hand is dedicated to special subpopulations and can be divided into *selective* and *indicated* prevention.
- *Selective* prevention implies treatments for risk groups that have a higher probability of developing aggression-related problems (selected by risk factors like impulsive temperament, low academic performance, rejection of peers, or influence of deviant peers).
- *Indicated* prevention refers to prevention efforts for those individuals that already show the early beginnings of aggression problems or a moderate expression of that behavior (e.g., children with disruptive behavior in class).

Violent offenders in particular are seen as a relevant target group for anger and aggression treatment. Indication therefore concerns individuals – adolescents as well as adults – who have been condemned because of criminal acts of violence. This indication is difficult to separate from the aforementioned clinical indication; for example, some violent offenders also fit into the category of antisocial personality disorders (Blackburn & Coid, 1999). Violent offenders are markedly heterogeneous (Blackburn, 1993).

Interventions have been designed for aggressive populations based on the assumption that highly aggressive people experience anger problems. It is not helpful to assume uniformly high anger levels within these populations. Offenders could be individuals with chronic dispositional problems of hostility, poor frustration tolerance, and angry, impulsive acting out (reactive aggression), or individuals who are reluctant to make hostile inferences, report low levels of anger, and control their aggressive impulses (proactive aggression; Howells, 1998). Anger management may be useful training for some people lacking the awareness and cognitive skills to cope with aggression, but it is not a magic bullet for all forms of aggression (Hollenhorst, 1998; e.g., batterers who are already controlling do not need to be more controlling).

Thus, the evaluation of anger management programs for violent offenders has demonstrated no consistent research findings. Anger treatments, especially with highly aggressive persons, are only partially effective (e.g., Howells, 1989; Watt & Howells, 1999). As anger is not a necessary condition for aggression, it can be argued that individual assessment is required primarily for allocation to a treatment, in order to ensure that the treatment is appropriate. Caution against indiscriminate referral of violent offenders to anger management programs is sorely needed. Thus, pretreatment assessment of anger regulation may be important to identify which offenders may benefit from particular treatment programs.

The question of differential indication for anger treatment as well as for aggression trainings for special target groups is to be addressed. Developmental aspects (age group) and gender are to be considered as well as disorder characteristics.

For specific disorders where anger and aggression are linked, a clarification of the role of anger and aggression is needed (e.g., posttraumatic stress disorder).

For instance, veterans with combat-related posttraumatic stress disorder (PTSD) have been found to be significantly more angry and aggressive and they often consider anger as their most salient problem (Kulka et al., 1990). The activation of anger can serve to activate the "survival mode" of functioning (characterized by the hyperactivation of cognitive structures which facilitate response – aggression – to life threatening situations). After the war, this reaction is activated maladaptively in response to threat.

The heightened arousal elements of anger activation serve to override inhibitory controls on aggression (Chemtob, Novaco, Hamada, Gross, & Smith, 1997). By conjoining the concepts of anger and aggression in this specific model (strong theoretical link), it is expected and shown that anger treatment also directly influences aggressive behavior (Chemtob, Novaco, Hamada, & Gross, 1997).

In conclusion, anger interventions are based on different objectives, and only partially is aggression reduction intended and indicated (see social indication) by these interventions. There is also only a partial overlap in target groups for both anger and aggression treatment.

Principles for Use of Anger Treatment to Reduce Aggressive Behavior

In summary, the previous comments suggest a close relationship between anger and aggression, and also suggest that anger treatments can influence aggressive behavior, but do not reduce aggression per se. If prevention or reduction of aggressive behavior by anger treatement is explicitly intended, some principles are to be taken into consideration:

1. The constructs of anger and aggression need to be defined clearly and accurately as distinct from each erther. Does the anger construct consist of action tendencies or behavior? Do the constructs of anger and aggression overlap? The differentiation between proactive and reactive aggression should also be considered in light of a need for different treatment approaches.

2. A clear description of the theory or model of anger that serves as the rationale for the treatment approach is indispensable (Edmondson & Conger, 1996; for aggression see Fields & McNamara, 2003).

3. The aims and goals of the treatment have to be named clearly. Which different aspects of aggression are intended to be influenced by the treatment?

4. Clear construct operationalization and valid assessement of different aspects of anger and aggression are to be mentioned. Both emotion-related and behavior-related elements have to be differentiated and included. Different anger and aggressive behavior components should be carefully assessed prior to, post, and as a follow-up to treatment. The level of specificity should be considered when evaluating outcomes.

5. Specific treatment components have to be included in an anger treatment program in order to reduce and change the anger experience, anger expression, and aggression. For example, for changing aggressive behavior, more behaviorally-oriented components (social skills, problem solving) should be integrated into a multicomponent treatment approach.

6. An indication for specific target groups is needed. Empirically supported programs should be developed for specific client populations.

It might be useful to recommend different treatment approaches for different aspects of anger and aggression problems and for different target groups (e.g., offenders). Anger prone persons have to be defined against a theoretical background. Without diagnostic criteria for anger problems there will be too much heterogenity in the target population to make accurate predictions about treatment.

In conclusion, the present review shows that there is some theoretical and empirical support for a relationship between anger and aggression. Anger can be a significant activator of aggression and is reciprocally influenced by aggression, but is neither necessary nor sufficient for aggression to occur. To some extent, specific treatment goals of anger or aggression interventions justify the necessity of different treatment approaches. However, in the field of overlapping of both constructs the application of parallel treatment strategies – especially cognitive behavior and social skills training – seems appropriate.

In consideration of the relationship between and the overlapping of the constructs of anger and aggression, by maintaining the described principles, a selective anger treatment could allow for the adequate evaluation of treatment effects and for influencing aggressive behavior more systematically.

References

American Psychiatric Association (1994). *Diagnostic and statistical manual for mental disorders* (DSM-IV, 4th ed.). Washington, DC: American Psychiatric Association.

Anderson, C. J., & Bushman, B. J. (2002). Human aggression. *Annual Review of Psychology, 53*, 27–51.

Averill, J. R. (1982). *Anger and aggression. An essay on emotion.* New York: Springer.

Bandura, A. (1973). *Aggression: A social learning analysis.* Englewood Cliffs, NY: Prentice Hall.

Baron, R. A., & Richardson, D. R. (1994). *Human aggression* (2nd ed.). New York, NY: Plenum.

Barton, C., & Alexander, J. F. (1981). Functional family therapy. In A. S. Gurman & D. P. Kniskern (Eds.). *Handbook of family therapy* (pp. 403–43). New York: Brunner/Mazel.

Barton, C., Alexander, J. F., Waldron, H., Turner, C. W., & Warburton, J. (1985). Generalizing treatment effects of functional family therapy: Three replications. *American Journal of Family Therapy, 13*, 16–26.

Beck, R., & Fernandez, E. (1998). Cognitive behavioural therapy in the treatment of anger: A meta-analysis. *Cognitive Therapy and Research, 22*, 63–74.

Berkowitz, L. (1962). *Aggression: A social psychological analysis.* New York: McGraw-Hill.

Berkowitz, L. (1989). Frustration-aggression hypothesis: Examination and reformulation. *Psychological Bulletin, 106*, 59–73.

Berkowitz, L. (1993). *Aggression: Its causes and consequences, and control.* New York, NY: McGraw-Hill.

Berkowitz L. (2003). Affect, aggression and antisocial behavior. In R. J. Davidson, K. R. Scherer, & H. H. Goldsmith (Eds.), *Handbook of affective sciences* (pp. 804–823). New York: Oxford University Press.

Blackburn, R. (1993). *The psychology of criminal conduct.* Chichester, UK: Wiley.

Blackburn, R., & Coid, J. W. (1999). Empirical clusters of DSM-III personality disorders in violent offenders. *Journal of Personality Disorders, 13*(1), 18–34.

Bor, W. (2004). Prevention and treatment of childhood and adolescent aggression and antisocial behaviour: A selective review. *Australian and New Zealand Journal of Psychiatry, 38*, 373–380.

Borduin, C. M. (1999). Multisystemic treatment of criminality and violence in adolescents. *Journal of the American Academy of Child and Adolescent Psychiatry, 38*(3), 242–249.

Buss, A. H. (1961). *The psychology of aggression.* New York: Wiley.

Chemtob, C. M., Novaco, R. W., Hamada, R. S., & Gross, D. M. (1997). Cognitive-behavioral treatment for severe anger in posttraumatic stress disorder. *Journal of Consulting and Clinical Psychology, 65*(1), 184–189.

Chemtob, C. M., Novaco, R. W., Hamada, R. S., Gross, D. M., & Smith, G. (1997). Anger regulation deficits in combat related posttraumatic stress disorder. *Journal of Traumatic Stress, 10*(1), 17–36.

Connor, D. F., & Steingard, R. J. (1996). A clinical approach to the pharmacotherapy of aggression in children and adolescents. In C. F. Ferris & T. Grisso (Eds.), *Understanding aggressive behavior in children* (pp. 290–307). New York: New York Academy of Sciences.

Connor, D. F., Steingard, R. J., Cunningham, J. A., Anderson, J. J., & Melloni, R. H. (2004). Proactive and reactive aggression in referred children and adolescents. *American Journal of Orthopsychiatry, 74*, 129–136.

Crick, N. R., & Dodge, K. A. (1994). A review and reformulation of social information-processing mechanisms in children's social adjustment. *Psychological Bulletin, 115*(1), 74–101.

Curtis, N. M., Ronan, K. R., & Borduin, C. M. (2004). Multisystemic treatment: A meta-analysis of outcome studies. *Journal of Family Psychology, 18*(3), 411–419.

Dahlen, E. R., & Deffenbacher, J. L. (2001). Anger management. In W. J. Lyddon, & J. V. Jones (Eds.), *Empirically supported cognitive therapies: Current and future applications* (pp. 163–181). New York: Springer Publishing Company.

Deffenbacher, J. L. (1988). Cognitive relaxation and social skills treatments of anger: A year later. *Journal of Counseling Psychology, 35*, 234–236.

Deffenbacher, J. L., Oetting, E. R., & DiGuiseppe, R. (2002). Principles of empirically supported interventions applied to anger management. *The Counseling Psychologist, 30*(2), 262–280.

Deffenbacher, J. L., Oetting, E. R., Lynch, R. S., & Morris, C. D. (1996). The expression of anger and its consequences. *Behavior Research and Therapy, 34*(7), 575–590.

Deffenbacher, J. L., Story, D. A., Brandon, A. B., Hogg, J. A., & Hazaleus, S. L. (1988). Cognitive and cognitive-relaxation treatments for anger. *Cognitive Therapy and Research, 12*, 167–184.

Deffenbacher, J. L., Story, D. A., Stark, R. S., Hogg, J. A., & Brandon, A. B. (1987). Cognitive-relaxation and social skills interventions in the treatment of general anger. *Journal of Counseling Psychology, 34*, 171–176.

Del Vecchio, T., & O'Leary, K. D. (2004). Effectiveness of anger treatments for specific anger problems: A meta-analytic review. *Clinical Psychology Review, 24*, 15–34.

DiGuiseppe, R. (1999). End Piece: Reflections on the treatment of anger. *Journal of Clinical Psychology, 55*(3), 365–379.

DiGuiseppe, R., & Tafrate, R. C. (2003). Anger treatments for adults: A meta-analytic review. *Clinical Psychology: Science and Practice, 10*, 70–84.

Dollard, J., Doob, L. W., Miller, N. E., Mowrer, O. H., & Sears, R. S. (1939). *Frustration and aggression.* New Haven, CT: Yale University Press.

Eckhardt, C. I., & Deffenbacher, J. L. (1995). Diagnosis of anger disorders. In H. Kassinove (Ed.), *Anger disorders: Definition, diagnosis, and treatment* (pp. 27–47). Washington, DC: Taylor and Francis.

Edmondson, C. B., & Conger, J. C. (1996). A review of treatment efficacy for individuals with anger problems: Conceptual, assessment, and methodological issues. *Clinical Psychology Review, 16*(3), 251–275.

Edmondson, C. D., Conger, J. C., & Tescher, B. (2000). Anger behavioral competence in anger-prone individuals. *Behavior Therapy, 31*, 463–478.

Ellis, A. (1977). *Anger: How to live with and without it.* New York: Citadel Press.

Feindler, E. L. (1990). Adolescent anger control: Review and critique. In M. Hersen, R. M. Eisler, & P. M. Miller (Eds.), *Progress in behavior modification* (Vol. 26, pp. 11–59). Newburry Park, CA: Sage.

Feindler, E. L., & Ecton, R. B. (1986). *Adolescent anger control: Cognitive behavioural techniques.* New York: Pergamon.

Feindler, E. L., & Scalley, M. (1998). Adolescent anger management groups for violence reduction. In K. C. Stoiber & T. R. Kratochwill (Eds.), *Handbook of group interventions for children and families* (pp. 100–119). Boston, MA: Allyn & Bacon.

Ferguson, T. J., & Rule, B. R. (1983). An attributional perspective on anger and aggression. In R. G. Green & E. L. Donnerstein (Eds.), *Aggression. Theoretical and empirical reviews* (Vol. 1, pp. 41–74). New York: Academic Press.

Feshbach, S. (1964). The function of aggression and the regulation of aggressive drive. *Psychological Review, 71*, 257–272.

Fields, S. A., & McNamara, J. R. (2003). The prevention of child and adolescent violence. A review. *Aggression and Violent Behavior, 8*, 61–91.

Freud, S. (1923). Das Ich und das Es [The Ego and the Id]. In S. Freud, *Gesammelte Werke* [Collected papers], Bd. XIII. London: Imago.

Gansle, K. A. (2005). The effectiveness of school-based anger interventions and programs: A meta-analysis. *Journal of School Psychology, 43*, 321–341.

Gordon, R. S. (1983). Operational classification of disease prevention. *Public Health Reports, 98*, 107–109.

Gottfredson, D. C. (1997). School-based crime prevention. In L. W. Sherman, D. Gottfredson, D. MacKenzie, J. Eck, P. Reuter, & S. Bushway (Eds.). *Preventing crime: What works, what doesen't, what's promising. A report to the united states congress.* Rockville, MD: National Institute of Justice. [available online: http://www.ncjrs.gov/works/chapter5.htm, retrieved 19.7.2006]

Greenberg, M. T., Domitrovich, C., & Bumbarger, B. (2001). The prevention of mental disorders in school-aged children: Current state of the field. *Prevention and Treatment, 4.* Available online: http://journals.apa.org/prevention/volume4/pre0040001a.html.

Harburg, E., Blakelock, E. H., & Roeper, E. J. (1979). Resentfull reflective coping with arbitary authority and blood pressure: Detroit. *Psychosomatic Medicine, 41*, 189–202.

Hart, K. E. (1984). Anxiety management training and anger control for Type A individuals. *Journal of Behavior Therapy and Experimental Psychiatry, 15*, 133–139.

Hazaleus, S. L., & Deffenbacher, J. L. (1986). Relaxation and cognitive treatments of anger. *Journal of Consulting and Clinical Psychology, 54*, 222–226.

Henggeler, S. W., Schoenwald, S. K., Borduin, C. M., Rowland, M. D., & Cunningham, P. B. (1998). *Multisystemic treatment of antisocial behavior in children and adolescents.* New York: Guilford.

Hollenhorst, P. S. (1998). What do we know about anger management programs in corrections? *Federal Probation, 62*, 52–64.

Howells, K. (1989). Anger-management methods in relation to the prevention of violent behaviour. In J. Archer & K. Browne (Eds.), *Human aggression: Naturalistic approaches* (pp. 153–181). London: Routledge.

Howells, K. (1998). Cognitive behavioural interventions for anger, aggression and violence. In N. Tarrier, A. Wells, & G. Haddock (Eds.), *Treating complex cases: The cognitive behavioural therapy approach* (pp. 295–318). Chichester, UK: Wiley.

Kassinove, H., & Eckhardt, C. I. (1995). An anger model and a look to the future. In H. Kassinove (Ed.), *Anger disorders: Definition, diagnosis, and treatment* (pp. 197–204). Washington, DC: Taylor and Francis.

Kassinove, H., & Sukhodolsky, D. G. (1995). Anger disorders: Basic science and practice issues. In H. Kassinove (Ed.), *Anger disorders: Definition, diagnosis, and treatment* (pp. 1–26). Washington, DC: Taylor and Francis.

Konecni, V. J. (1975). The mediation of aggressive behavior: Arousal level versus anger and cognitive labeling. *Journal of Personality and Social Psychology, 32*, 706–712.

Kornadt, H.-J. (1984). Motivation theory of aggression and its relation to social psychological approaches. In A. Mummendey (Ed.), *Social psychology of aggression* (pp. 21–32). Berlin: Springer.

Krahé, B. (2001). *The social psychology of aggression.* Hove: Psychology Press.

Kulka, R. A., Shlenger, W. E., Fairbank, J. A., Hough, R. L., Jordan, B. K., Marmar, C. R., & Weiss, D. S. (1990). *Trauma and the Vietnam War generation.* New York: Brunner/Mazel.

Lazarus, R. S. (1966). *Psychological stress and the coping process.* New York: McGraw-Hill.

Lindsay, J. J., & Anderson, C. A. (2000). From antecedent conditions to violent actions: A general affective aggression model. *Personality and Social Psychology Bulletin, 26*, 533–547.

Little, T. D., Henrich, C. C., Jones, S. M., & Hawley, P. H. (2003). Disentangling the 'whys' from the 'whats' of aggressive behavior. *International Journal of Behavioral Development, 27*(2), 122–133.

Lochman, J. E., & Wells, K. C. (2004). The coping power program for preadolescent aggressive boys and their parents: Outcome effects at the 1-year follow-up. *Journal of Consulting and Clinical Psychology, 72*(4), 571–578.

Lochman, J. E., Nelson, W. M., & Sims, J. P. (1981). A cognitive-behavioral program for use with aggressive children. *Journal of Clinical Child Psychology, 10*, 146–148.

Lorenz, K. (1963). Das sogenannte Böse [The so-called evil]. Vienna: Borotha-Schoeler.

Mayne, T. J., & Ambrose, T. K. (1999). Research review on anger in psychotherapy. *Journal of Clinical Psychology, 55*(3), 353–363.

Moon, J. R., & Eisler, R. M. (1983). Anger control: An experimental comparison of three behavioural treatments. *Behavior Therapy, 14*, 493–505.

Nangle, D. W., Erdley, C. A., Carpenter, E. M., & Newman, J. E. (2002). Social skills training as a treatment for aggressive children and adolescents: A developmental-clinical integration. *Aggression and Violent Behavior, 7*, 169–199.

Nomellini, S., & Katz, R. C. (1983). Effects of anger control training on abusive parents. *Cognitive Therapy and Research, 7*, 57–67.

Novaco, R. W. (1975). *Anger control: The development and evaluation of an experimental treatment.* Lexington, MA: Heath.

Novaco, R. W. (1976). The functions and regulation of the arousal of anger. *Journal of Psychiatry, 133*, 124–128.

Novaco, R. W. (1977). Stress inoculation: A cognitive therapy for anger and its application to a case of depression. *Journal of Consulting and Clinical Psychology, 45*, 600–608.

Novaco, R. W. (1978). Anger coping with stress. In J. Foreyt & D. Rathjen (Eds.), *Cognitive behaviour therapy* (pp. 135–173). New York, NY: Plenum Press.

Novaco, R. W. (1986). Anger as a clinical and a social problem. In R. J. Blanchard & D. C. Blanchard (Eds.), *Advances in the study of aggression* (Vol. 2, pp. 1–67). Orlando, FL: Academic Press.

Novaco, R. W. (1994). Anger as a risk factor for violence among the mentally disordered. In J. Monahan & H. Steadman (Eds.), *Violence and mental disorder: Developments in risk assessment* (pp. 21–56). Chicago, IL: University of Chicago Press.

Salisch, M. von, & Pfeiffer, I. (1998). Ärgerregulierung in den Freundschaften von Schulkindern – Entwicklung eines Fragebogens [Regulation of anger in children's friendships: Development of a questionnaire]. *Diagnostica, 44*, 41–53.

Scheithauer, H., & Petermann, F. (2000). Aggression. In F. Petermann (Ed.). *Lehrbuch der Klinischen Kinderpsychologie und -psychotherapie* [Textbook of clinical childpsychology and -psychotherapy] (4th ed). Göttingen: Hogrefe.

Scheithauer, H., & Petermann, F. (2004). Aggressiv-dissoziales Verhalten [Aggressive-dissocial Behavior]. In F. Petermann, K. Niebank, & H. Scheithauer (Eds.), *Entwicklungswissenschaft. Entwicklungspsychologie – Genetik – Neuropsychologie* [Developmental science. Developmental psychology – genetics – neuropsychology] (pp. 367–410). Berlin: Springer.

Schwenkmezger, P., Steffgen, G., & Dusi, D. (1999). *Umgang mit Ärger. Ärger und Konfliktbewältigungstraining auf kognitiv-verhaltenstherapeutischer Grundlage.* [To cope with anger. Anger and conflict regulation training on cognitive-behavioral basis] Göttingen: Hogrefe.

Sherif, M., Harvey, O. J., White, B. J., Hood, W. R., & Sherif, C. W. (1961). *Intergroup conflict and cooperation: The robber's cave experiment.* Norman, OK: University of Oklahoma.

Spielberger, C. D. (1988). *Professional Manual for the State-Trait Anger Expression Inventory.* Odessa, FL: Psychological Assessment Resources.

Spielberger, C. D., Johnson, E. H., Russell, S. F., Crane, R. J., Jacobs, G. A., & Worden, T. (1985). The experience and expression of anger: Construction and validation of an Anger Expression Scale. In M. A. Chesney & R. H. Rosenman (Eds.), *Anger and hostility in cardiovascular and behavioural disorders* (pp. 5–30). Washington, DC: Hemisphere.

Spielberger, C. D., Reheiser, E. C., & Sydeman, S. J. (1995). Measuring the experience, expression, and control of anger. In H. Kassinove (Ed.), *Anger disorders: Definition, diagnosis, and treatment* (pp. 49–67). Washington, DC: Taylor and Francis.

Spivack, G., & Shure, M. B. (1974). *Social adjustment of young children: A cognitive approach to solving real-life problems.* San Francisco: Jossey-Bass.

Steffgen, G. (1993). *Ärger und Ärgerbewältigung. Empirische Überprüfung von Modellannahmen und Evaluation eines Ärgerbewältigungstrainings* [Anger and coping with anger. Empirical testing of model hypothesis and evaluation of an anger regulation training]. Münster, Germany: Waxmann.

Steffgen, G., & Dusi, D. (2006). Ärgerbewältigungstraining [Anger regulation training]. In F. J. Schermer & A. Weber (Eds.), *Methoden der Verhaltensänderung: Komplexe Interventionsprogramme* [Methods of behavioral change: Complex intervention programs] (pp. 37–64). Stuttgart, Germany: Kohlhammer.

Steffgen, G., & Schwenkmezger, P. (1990). Zur Gültigkeit eines interaktionistischen Ärgermodells: Untersuchungen zum Management und Leistungssport [Validity of the interaction model of anger: Studies in management and competitive sport]. *Zeitschrift für experimentelle und angewandte Psychologie, 37*, 78–99.

Steffgen, G., & Schwenkmezger, P. (1993). Psychologische Interventionsverfahren zur Modifikation von Ärger und Ärgerausdruck [Psychological interventions concerning anger and anger expression]. In V. Hodapp & P. Schwenkmezger (Eds.), *Ärger und Ärgerausdruck* [Anger and anger expression] (pp. 277–297). Bern: Hans Huber.

Stouffer, S. A., Suchman, E. A., DeVinney, L. C., Star, S. A., & Williams, R. M. (1949). *The American Soldier: Adjustment during Army Life* (Volume I). Princeton, NJ: Princeton University Press.

Sukhodolsky, D. G., Kassinove, H., & Gorman, B. S. (2004). Cognitive-behavioral therapy for anger in children and adolescents: A meta-analysis. *Aggression and Violent Behavior, 9*, 247–269.

Tafrate, R. C. (1995). Evaluation of treatment strategies for adult anger disorders. In H. Kassinove (Ed.), *Anger disorders: Definition, diagnosis, and treatment* (pp. 109–129). Washington, DC: Taylor and Francis.

Tate, D. C., Reppucci, N. D., & Mulvey, E. P. (1995). Violent juvenile delinquents. Treatment effectiveness and implications for future action. *American Psychologist, 50*(9), 777–781.

Tedeschi, J. T., & Felson, R. B. (1994). *Violence, aggression, and coercive actions.* Washington, DC: American Psychological Association.

Turner, K. M., & Sanders, M. R. (2006). Dissemination of evidence-based parenting and family support strategies: Learning from the Triple P-Positive Parenting Program system approach. *Aggression and Violent Behavior, 11*, 176–193.

Watt, B. D., & Howells, K. (1999). Skills training for aggression control: Evaluation of an anger management programme for violent offenders. *Legal and Criminological Psychology, 4*, 285–300.

Weber, H. (1994). *Ärger. Psychologie einer alltäglichen Emotion* [Anger. Psychology of a common emotion]. Weinheim, Germany: Juventa.

Weber, H. (1999). Ärger und Aggression [Anger and aggression]. *Zeitschrift für Sozialpsychologie, 30*(2/3), 139–150.

Weber, H., & Titzmann, P. (2003). Ärgerbezogene Reaktionen und Ziele: Entwicklung eines neuen Fragebogens [Anger related reactions and goals: Development of a new questionnaire]. *Diagnostica, 49*, 97–109.

Wilson, E. O. (1978). *On human nature.* Cambridge, MA/London: Harvard University Press.

Wilson, S. J., Lipsey, M. W., & Derzon, J. H. (2003). The effects of school-based intervention programs on aggressive behavior: A meta-analysis. *Journal of Consulting and Clinical Psychology, 71*(1), 136–149.

World Health Organization (1992). *International Statistical Classification of Diseases and Health Related Problems* (ICD-10): Clinical descriptions and diagnostic guidelines. Geneva, Switzerland: World Health Organization.

Zillmann, D. (1988). Cognition-excitation interdependencies in aggressive behaviour. *Aggressive Behavior, 14*, 51–64.

How Affective is Revenge?
Emotional Processes Involved in Vengeful Reactions to Experienced Injustice

Mario Gollwitzer

> Vindictive persons live the life of witches; who, as they are mischievous,
> so end they infortunate. (Francis Bacon)

Revenge and retribution are important topics in our daily lives. Numerous novels, movies, theatre plays, fairy tales, myths, and legends tell dramatic stories of injustice and, accordingly, of revenge. Even as neutral observers, we have a desire to see the offender pay for what he did (French, 2001; Miller, 1998). Strong, passionate emotions accompany a revenge-related social episode: Witnessing acts of injustice makes us angry, morally outraged; sometimes we also experience anxiety or disgust. But as soon as revenge is carried out, as soon as the offender got what he deserves, we experience moral satisfaction, contentment, and gratification. On the other hand, we are deeply frustrated when the injustice cannot be redressed and when evil prevails (Solomon, 1999).

Some authors assume that vengeance is a passion, that we all have a deeply rooted desire for vengeance (Frijda, 1994), and that this desire is immoderate in quality and quantity (e.g., Jacoby, 1983). Legal philosophers argue that curtailing victims' desire to avenge is one of the most important functions of criminal law. Potter Stewart, one of the U.S. Supreme Court judges in the Furman v. Georgia case (1972), which led to a temporary suspension of capital punishment in the U.S. between 1972 and 1976, explicitly refers to this notion in his explanatory statement:

> The instinct for retribution is part of the nature of man, and channeling that
> instinct in the administration of criminal justice serves an important purpose in promoting the stability of a society of government by law. (Furman v. Georgia, 1972).

Indeed, numerous examples seem to prove that vengeful acts can be rampant and excessive (e.g., Frijda, 1994; Jacoby, 1983). But do these examples also prove that the desire for vengeance is irrational, primitive, a "deep-seated urge" (de Waal, 1996), a "kind of wild justice" (Bacon, 1601/1986)?

Revenge and Retribution

If we subscribe to the opinion that interpersonal revenge is inherently primitive, irrational, and immoderate in nature, we logically come to the conclusion that the right to punish wrongdoers should be taken away from the individual and granted to legal institutions only in order to protect and promote social order. The idea that the desire for revenge needs to be channeled and shaped in accordance with principles of appropriateness is even older than the Old Testament, where we find the often-cited phrase "an eye for an eye, a tooth for a tooth" (Exodus 21:23–25, Leviticus 24:18–20, Deuteronomy 19:21). Legal scholars, criminologists, and philosophers have elaborated the idea that revenge and retribution are two sides of the same coin. Whereas the latter can be described as rational, fair, enlightened, the former is described as primitive, irrational, excessive. One of the most systematic attempts to distinguish revenge from retribution on an empirical level has been put forth by American philosopher Robert Nozick. His revenge-retribution distinction rests on five criteria; three of which are briefly summarized in the following:

  (a) Retribution sets an internal limit to the amount of the punishment, according to the seriousness of the wrong, whereas revenge internally sets no limit.
  (b) Revenge involves pleasure in the suffering of another, while retribution involves pleasure in justice being done.
  (c) Vengeance will depend on how the avenger feels at the time about the act of injury, whereas the imposer of retribution is committed to general principles (Nozick, 1981; pp. 366-368).

These criteria can be transformed into empirically testable hypotheses. For example, the first criterion (a) suggests that vengeful actions are excessive and limitless, as long as they are not shaped by legal or social boundaries or norms. However, looking at a large body of empirical findings in the aggression literature reveals that this does not seem to be true for most kinds of observable vengeful reactions. On the contrary, retaliatory reactions are largely proportionate to the (subjectively perceived) initial provocation, even outside the influence of legal or social norms (e.g., Johnson & Rule, 1986; Kelln & Ellard, 1999; Ohbuchi & Ogura, 1985; Ohbuchi, Kameda, & Agarie, 1989). Second, mitigating circumstances are taken into account when retaliatory reactions are carried out (Craig et al., 1993). Third, social norms strongly shape the quality and quantity of retaliatory reactions (e.g., Lee & Tedeschi, 1996). Thus, it seems that even revenge appears to have its limits of appropriateness, and that retaliation and revenge are – at least in the context of minor provocations investigated in the laboratory or in everyday life – not as irrational and excessive as they are usually portrayed.

Revenge, Aggression, and Justice-Related Emotions

The second and the third distinctive criteria (b and c) can also be transformed into empirically testable hypotheses. They are concerned with the connection between revenge (or retribution) and emotional processes and reactions. Slightly reformulated, argument (b) states that vengeful acts are aimed at seeing the harm-doer suffer, whereas retributive punishment predominantly aims at reestablishing justice. Argument (c) implies that the willingness to engage in vengeful reactions depends on the avenger's negative emotional state evoked by the initial provocation, but not on the appropriateness of general principles of retributive justice; any positive emotional reactions that arise in the context of committed acts of revenge are not related to justice-based perceptions, but merely to seeing the offender suffer. Meanwhile, several researchers have adopted this concept of a hot–cold, irrational–rational, unfair–fair dichotomy in order to empirically distinguish revenge and retribution as different motives (e.g., Ho, ForsterLee, ForsterLee, & Crofts, 2003; Stuckless & Goranson, 1992).

Interestingly, pleasure in seeing someone suffer is also a defining element of "hostile aggression," a concept that was originally put forth by Feshbach (1964) in order to distinguish it from aggressive behavior in which harming a person is not a goal in itself, but rather a means to achieve higher-order goals ("instrumental aggression"). For a long time, this distinction was prominent in social psychological theories of aggression (e.g., Berkowitz, 1993; Buss, 1961; Hartup, 1974). An attempt to prove the existence of "hostile aggression" empirically was made by Betsch, Schmid, Glaubrecht, Kurzenhäuser, and Dondelinger (1999). In this study, participants read a vignette in which a woman jumped a queue at a bakery store. Taking the perspective of another customer in the store, participants were asked to indicate (a) to what degree they would like to see the woman's emotional state change (i.e., decrease or increase) and (b) to what degree they would like to see their own emotional state change. In general, participants wished their own emotional state would increase, and the woman's emotional state would decrease. This relative change in emotional state was augmented in an experimental condition in which participants were primed with anger-related words by means of a scrambled-sentence technique. According to Betsch et al. (1999), this can be seen as indirect evidence that "hostile aggression" was evoked by the queue-jumping vignette. In an attempt to replicate these findings, Schmid (2005) used a similar measure for hostile aggression and a similar priming procedure, but different vignettes. Although she failed to find a priming main effect, another interesting effect emerged with regard to the harm-doer's motives in the four vignettes she used. In two of these vignettes, the harm-doer's motives were clearly egoistic; in the two other vignettes, his motives for doing harm were rather unclear. In the egoistic vignettes, participants wished that the harm-doer felt significantly worse than in the nonegoistic vignettes.

Although these findings seem to corroborate the notion that revenge is associated with a desire to see the harm-doer suffer (or at least feel worse), they do not prove that revenge is identical to "hostile aggression," that is, that there are no higher-order goals connected to this aggression. As Bushman and Anderson (2001) in their insightful critique on the "hostile"/"instrumental" dichotomy put it:

> intention to harm is still a necessary feature of all aggression, but only as a proximate goal. [...] Because aggression can be motivated by many different goals, much hostile aggression can alternatively be viewed as instrumental aggression. (pp. 274-275)

Such higher-order goals can be (a) reestablishing self-esteem and self-worth, (b) redressing the power inequality between victim and harm-doer and reinforcing one's social status, (c) reestablishing an equilibrium between gains and losses (equity), (d) preventing future threats and harm (prevention), or (e) obtaining other personal benefits, such as reputation, money, or information (Frijda, 1994; Tedeschi & Felson, 1994; see also Montada, this volume). These goals are not mutually exclusive, any aggressive reaction can serve one or more or even all of them. Moreover, we do not know anything about the dimensionality of these goals. For example, it might well be that defending one's social status and reestablishing one's self-esteem are psychologically redundant. In a similar vein, one can argue that the desire to decrease the offender's emotional state while, at the same time, increasing one's own state, reflects a desire to see justice reestablished. Thus, if emotional state is conceptualized as a resource that can be distributed according to fairness principles, rebalancing emotional states (by making the offender feel worse and oneself feel better) is nothing other than restoring "emotional equity":

> Vengeance actually works in equalizing the suffering. It makes part of the suffering disappear [...]. All this is personal and emotional. It has nothing to do with a sense of justice. But the dolorous inequalities can be transformed onto an abstract and general plane and become formulated in a moral way, and so can the restoration of the balance of suffering. Then it indeed becomes a sense of justice. (Frijda, 1994; p. 274f.)

Given these communalities between different aggression goals, Nozick's (1981) argument that revenge and retribution can be differentiated on the basis of emotional perceptions involved in the vengeful act (i.e., pleasure about seeing the offender suffer vs. pleasure about justice being reestablished) becomes conceptually weak, if not untenable. Nevertheless, the question of how many different goal dimensions can be empirically differentiated and how the different revenge goals are interrelated remains an important empirical question.

Another open question is which goals actually predict vengeful behavior. If Nozick's (1981) analysis was correct, then the predominant goal should be to see the harm-doer suffer; thus, an avenger should be more likely to engage in vengeful behavior if the particular behavior is instrumental for achieving that goal.

Overview of the Present Research

These open questions were addressed in a study that will be described in the remainder of the present chapter. Taken together, the study sought to investigate:

1. How different revenge goals are related to each other.
2. Which revenge goal is most important to a victim (or an avenger).
3. Whether these goals can be understood as motives for vengeful behavior.
4. Whether the intensity of anger experienced by the injustice is indeed a powerful predictor of engaging in vengeful behavior, as Nozick's (1981) hypothesis (c) suggests.

As with many other studies on revenge, a questionnaire approach was pursued here. Participants were confronted with four vignettes describing a harmful and unfair offense, in which they were supposed to take the victim's perspective. Vignettes were constructed by reviewing published studies that used similar material (e.g., Cota-McKinley, Woody, & Bell, 2001; Schmid, 2005), and by reviewing empirical findings about which scenarios usually evoke the most intense anger and moral outrage (Bies & Tripp, 1996; Mikula, Petri, & Tanzer, 1990). This approach led to the construction of seven vignettes describing cases of egoistic behavior (e.g., queue-jumping, snapping up a parking space by disregarding safety and respect, uncooperative behavior in the context of a student learning group, unfair treatment by one's supervisor, and disloyal behavior displayed by colleagues and friends). Out of these seven vignettes, four were finally selected on the basis of a pretest: A group of 14 students were asked to read all seven vignettes and rate (a) the unfairness of the offender's action, (b) their perceived intensity of anger and moral outrage, and (c) their desire to make the offender pay for what he did. Averaged across these three indicators, the highest values were obtained for the disloyal colleague scenario, the parking lot scenario, the unfair supervisor scenario, and the disloyal friend scenario (for details, see Gollwitzer, 2005).

As an example, the disloyal colleague scenario reads as follows:

You are working together with eight other people from your company on an important project. [...] One of your working team members seems to pick out only the most convenient tasks for himself while leaving the more boring tasks to others, especially to you. [...] One day, he comes to your desk and tells you to pick up a package from the post office for him, since he had to meet the boss for an "extraordinarily important meeting."

Dependent Variables

Cognitive and emotional reactions. Participants' immediate reactions to these scenarios were assessed via self-reports. Specifically, cognitive reactions (perceived injustice) and emotional reactions (anger, moral outrage) were assessed with three items each (cognitive: "I consider the offender's behavior to be unfair," $.56 \leq \alpha \leq .79$; emotional: "The offender's behavior makes me angry," $.59 \leq \alpha \leq .72$). Participants were asked to indicate their agreement with each of these statements on six-point rating scales ranging from 0 (*not at all*) to 5 (*absolutely*).

Willingness to take revenge. One important goal of the present study was to investigate participants' willingness to engage in a vengeful action. Unlike Betsch et al. (1999) or Schmid (2005), this willingness was not measured abstractly (i.e., "I would like the other person to feel [very bad] ... [very good]"), or via open-format questions (Cota-McKinley et al., 2001). Instead, specific revenge opportunities were constructed; participants were asked to what extent they would be willing to engage in each of these opportunities. By constructing the revenge opportunities, an attempt was made to acknowledge the "aesthetic" vengeance criteria that had been identified by Tripp, Bies, and Aquino (2002). These aesthetic criteria can be briefly described as follows: (a) the revenge should have an altruistic or humorous component; (b) the revenge should have a "poetic quality," which points to the fact that an appropriate revenge should qualitatively fit the initial provocation, ideally by making the harm-doer's own evil behavior the cause for his later suffering; (c) the consequences of the revenge as well as its method should be symmetrical to the initial harm.

For example, the revenge option in the disloyal colleague scenario reads as follows:

You know that there will be a team meeting the following day. Your coworker has to present this week's proceedings [...]. Through your company's intranet you have access to your coworker's computer. You could insert some small errors in your coworker's presentation, which would leave him unable to proceed. Then you could "stand in" spontaneously and take over with the presentation using some slides of your own.

The revenge option in the parking lot scenario was putting a small hump behind the back wheel of the egoistic driver's car. In the unfair supervisor scenario, revenge could be executed by installing a nonharmful (but nevertheless irritating) virus on the manager's computer. Finally, in the disloyal friend scenario, the revenge option was about sending a parcel with embarrassing pictures of the friend anonymously to his wife. Participants were asked, "Please indicate how likely you are to take on the described revenge opportunity" on a eleven-point rating scale ranging from 0% (*I will certainly not do it*) to 100% (*I will certainly do it*), ascending in 10%-steps.

Importance of revenge goals. Revenge goals were adopted from Frijda (1994) and enriched by research on punishment goals in legal contexts (Orth, 2003; Oswald, Hupfeld, Klug, & Gabriel, 2002). The final list of goals consisted of (a) preventing future harm, (b) restoring one's social esteem, (c) demonstrating powerfulness to the offender, (d) relief from anger, (e) inducing feelings of guilt in the offender, (f) restoring personal self-worth, (g) reestablishing justice, and (h) making the offender suffer. In order to assess the subjective importance of each of these eight revenge goals, participants were asked, "If you had the opportunity to make the offender pay for what he did, what would be important for you to achieve?" Each goal had to be rated with regard to its subjective importance on a six-point scale from 0 (*not at all important*) to 5 (*very important*).

Instrumentality. Participants were also asked to what extent they considered it likely that the described revenge option was able (a) to prevent future harm, (b) to restore one's social esteem, (c) to demonstrate powerfulness to the offender, (d) to reduce anger, (e) to induce guilt, (f) to restore one's self-worth, (g) to reestablish justice, and (h) to make the offender suffer. The likelihood ratings were made on a six-point rating scale ranging from 0 (*very unlikely*) to 5 (*very likely*).

Occasions of Measurement

In order to eliminate artificial findings due to carry-over effects between the dependent variable (likelihood of engaging in the vengeful behavior) and the other variables (emotional and cognitive reactions to the offense, subjective importance of revenge goals, revenge option's instrumentality for each revenge goal), variables were measured on two different occasions of measurement. More specifically, the likelihood of engaging in the vengeful reaction was measured on the first occasion of measurement. Reactions to the offense, importance of revenge goals, and instrumentality ratings were measured six months later, on the second occasion of measurement. Since the sample partly consisted of students in introductory psychology classes (see below), it was not too complicated to approach them twice with a relatively large time interval between the two measurement occasions. In order to make the sample more heterogeneous, students were asked to take as many questionnaires as they wanted and distribute them among friends, family, neighbors, and relatives. Cases from the two occasions were matched by using a personalized six-digit code.

Sample

On the first measurement occasion, 134 questionnaires were returned (26 men, 108 women). A majority of participants (80%) were students, mostly students of psychology in introductory classes. Ages ranged from 17 to 70 years ($M = 26.4$; $SD = 10.77$). At the second measurement occasion, 187 questionnaires were returned (38 men, 149 women). Again, a majority of them (75%) were students. Ages ranged from 18 to 75 years ($M = 29.1$; $SD = 12.91$). On the basis of the personalized code, 80 cases from both measurement occasions could be unequivocally matched. Four of these cases had to be removed from the data set because of language problems and/or too much missing data. In the final data set ($N = 76$), women were largely overrepresented (83%), and so were students (78%).

Consistency Across Vignettes

In order to increase generalizability and reliability, importance ratings for each revenge goal were aggregated across the four offense vignettes. Such aggregation, however, demands that internal consistency across the vignettes is sufficiently high. Table 1 reports mean values and Cronbach's alphas for all eight revenge goals. These analyses were conducted with the complete data set obtained at the second measurement occasion ($N = 180$ complete cases). In sum, consistency coefficients were rather low ($\alpha \geq .60$). Restoring one's social status and making the offender suffer are the two most consistent (that is, situation-unspecific) variables.

Table 1. Importance of Revenge Goals Across the Four Offense Vignettes

Revenge goal	Means				Alpha
	Disloyal Colleague	Parking Lot	Unfair Supervisor	Disloyal Friend	
Preventing future harm	4.09	3.55	3.87	3.64	.60
Restoring social esteem	3.43	1.55	3.89	3.12	.77
Demonstrating powerfulness	3.87	3.18	4.25	3.46	.60
Reducing anger	3.58	3.95	3.92	3.22	.62
Inducing guilt	4.03	3.43	4.14	3.99	.76
Restoring self-worth	2.11	1.51	2.99	1.54	.75
Reestablishing justice	3.28	2.68	3.30	2.17	.60
Making offender suffer	1.25	1.04	1.47	1.08	.79

Note: $N = 180$. Response scale ranges from 0 to 5, with higher values indicating higher importance.

Dimensionality of Revenge Goals

First, the dimensionality of the eight revenge goals was investigated. This was done by conducting a principal axis factor analysis. The first factor had an eigenvalue of 3.07

Table 2. VARIMAX-Rotated Factor Loading Matrix of the Three-Factor Solution

Revenge goal	Factor 1	Factor 2	Factor 3
Preventing future harm	**.76**	.08	.13
Restoring social esteem	.27	**.60**	.08
Demonstrating powerfulness	**.49**	**.50**	.23
Reducing anger	.29	.30	**.38**
Inducing guilt	**.70**	.04	.18
Restoring self-worth	−.14	**.64**	.17
Reestablishing justice	.33	.25	**.65**
Making offender suffer	.05	.07	**.64**

Note: N = 180. Loadings higher than *a* = .35 are printed in bold type.

and explained 38.32% of the total item variance. The second factor had an eigenvalue of 1.30 and explained another 16.22% of the variance. The third factor had an eigenvalue of 1.05 and explained another 13.15% of the variance. All other factors had eigenvalues below 1. The loading structure of the three-factor solution was clearly interpretable, independent of which rotation procedure was employed. For reasons of simplicity of interpretation, the VARIMAX rotation is presented in Table 2.

Factor 1 can be described as tapping a utilitarian aspect of punishment, that is, reducing the probability of future harm by inducing guilt and by demonstrating one's power. Factor 2 consists of goals that indicate the desire to repair one's intrapersonal identity (self-worth), one's interpersonal identity (powerfulness), and one's social identity (esteem/status). Factor 3 indicates the desire to reestablish justice by making the offender suffer. Reducing anger has a relatively minor loading on this factor (.38). However, since this item has no higher loading on any other factor, and since making the offender suffer and relieving oneself from anger are usually considered as two sides of the same coin (cf. Betsch et al., 1999; Schmid, 2005), reducing anger was added to the third factor. Demonstrating powerfulness has a double loading on the first and on the second factor. Nevertheless, it was added to the second factor for conceptual reasons: Demonstrating one's powerfulness might rather be considered a tool to restore one's identity than to reeducate the offender.

Relative Importance of Revenge Goals

Second, the relative importance of the three revenge goal factors was investigated. According to Nozick (1981), affect regulation should be the most important revenge goal. In order to test this hypothesis empirically, mean ratings were compared across revenge goal factors. Additionally, participants' gender was included in the model as a second factor. A 3 (revenge goal factor) by 2 (gender) mixed-model ANOVA revealed a highly significant main effect of revenge goal factor, $F(2,368) = 117.26$; $p < .001$; $\eta^2 = .39$. The

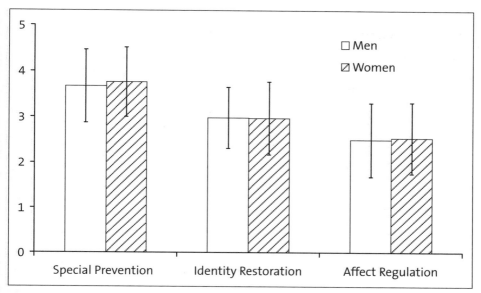

Figure 1. Mean importance ratings for each revenge goal factor, given for men and women, separately. Vertical lines denote standard deviations.

main effect of gender and the goal factor × gender interaction were not significant, $F <$ 1 (see Figure 1). Post-hoc repeated contrasts revealed that all three revenge goal factors were significantly different from each other: Prevention was significantly more important than identity restoration, $F(1,184) = 78.55$; $p < .001$; $\eta^2 = .30$; and identity restoration was more important than affect regulation, $F(1,184) = 37.55$; $p < .001$; $\eta^2 = .17$.

Revenge Goals and Revenge Probabilities

Third, the relation between each of the eight revenge goals and participants' willingness to engage in vengeful actions was investigated by inspecting correlations between revenge likelihood ratings (measured at t_1) and revenge goal instrumentalities (measured at t_2). This was done for each of the four vignettes, separately. For example, if probability to take revenge on the disloyal colleague was uncorrelated with the instrumentality rating for preventing future harm, then preventing future harm does not appear to be an important motive underlying participants' willingness to take revenge. If, on the other hand, revenge probability was positively correlated with demonstrating powerfulness, then those participants who believe that inserting errors into one's coworker's presentation demonstrates powerfulness are more likely to do it. In this case, demonstrating powerfulness can be considered an important goal underlying the particular vengeful behavior.

The percent ratings with which participants indicated their willingness to engage in a particular vengeful action were strongly skewed, that is, most people reported that they

Table 3. Correlations Between Instrumentalities and Revenge Likelihood

Revenge goal instrumentality	Correlations (r)				M(r)
	Disloyal Colleague	Parking Lot	Unfair Supervisor	Disloyal Friend	
Preventing future harm	.11	.18	.14	.18	.15
Restoring social esteem	-.07	.11	.06	.11	.05
Demonstrating powerfulness	.25*	.32**	.28*	.25*	.27*
Reducing anger	.21	.41**	.39**	.32**	.33**
Inducing guilt	.01	.11	.14	.26*	.13
Restoring self-worth	-.08	.50**	.21	.13	.20
Reestablishing justice	.18	.38**	.30**	.36**	.31**
Making offender suffer	.06	-.27*	.12	.07	.00

Note: $N = 76$. $* = p \leq .05$; $** = p \leq .01$. $M(r)$ = Mean correlation coefficient (aggregated across vignettes on the basis of a Fisher Z-transformation).

would rather *not* take the specific opportunity to avenge. More specifically, the average revenge likelihood in the disloyal colleague scenario was 9.74% ($SD = 16.44\%$), in the parking lot scenario, it was 18.73% ($SD = 29.80\%$), in the unfair supervisor scenario, it was 20.59% ($SD = 25.72\%$), and in the disloyal friend scenario, it was 20.87% ($SD = 27.13\%$). Since these distributions may weaken the robustness of certain statistical procedures, likelihood ratings were log-transformed in order to reduce skewness. Such transformation is usual when, for example, reaction time data are analyzed (cf. Fazio, 1990). The correlations between instrumentality ratings and log-transformed likelihood ratings are depicted in Table 3.

   Taken together, it appears that, across vignettes, demonstrating powerfulness, reducing anger, and reestablishing justice are the most important revenge goals: The more a specific revenge option is perceived as instrumental for achieving each of these goals, the higher the reported revenge probability. Making the offender suffer, on the other hand, is not an important goal underlying vengeful actions. Contrary to Nozick's (1981) hypothesis, making the offender suffer even had a negative effect on revenge likelihood in one of the four scenarios: The more participants thought that putting a small hump behind the bad guy's back wheel will make him suffer, the *less* likely they actually engaged in this behavior.

Does Anger Predict Revenge Likelihood?

Finally, the hypothesis that it is the magnitude of anger and moral outrage experienced in the harmful situation which predicts participants' likelihood of taking revenge was investigated. This hypothesis was tested by the regression of log-transformed revenge

Table 4. Regression of Revenge Likelihood on Cognitive and Emotional Reactions

Predictor	Beta Coefficients			
	Disloyal Colleague	Parking Lot	Unfair Supervisor	Disloyal Friend
Perceived injustice	.07	.09	−.10	−.08
Anger and moral outrage	.02	.17	.11	.06
Explained variance (R^2)	*.006*	*.06*	*.01*	*.007*

Note: $N = 76$. All beta coefficients were nonsignificant ($p \leq .30$).

likelihood ratings for each scenario on the amount of perceived injustice (cognitive reactions) and on anger and moral outrage (emotional reactions), which were evoked by the respective scenarios. Regression coefficients are reported in Table 4.

All beta coefficients were low and nonsignificant; accordingly, only a small portion of the variance of revenge likelihood could be explained by immediate cognitive and emotional reactions ($R^2 \leq .06$). Although the sample size for these regressions is relatively small, the analysis had a power of $1 - \beta = .85$ given a medium effect size ($f^2 = .15$; cf. Cohen, 1992). Thus, our findings suggest that, contrary to Nozick's (1981) third hypothesis, emotional reactions do − by and large − *not* predict the desire to take revenge.

Discussion

In many popular and philosophical writings, vengeance and retribution are displayed as opposite sides of the same coin: Whereas retributive sanctions are conceived of as justice-based, rational, utilitarian in nature, and beneficial to society, vengeful reactions are said to be irrational, limitless, affective, and unconnected to general principles of fairness or proportionality. The present chapter attempted to put this notion to a conceptual and an empirical test. First, the question of how different goals and functions underlying vengeful reactions can be empirically dimensionalized was addressed. The results from the present study suggest a three-factor structure: One factor comprises utilitarian goals, the second factor comprises identity-related goals, and the third factor comprises affect-related goals, such as making the offender suffer and wishing to feel better. A descriptive analysis of the relative relevance that participants attached to these goals suggests that utilitarian goals are most important, followed by identity-related goals. Affect-related goals are relatively less important.

Second, the relation between each of these eight revenge goals and the reported likelihood of actually engaging in particular vengeful behavior was investigated. More specifically, we asked to what extent the particular option was instrumental for achieving each of the formerly specified revenge goals; these instrumentality ratings were then correlated with (log-transformed) revenge likelihoods. Across the four scenarios, demonstrating powerfulness, reducing anger, and reestablishing justice were most highly correlated with vengeful behavior. The subjectively perceived probability that a vengeful action is more or less likely to make the offender suffer was, on the other hand, unrelated to participants' self-reported willingness to engage in a particular vengeful reaction. Rather, participants were unlikely to take revenge if the particular action was likely to do harm to the offender (at least in one out of four vignettes).

This pattern of results suggests that the conceptual relations between emotions and revenge are more complex than assumed by some legal scholars, criminologists, and philosophers. Contrary to Robert Nozick's (1981) intuition that revenge involves pleasure in the suffering of another, it seems that making the offender suffer is not a relevant goal underlying vengeful reactions. Likewise, the hypothesis that vengeance depends on how the avenger feels about the act of injury is empirically not tenable. Nevertheless, reducing anger – as a revenge goal – is positively correlated with revenge probability. If a particular revenge option is not instrumental in reducing anger, then people are less likely to engage in this option. This finding corresponds with other research that has been investigating motivational principles of retaliatory aggression: In the Betsch et al. (1999) study, participants' wished for a significant decrease of their self-reported anger in response to the queue-jumping vignette, independent of experimental condition (i.e., priming manipulation). Bushman, Baumeister, and Phillips (2001) have demonstrated in a series of experiments that if people are led to believe that they will not feel better by aggressing, they are less likely to aggress (see also, Baumeister & Bushman, this volume). A recent neurobiological study conducted by de Quervain et al. (2004) suggests that punishing offenders for egoistic behavior is connected to an activation of reward-related brain areas.

At first glance, these findings seem to support a simple affect-regulative model of retaliatory aggression and vengeful reactions. However, they do not rule out that the psychological processes involved in such reactions are a little more complex: Research has not yet proven that anticipating reward and emotional well-being are goals per se; it might well be that emotional well-being is an epiphenomenon of some higher-order goal, such as reestablishing justice or preventing future harm. Regarding the neurobiological findings reported by de Quervain et al. (2004), we cannot say for sure what exactly the punisher anticipated being rewarded for. And although the experimental findings reported by Bushman et al. (2001) suggest that people aggress in the hope that doing so will enable them to feel better, we do not know whether they considered the particular aggressive option that they had in this experiment (giving uncomfortable noise blasts to an ostensible opponent) instrumental for achieving any higher-order goal, such as reestablishing justice or preventing future harm. This view is also supported by the factor loading matrix reported in Table 1: The revenge goal "reducing anger" had nontrivial loadings on all three factors. This means that reducing anger is connected both to preventing future harm and to restoring one's identity. Future research needs to clarify the role of participants' desire to reduce their anger (or, to improve their mood) in the context of other goals and instrumentalities underlying retaliatory aggression and vengeful behavior.

Of course, the empirical approach that was pursued here is subject to methodological criticism. First, one might doubt whether self-reports concerning goal importance, instrumentality, and revenge likelihood are valid indicators of the respective latent constructs. Despite the fact that anonymity was guaranteed, participants might have been motivated to display socially desirable responding. Second, self-reports are usually considered unable to tap any spontaneous, automatic aspects of behavior. Thus, they can only predict a part of the variance of actual behavior. The size of this part, that is, the validity of self-reports, is subject to a long-lasting debate. For the present purpose, one can reasonably doubt whether the research paradigm employed here was actually able to put the central hypothesis ("revenge is merely affective") to a proper test. Third, one might question the practice of providing *specific* vengeful options. Fourth, revenge probabilities were admittedly low and strongly skewed to the left in all four scenarios. This means that a relatively low percentage of participants were actually willing to engage in that particular behavior. Fifth, our sample is largely selective with regard to occupation (and all psychologically relevant factors related to it, such as intelligence, attitudes etc.) and gender. And finally, the fact that there was a 6-month interval between the two measurement occasions has, despite its strengths (i.e., control of carry-over effects), some inherent weaknesses: Participants' attitudes toward revenge or toward revenge goals could have shifted, or some other systematic or unsystematic incident could have blurred the pattern of results. Nevertheless, the amounts of explained variance in log-transformed revenge probabilities can still be considered reasonable in size.

Taken together, the role of affect and emotions in vengeful episodes still needs to be clarified. The various sources of variance that influence whether and how people take revenge should be more systematically elucidated. Situational aspects (e.g., the social context, the cost-benefit ratio of a particular revenge option), personal aspects (e.g., justice-related attitudes, goal preferences), and their interactions should be taken into account. An important question might be which kinds of provocations evoke which revenge goals. The assumption that revenge is an evil, irrational, affective, and primitive reaction that should be eliminated by criminal law does not account for the complex psychological function that vengeful behavior has for the individual and for the social system we are living in.

References

Bacon, F. (1601/1986). On revenge. In F. Bacon & J. Pitcher (Eds.), *Francis Bacon – The essays*. New York: Viking Press.

Baumeister, R. F., & Bushman, B. J. (2007). Angry emotions and aggressive behaviours. In G. Steffgen & M. Gollwitzer (Eds.), *Emotions and aggressive behavior* (pp. 59-73). Cambridge, MA: Hogrefe & Huber Publishers.

Berkowitz, L. (1993). *Aggression: Its causes, consequences, and control*. New York: McGraw-Hill.

Betsch, T., Schmid, J., Glaubrecht, M., Kurzenhäuser, S., & Dondelinger, A. (1999). Zur empirischen Fundierung des Konzepts der feindseligen Aggression [An empirical test of the concept of hostile aggression]. *Zeitschrift für Sozialpsychologie, 30*, 194–206.

Bies, R. J., & Tripp, T. M. (1996). Beyond distrust: "Getting even" and the need for revenge. In R. M. Kramer & T. R. Tyler (Eds.), *Trust in organizations: Frontiers of theory and research* (pp. 246–260). Thousand Oaks, CA: Sage.

Bushman, B. J., & Anderson, C. A. (2001). Is it time to pull the plug on the hostile versus instrumental aggression dichotomy? *Psychological Review, 108*, 273–279.

Bushman, B. J., Baumeister, R. F., & Phillips, C. M. (2001). Do people aggress to improve their mood? Catharsis beliefs, affect regulation opportunity, and aggressive responding. *Journal of Personality and Social Psychology, 81*, 17–32.

Buss, A. H. (1961). *The psychology of aggression.* New York: Wiley.

Cohen, J. (1992). A power primer. *Psychological Bulletin, 112*, 155–159.

Cota-McKinley, A. L., Woody, W. D., & Bell, P. A. (2001). Vengeance: Effects of gender, age, and religious background. *Aggressive Behavior, 27*, 343–350.

Craig, K. M., O'Neal, E. C., Taylor, S. L., Yost, E. A., Langley, T., Rainbow, R. et al. (1993). Equity and derogation against whom we have aggressed. *Aggressive Behavior, 19*, 355–360.

de Waal, F. (1996). *Good natured: The origins of right and wrong in humans and other animals.* Cambridge, MA: Harvard University Press.

de Quervain, D. J.-F., Fischbacher U., Treyer, V., Schellhammer M., Schnyder, U., Buck, A., & Fehr, E. (2004). The neural basis of altruistic punishment. *Science, 305*, 1254–1258.

Fazio, R. H. (1990). A practical guide to the use of response latency in social psychological research. In C. Hendrick & M. S. Clark (Eds.), *Research Methods in Personality and Social Psychology* (pp. 74–97). Newbury Park, CA: Sage.

Feshbach, S. (1964). The function of aggression and the regulation of aggressive drive. *Psychological Review, 71*, 257–272.

French, P. A. (2001). *The virtues of vengeance.* Lawrence, KS: The University Press of Kansas.

Frijda, N. H. (1994). The Lex Talionis: On vengeance. In S. H. M. van Goozen, N. E. van der Poll, & J. A. Sergeant (Eds.), *Emotions: Essays on emotion theory* (pp. 263–289). Hillsdale, NJ: Erlbaum.

Furman v. Georgia, 408 U.S. 238 (1972).

Gollwitzer, M. (2005). *Ist „gerächt" gleich „gerecht"? Eine Analyse von Racheaktionen und rachebezogenen Reaktionen unter gerechtigkeitspsychologischen Aspekten* [Does "avenged" equal "just"? An analysis of vengeful reactions and revenge-related reaction from a psychology of justice perspective]. Berlin, Germany: wvb.

Hartup, W. W. (1974). Aggression in childhood: Developmental perspectives. *American Psychologist, 34*, 944–950.

Ho, R., ForsterLee, L., ForsterLee, R., & Crofts, N. (2003). Justice versus vengeance: Motives underlying punitive judgements. *Personality and Individual Differences, 33*, 365–378.

Jacoby, S. (1983). *Wild justice: The evolution of revenge.* New York: Harper and Row.

Johnson, T. E., & Rule, B. G. (1986). Mitigating circumstances information, censure, and aggression. *Journal of Personality and Social Psychology, 50*, 537–542.

Kelln, B. R. C., & Ellard, J. H. (1999). An equity theory analysis of the impact of forgiveness and retribution on transgressor compliance. *Personality and Social Psychology Bulletin, 25*, 864–872.

Lee, S.-J., & Tedeschi, J. T. (1996). Effects of norms and norm-violations on inhibition and instigation of aggression. *Aggressive Behavior, 22*, 17–25.

Mikula, G., Petri, B., & Tanzer, N. (1990). What people regard as unjust: Types and structures of everyday experiences of injustice. *European Journal of Social Psychology, 20*, 133–149.

Miller, W. I. (1998). Clint Eastwood and equity: Popular culture's theory of revenge. In A. Sarat & T. R. Kearns (Eds.), *Law in the domains of culture.* (pp. 161–202). Ann Arbor, MI: The University of Michigan Press.

Montada, L. (2007). Emotion-based motives for aggressive behaviour. In G. Steffgen & M. Gollwitzer (Eds.), *Emotions and aggressive behaviour* (pp. 19-36). Cambridge, MA: Hogrefe & Huber Publishers.

Nozick, R. (1981). *Philosophical explanations.* Cambridge, MA: Harvard University Press.

Ohbuchi, K., & Ogura, S. (1985). Motives of anger: Their structure, factors, and relationships with responses. *Japanese Journal of Psychology, 56*, 200–207.

Ohbuchi, K., Kameda, M., & Agarie, N. (1989). Apology as aggression control: Its role in mediating appraisal of and response to harm. *Journal of Personality and Social Psychology, 56,* 219–227.

Orth, U. (2003). Punishment goals of crime victims. *Law and Human Behavior, 27,* 173–186.

Oswald, M. E., Hupfeld, J., Klug, S. C., & Gabriel, U. (2002). Lay perspective on criminal deviance, goals of punishment, and punitivity. *Social Justice Research, 15,* 85–98.

Schmid, J. (2005). The vengeance puzzle – retributive justice or hostile aggression? *Aggressive Behavior, 31,* 589–600.

Solomon, R. C. (1999). Justice v. vengeance: On law and the satisfaction of emotion. In S. A. Bandes (Ed.), *The passions of law* (pp. 123–148). New York: University Press.

Stuckless, N., & Goranson, R. (1992). The vengeance scale: Development of a measure of attitudes toward revenge. *Journal of Social Behavior and Personality, 7,* 25–42.

Tedeschi, J. T., & Felson, R. B. (1994). *Violence, aggression and coercive actions.* Washington, DC: American Psychological Association.

Tripp, M., Bies, R. J., & Aquino, K. (2002). Poetic justice or petty jealousy? The aesthetics of revenge. *Organizational Behavior and Human Decision Processes, 89,* 966–984.

Part 4

Emotions and Aggression in Intergroup Contexts

Intergroup Aggression and Emotions: A Framework and First Data

Ulrich Wagner and Oliver Christ

The significance of intergroup aggression in the world becomes obvious by a mere superficial screening of the media: War, civil war, genocide, pogroms, terrorism, ethnic violence, gang violence, and hooligan aggression are seen in the primary headlines. The kind of aggression that involves the interaction of two or more groups often exceeds the intensity of interindividual aggression (Jaffe & Yinon, 1979; Jaffe, Shapiro, & Yinon, 1981). Thus, psychological explanations are in high need. However, psychological research has made only few contributions to our understanding of these kinds of extreme violence and aggression (for the few examples see e.g., Christie, Wagner, & Winter, 2001; Sommer & Fuchs, 2004; Staub, 1989). Aim of the present chapter is to review some of the available research in the field of intergroup aggression and to develop a heuristic model that combines different levels of explanations to understand intergroup aggression and violence.

The chapter starts with a definition of intergroup aggression. Then the sparse empirical results on intergroup aggression, primarily coming from research focusing on aggression against ethnic minorities, will be summarized. Based on these empirical data, a general framework of intergroup aggression is presented that allows for the combining of a social psychological perspective with insights from proximate disciplines such as, e.g., history, sociology, and political sciences, as well as physiology and biology. The third section will focus primarily on the social psychological kernel of the model. Here, an intergroup perspective based on the social identity approach is introduced. Based on this perspective, the model differentiates ingroup-outgroup categories which are located on a societal level and lower level categorization. The first incorporates, e.g., distinctions between different ethnic and national categories. An example for lower level categorizations is the categorization into a peer-ingroup and an antagonist outgroup in which both are involved in a case of intergroup aggression. Thus, lower level categorizations reflect the importance of small group processes. A matter of special importance in aggressive intergroup encounters can be found in emotional processes, especially in the form of intergroup emotions. The fourth section of the paper uses data from two representative surveys and a panel of German adult respondents. It will be shown that in fact, prejudice causes intergroup aggression which is directed against foreigners living in Germany. In addition, this relationship is mediated and moderated by intergroup emotions, especially anger. The fifth and final part of the chapter will provide an outlook on future research based on the general framework of intergroup aggression and its social psychological specifications.

Facts and Definitions

We will confine ourselves here to physical aggression against people, thus following the classical definition of aggression given by Zillmann (1979, p. 33) who stated that "any and every activity by which a person seeks to inflict bodily damage or physical pain upon a person who is motivated to avoid such infliction constitutes aggressive behavior." The phenomenon we will discuss here is aggression between groups of individuals. This also incorporates aggression between single individuals if this behavior is based on, motivated and driven by the opponents' membership in different groups. We will call these phenomena *intergroup aggression*. Our understanding of groups in this context is adopted from social identity theory (Tajfel & Turner, 1979; see also Turner, Hogg, Oakes, Reicher, & Wetherell, 1987), according to which "a group exists when two or more people define themselves as members of it and when its existence is recognized by at least one other" (Brown, 2000, p. 3). The term "group" can thus refer to different entities such as national or ethnic groups, religious societies, groups of fans attached to a sports club, peer groups, etc.

Intergroup aggression is conducted on the background of targets' and perpetrators' group memberships. Even if a single person becomes the target, intergroup aggression is often aimed at the whole outgroup (Schneider, 2001): Rape in war, for example, is a form of aggression that dramatically affects an individual outgroup member but really intends to devalue the outgroup as a whole. Thus, the conduct of intergroup aggression often includes messages: Aggression directed against a single ethnic minority member is intended to signal to the whole ethnic outgroup that it is not welcomed. And intergroup aggression can be a means of sending messages to fellow ingroup members about how to defend territory, culture, economic status, etc. Terrorism often contains the same kind of messages.

A special kind of intergroup aggression is violence against minorities in societies, also denoted as hate crimes[1]. A closer look at hate crimes as an example of intergroup aggression may help to get some information about covariates and causes of this kind of aggressive behavior. Comparing the phenomenon of hate crimes in Germany and in the U.S. on the basis of official statistics (Bundesministerium des Inneren und Bundesministerium der Justiz, 2001; APA, 1998; Craig, 2002), a number of similarities can be observed: Perpetrators are primarily male, adolescent, lower educated, unemployed, and are known to the police for former offences. Contrary to expectations, most of the perpetrators are not members of established hate groups, such as right wing political organizations or political parties. There is an increase in incidences on weekends, offences are conducted spontaneously and perpetrators are often drunk. Victims are as young as their offenders. Victims usually have not been personally known to their attackers before, a fact that excludes interpersonal revenge as an explanation. Furthermore, offences are conducted in small groups.

---

[1] The term hate crime can be misleading because it gives the impression that the individual emotion of hate should be a constituent element of this form of intergroup aggression (cf. Craig, 2002, p. 86; but see also the APA, American Psychological Association, 1998, p. 1, that defines hate crimes as "violent acts against people, property, or organizations because of the group to which they belong to or identify with" and which goes along with the understanding of group focused aggression as defined here): The description of types of perpetrators below will demonstrate that some of them, the so-called thrill seekers and fellow members, are ostensibly not driven by the emotion of hate directed against the outgroup. If hate plays the role of an explanatory concept for understanding the empirical emergence of intergroup aggression, then this is often because the specific target groups are defined by society as groups that society/ingroup members perceive should be hated. An example is how German Jews were presented in Nazi propaganda (see Hoffmann, Bergmann, & Walser Smith, 2002).

A review of available research and (theoretical) perspectives used to explain aggression against (ethnic) minorities shows that most of the research starts from a macro- or societal perspective. For example, some studies aim to predict the occurrence of hate crimes from a country's economic development, thus arguing that hate crimes are a consequence of *economic competition, threat* and *frustration*. Hovland and Sears (1940), for example, analyzed the relationship between economic well being in the Southern United States, operationalized as cotton price, and rates of lynching of African Americans for the time period of 1882 to 1930. They found a significant negative covariation supporting their expectations (for a critical discussion see Green, Glaser, & Rich, 1998). Green, Strolovitch, and Wong (1998) analyzed registered incidents of hate crimes between 1987 and 1995 in New York City and set these into relation to the region's monthly unemployment rate. They did not find any relationship. According to their analyses, it is the influx of ethnic minorities into formerly homogeneous neighbourhoods that evokes hate crimes. Green, Abelson, and Garnett (1999) show a similar result on the basis of data from people known to have participated in hate crime activities between 1986 and 1995. According to their analyses, it is fear of diversity that motivates hate crime perpetrators.

A number of studies based on German data demonstrate the influence of *media coverage* of topics like immigration and ethnic minorities in a country on the incidence rate of hate crimes. Two of these studies focus on the dramatic increase of hate crimes in Germany in the early nineties (cf. Wagner & van Dick, 2001). Brosius and Esser (1995), using the method of time lagged correlations, show that reports of hate crimes on television and in the newspaper are significantly correlated with the number of hate crimes in the following week, indicating a causal influence from media coverage following imitating acts. In a similar vein, Koopmans and Olzak (2004) demonstrate that the number of newspaper articles reporting negative comments on immigration and ethnic groups covaries positively with the number of hate crimes (see also Waddington, Jones, & Critcher, 1987).

In interviews, perpetrators of hate crimes often utter their conviction to act in accordance with the silent majority. Ohlemacher (1994) correlated the attitudes of the autochthonous German population obtained from representative surveys and the number of hate crime attacks. He shows that a higher rejection of immigrants in the public opinion is related to the hate crime numbers registered a month later. This finding supports the assumption that the *social climate* in a society has an influence on single hate crime conduct. In a multilevel analysis of recent German survey data Wolf, Stellmacher, Wagner, and Christ (2003) show that the relationship between individual prejudice and the readiness to behave violently against ethnic minorities is moderated by the acceptance of violence in the district in which the respondent lives. Only if the acceptance of violence in the district (mean acceptance score on the district level) is high, does prejudice relate substantially to the readiness to act violent (see also Horowitz, 1987; Spergel, 1964).

To summarize, we can infer from the available research that the societal economic development, political discourse, and media coverage of topics related to ethnic minorities, as well as the social climate regarding the treatment of ethnic groups, are likely to have an influence on aggression and violence against ethnic minorities. Thus, the societal context influences this kind of intergroup aggression. Further research uses interviews with convicted delinquents of hate crimes and focuses on psychological attributes of hate crime perpetrators. For example, Dunbar (2003) analyzed interviews of 58 convicted hate crime offenders to detect *psychiatric pathologies*. Sixty percent of the offenders are reported to have a history of substance abuse. In addition, the results indicate that a higher bias motivation predicts higher rates of instrumental aggression and the targeting of racial or ethnic minority victims. In other words, the more prejudiced respondents' perspectives on ethnic minorities, the more they tend to attack ethnic minorities. Despite these results, very little is known about psychological deficits and physiological or neurological anomalies of people conducting hate crimes.

Based on interviews with experts and convicted perpetrators, *typologies* of hate crimes have been developed which differentiate perpetrators mainly on the basis of their underlying motives. One such typology is based on German data (Willems, Eckert, Würtz, & Steinmetz, 1993; Willems, 2002). For another typology, interviews of American convicts were conducted (Levin & McDevitt, 1993; McDevitt, Levin, & Bennett, 2002). Both typologies show only a low percentage of perpetrators possessing an elaborated right wing political ideology. A much higher percentage, about one third of the interviewed, are highly prejudiced against minorities, however, without being able to express further attributes of a clear right wing ideological system. The American study differentiates these perpetrators further into those who argue for defensive behavior against intruders and those who retaliate. Thrill seekers compose the largest perpetrator group. They are best described as criminal fun seekers with a high degree of aggression potential. A fourth type of perpetrator is defined only in the German data: These are fellow group members who are neither highly prejudiced nor aggressive and who probably join youth gangs to fulfill their affiliation motivation. These people would probably just as well search for membership in many other groups. Summarizing these typologies, one can assume that ideologically motivated and prejudiced perpetrators act on the basis of their prejudice against the outgroup. For thrill seeking perpetrators, the display of aggression and power – independent of its target – seems to be the most prominent underlying motivation. And last, the fellow group members constitute a category of perpetrators who participate in violent group acts due to their motivation to be an accepted group member.

A Framework for Understanding Hate Crimes

In Figure 1 we present a heuristic model which aims to combine the aforementioned multiple facets of intergroup aggression. The model should be read from left to right, i.e., concepts on the left are assumed to have emerged historically earlier and to influence concepts located more to the right side of the figure. The model is comprised of two dimensions. The vertical dimension describes relevant levels of explanations (cf. Pettigrew, 1996), ranging from microlevel explanations and processes, such as, e.g., incorporating biological and physiological variables, to macrolevel or societal processes at the top, such as, e.g., historical events incorporating the whole society. The horizontal axis represents time dimensions for the different levels, as, e.g., for individual developmental processes as well as for societal changes[2].

---

[2] Strictly speaking, individual and societal developments have to be located on different time dimensions due to their different developmental gradients.

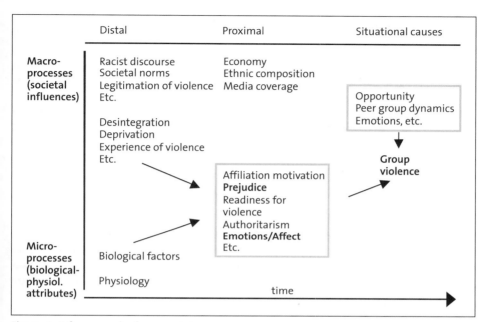

Figure 1. A framework of group violence.

According to the model, a full understanding of intergroup aggression is possible only when the different levels and their developmental backgrounds are taken into account. This includes features of the society, within which intergroup aggressive acts are embedded, and the history of the intergroup relations – the upper part of the figure: For example, target groups of hate crime are defined as targets by society, i.e., society stigmatizes certain groups as possible targets of devaluation, discrimination, and aggression. From a historical point of view, racism in the Western world has its roots in the history of colonization, slavery, and their legitimization (Fredrickson, 2002). In the same way, anti-Semitism is a product of centuries of discrimination against Jews (Hoffmann, Bergmann, & Walser Smith, 2002). These historical backgrounds have their influence on proximal societal influences of relevance, such as the current economic development of society and its public interpretation, society's ethnic composition and the media coverage of the topic.

In the middle of the left side of the model, a number of possible variables in the individual's ontological development are specified. It is known, e.g., that a person's own experience of violence in the family is an important predictor of his or her later aggressive tendencies (Krahe, 2001, p. 151ff.). In the lower left part of the model, biological preconditions are located. Even if one attempts to describe intergroup aggression in a nonreductionist way, perpetrators' biological and physiological equipment should be taken into account as relevant preconditions and moderators of group aggressiveness. A relevant biological background variable might be a person's impulsiveness that may provide the basis for his or her later aggressive tendencies (Scarpa & Raine, 2000). Thus, intergroup aggression against ethnic minorities conducted by thrill seeking perpetrators could be explained, among other behavioral tendencies, as a consequence of a society's presentation of ethnic minorities as a relevant outgroup in interaction with the thrill-seeking person's impulsiveness.

The middle column of the model lists a number of proximal determinants of intergroup aggression. On the side of the individuals, these include prejudice and willingness to use violence as important proximal predictors of intergroup aggression. Both factors can be assumed to depend on the interaction of certain societal features and underlying biological and physiological factors. Further proximal personal variables are, e.g., general affectivity and the individual's motivation to affiliate with certain relevant peer groups.

Besides the proximal societal and psychological determinants of intergroup aggression, the heuristic model also considers relevant situational triggers of intergroup aggression. These include group processes that take place within the peer group that is involved in the intergroup aggressive acts. As described above, most intergroup aggression occurs between small groups. Thus, group dynamics and their consequences are influential and these include phenomena like deindividuation (Zimbardo, 1969), depersonalization (Turner, Hogg, Oakes, Reicher, & Wetherell, 1987), group pressure (Schachter, 1951) and group polarization (Moscovici & Zavalloni, 1969). Affective factors and emotions, instigated by peer group interaction and outgroup confrontation, are of importance as well (Hess & Kirouac, 2000). This emotional involvement might be further enforced by alcohol or drug consumption.

The term "opportunity" points to the fact that intergroup aggression often has a causal character: Given all the preconditions described above, no intergroup aggressive act will emerge as long as no outgroup member is available. And, last but not least, the phenomenology of the aggressive intergroup encounter depends on the behavior of the opponent, i.e., the reaction of the target person or the target group. To understand their behavior, similar underlying processes as described for perpetrators have to be considered. And at least for the situational factors, mutual influences between perpetrators and targets have to be assumed, as, e.g., for group dynamic processes between the involved peer groups. Such kinds of feedback allow for an understanding of the accelerated dynamic of aggressive intergroup encounters (cf. Baron, Kerr, & Miller, 1992; Horowitz, 2001; Marsh, Rosser, & Harre, 1978).

If one compares the available empirical data on intergroup aggression with the elements of the heuristic model, one can see that most of the research focuses on effects of proximal societal factors on hate crime conduct (e.g., economic changes, ethnic compositions of neighbourhoods, and media coverage of intergroup relations). In comparison to that, research on other elements of the model and their interrelationships is barely developed. We do not really know much about proximal conditions of intergroup aggression. Implicitly, research seems to assume that prejudice is a precondition of all intergroup aggression, contrary to the results coming from typologies of perpetrators. Also, we know nearly nothing about the relationship of perpetrators' individual aggressive tendencies and their proneness to intergroup aggression. The same holds true for biological and physiological processes related to intergroup aggression. Furthermore, relevant peer group dynamics have almost never been focused on in relationship to intergroup aggression. And finally, almost no research exists on emotions as an explanatory concept for intergroup aggression.

A Social Identity Model of Hate Crime Behavior

The model presented in Figure 1 has at its core a social psychological perspective, incorporating proximal personal determinants of group aggression as well as situational triggers. We will now further elaborate this central social psychological part of the model on the basis of a social identity perspective of group membership (Tajfel & Turner, 1979; Turner et al., 1987; for a social identity perspective of aggression against gay men, see Hamner, 1992). An important precondition of group membership is – according to the social identity approach – a person's identification with a social category. Social identity theory assumes that if a person identifies with a social category, the person defines part of his- or herself in terms of that group membership, forming a certain group-related social identity. Group members try, as has been repeatedly shown in the so-called minimal group experiments (Tajfel, Billig, Bundy, & Flament, 1971), to improve the status of their ingroup and relatively devaluate the outgroup in order to bolster or improve their group-bounded social identity. From this perspective even intergroup aggression can be considered an attempt to heighten ingroup status and group-related self esteem (but see also Brewer, 2001).

Aggression and violence are importantly instigated and directed by normative concerns (Huesmann & Guerra, 1997). These include both individual standards (Bandura, 1999) as well as norms prescribed by society as a whole or by a certain subgroup. The conduct of aggressive acts also often has the consequence of changing individual standards and group norms as a means to legitimize the group's own behavior "after the fact" (Castano & Giner-Sorolla, 2006; Festinger, 1957). This process of legitimization can be assumed to be strongly supported by intergroup dynamics. One assumption derived from self-categorization theory (an extension of social identity theory primarily developed to explain intragroup processes and their relationship to the intergroup context, see Turner et al., 1987) is that a confrontation with a relevant outgroup not only evokes a tendency to relatively devalue the outgroup, but that this confrontation also affects the standards of appropriate group behavior. If ingroup members perceive their group to be in opposition to a relevant outgroup, ingroup standards and norms about appropriate ingroup behavior are modified in such a way that both homogeneity within the ingroup and contrast to the outgroup position are maximized (see Oakes, 1987, for a detailed description of the metacontrast principle). Within the intergroup encounter, signals from the outgroup can easily be (mis)perceived as hostile and aggressive, thus legitimizing a change in ingroup norms that allows or even prescribes hostile behavior towards the outgroup. This means that norms about the appropriate behavior and aggression towards in- and outgroup members are modified in the intergroup encounter (Short & Strodtbeck, 1965; Wagner & Ward, 1993). In fact, the tendency to relatively derogate the outgroup, the legitimization of one's own aggression tendencies and the emergence of devaluative norms within the ingroup, reinforce each other.

Aggression and violence are not only cognitively driven. Many forms of aggression and violence are strongly under the influence of affect. Affect emerges from the hostile encounter itself. In intergroup aggression this effect is further influenced by the emotional experience and the presentation of these emotions by fellow ingroup members as well as their common discursive interpretations within the ingroup, thus promoting a process of contagion of negative affect towards the outgroup and arousal among members (Hatfield, Cacioppo, & Rapson, 1994).

In many incidents of intergroup aggression, intergroup processes are relevant in two ways: First, in the construction and definition of large scale groups or categories. These include, e.g., such categories as national groups and ethnic minorities. Such a categorization into ingroup and outgroup can only be understood by considering societal historical events and developments. From the perspective of this intergroup constellation, group-focused aggression is an intergroup act directed against an outgroup member whereby the perpetrator behaves as a member of a certain ethnic, national, political, sexual, etc. ingroup with which he identifies. For example, aggression against an ethnic minority member focuses on that target only because he or she is a member of a relevant outgroup (the ethnic outgroup) from the perspective of the perpetrators' national ingroup. We will call this kind of intergroup encounter: *societal level (sl) intergroup processes*. Second, small groups are often relevant, too. As described above, hate crimes are often conducted by a small group or gang focusing on an opposing small group or gang and its members. Violence in war, civil war, and genocide, for example, is often conducted by marauding groups of soldiers. The same holds true for interethnic violence as well as hooligan violence in sports. We will call this *peer group level (pl) intergroup processes*.

Depending on the concrete case, actors involved in intergroup aggression are more or less aware of sl and pl intergroup processes. Categorization as sl or pl affects both ingroup and outgroup memberships. That means, at first, that a person can define his- or herself primarily according to sl or to pl memberships or both. Secondly, in many cases as, e.g., in gang youth violence, even opponents can be defined according to different levels of categorization. A hypothesis to be tested empirically is that ascription of opponents to groups located at different levels is less vivid than the different levels of ingroup membership (see the outgroup-homogeneity effect, Simon, 1992). Thus, outgroups tend to be perceived as simply "the opponents."

The importance of the group memberships located at the social and peer group level varies over different incidents of intergroup aggression and for different persons. Applied to the explanation of hate crimes, it might depend on the type of perpetrator motivation (cf. McDevitt et al., 2002; Willems, 2002), whether sl intergroup relations or pl intergroup embeddedness have a stronger influence. Thus, main effects of both sl intergroup processes and pl processes on intergroup aggression can be expected, moderated by perpetrators' motivations. In addition, an interaction of both kinds of intergroup relationships can be assumed, especially if pl categorization is nested within the sl categorization, which usually is the case in intergroup aggression that incorporates ethnic groups. Then a perpetrator perceives a target as an outgroup member both from his sl as well as from his pl group membership. As experimental intergroup research has shown, such a double outgroup membership of a target person evokes extreme forms of outgroup derogation and can be seen as the worst case of escalating hostile intergroup relations (Vanbeselaere, 1987).

Social identity theory and especially self categorization theory focus strongly on cognitive processes. What is missing from the explanation of intergroup aggression is an analysis of the influences of arousal and emotions (Smith & Mackie, 2005). Arousal and emotions are influenced by individual variables like strong affectivity as a correlate of perpetrators' aggressiveness (Scarpa & Raine, 2000), by perceived sl and pl intergroup relations like the negative affect produced by prejudice, as well as by pl intergroup processes like emotional contagion (Zimbardo, 1969) and situational factors, like alcohol (Krahe, 2001, p. 69 ff.). Recent theoretical developments have shown that especially the consideration of intergroup emotions, i.e., emotions connected with an outgroup as one dimension of prejudiced attitudes, helps to significantly improve the understanding of intergroup processes and the attitude-behavior relationship in intergroup encounters (Smith, 1993). According to intergroup emotion theory, the specific intergroup emotion experienced in hostile intergroup relations is dependent on ingroup power. If the outgroup is perceived as strong, the resulting intergroup emotion is fear and the behavioral consequence is outgroup avoidance. On the other hand, if the ingroup is perceived as relatively strong in comparison to the outgroup, hostile intergroup encounters evoke anger which results in aggressive tendencies against the outgroup (Mackie, Devos, & Smith, 2000). Thus, one can propose that intergroup aggression and violence can be better predicted in many cases by taking emotions like anger into account.

To summarize, we have shown that a social identity perspective helps to explain how in- and outgroup memberships emerge as a consequence of group identifications and how these affect intergroup evaluation. Applying self categorization theory to intergroup aggression also allows for a theoretical prognosis of how ingroup norms concerning aggression against outgroup members might change. And finally, combining considerations about affect and emotions with intergroup theories offers an opportunity to get a deeper insight into specific escalating characteristics of intergroup aggression. In the following, we will present data from a survey study that illustrates the explanatory power of intergroup theories and emotions for predicting intergroup aggression.

A Partial Test of the Influence of Prejudice and Emotions on Aggression Against Foreigners in Germany

Based on data from three representative German surveys (N = 2,722, N = 1,383, and N = 1,778, respectively, data collection summer 2002, 2004, and 2005) as well as a three wave panel survey (N = 825; summer 2002, 2003, 2004; all respondents older than 15 without migration background)[3], we will analyze the influence of societal level (sl) intergroup relations and intergroup emotions on intergroup aggression directed against ethnic minorities in Germany (see also Wagner, Christ, & Pettigrew, 2006). All datasets include a two-item prejudice scale (Items: "If jobs become scarce, foreigners should be sent back to their home countries," and "There are too many foreigners in Germany.") as well as different indicators measuring respondents' intention to use violence against

---

[3] The data presented here stem from the research project "Group focused enmity," financially supported by the Volkswagen Stiftung, the Freudenberg Stiftung and Möllgaard-Stiftung given to Wilhelm Heitmeyer, The University of Bielefeld.

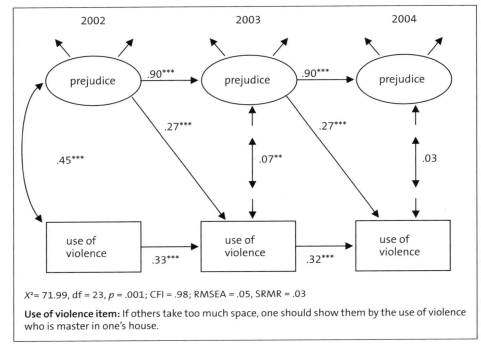

Figure 2. The prejudice-violence (causal) relation (Wagner, Christ, & Pettigrew, 2006).

foreigners living in Germany[4]: In the survey 2002 as well as in the panel survey, only one indicator is available ("If others take too much space we should show them by the use of violence who is master in one's house."). The survey in 2004 includes a two-item scale measuring willingness to use violence directed against Turks ("If a Turk insults me, it might happen that I will attack him," and "If it really matters, I am prepared to gain a Turk's respect by using violence."). And finally, in 2004, items measuring inter-group anger ("The Turks living in Germany sometimes make me angry") and intergroup fear ("The Turks living in Germany make me anxious," answering scales as above) are available. All indicators were answered on a four-point scale; higher values indicate higher scores on the respective construct.

---

[4] Germany has been a country of immigration for more than 50 years. Starting in the late 1950s, foreigners were recruited from Italy, Spain, Turkey, and many other states to come to work in the growing German industry. They were expected to stay for a while, earn their money, and then go back home. This is the reason for calling these migrant workers guest workers (Gastarbeiter). However, many of the guest workers decided to stay and invited their families to follow them. Due to the expec-tation of having guest workers and due to restrictive naturalization laws, which among others, do not allow double citizenship, the majority of these guest workers and their offspring did not get German citizenship and were considered and consider themselves to be foreigners, even if they have lived in Germany now for decades or were even born in Germany. Today, about 9% of the German popula-tion of about 82 million people does not hold German citizenship, the majority of them coming from Turkey. Cognitive pretests show that respondents primarily think of Turks when answering questions about foreigners.

As a first step, using the panel data, we analyzed the causal relationship between prejudice and intergroup aggression. In Figure 2, the result of a cross-lagged analysis is summarized. The significant cross-lagged paths from prejudice measured in 2002 and 2003 to use of violence measured in 2003 and 2004, respectively, confirm the assumed causal relationship: Prejudice can be considered to be one cause of intergroup aggression, at least for the German autochthonous population's willingness to use violence against foreigners living in Germany.

In the next step, we regressed the willingness to use violence on prejudice, including a number of additional variables in order to control for possible confounding influences. This was done on the basis of the 2002 and 2004 survey data. Regression analyses show that besides significant effects of prejudice, further influences on the willingness to use violence exist: There are covariations (significant betas) with age (.09 for 2002 and .17 for 2004), gender (–.17/–.17; females being less aggressive), West-East place of living (not significant for 2002/.07 for 2004; higher aggression in East Germany), social dominance orientation (.18/.19; see Sidanius & Pratto, 1999), and collective threat (not assessed in 2002/.16). In addition, there is a gender by prejudice interaction (–.07/–.09, indicating a covariation of prejudice and aggression primarily for male respondents). Most of these covariations are theoretically sensible. Most relevant in the given context, however, is that even after including these controls, the prejudice-aggression covariation remains significant (.19/.11), showing that the relationship does not artificially originate in the mediation of another confounding factor (see also Wagner et al., 2006).

Based on the 2005 data, we analyzed the influence of intergroup emotions on the prejudice-aggression relationship. Regressing the aggression scale simultaneously on

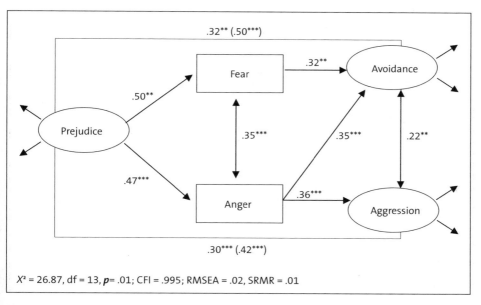

X^2 = 26.87, df = 13, p = .01; CFI = .995; RMSEA = .02, SRMR = .01

Figure 3. Emotions as mediatiors of the prejudice-behavior intention relationship (Asbrock et al., 2006).

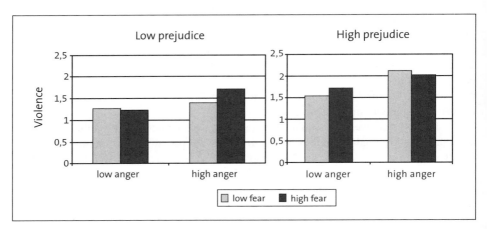

Figure 4. Emotions as moderators of the prejudice-aggression intention relationship.

prejudice as well as anger and fear as indicators of intergroup emotions, prejudice (β = .27) and anger (β = .22) show a significant influence on the use of violence scale. Figure 3 presents the results of a mediation analysis using the latent variable use of violence in comparison to another variable measuring intergroup discrimination, namely avoidance of Turks ("If a Turk tries to come in contact with me, I try to keep a distance from him or her," and "When using the bus I avoid sitting down next to a Turk."). As can be seen, anger regarding Turks in Germany mediates at least part of the prejudice aggression relationship (see also Asbrock et al., 2006), indicating the importance of emotional processes for understanding intergroup aggression.

As a final step, we tested the interactive effect of the intergroup emotions anger and fear and prejudice on the willingness to use violence. In a moderated regression analysis, a significant three-way-interaction (β = −.12, $p < .01$) emerged. Assessed means for one standard deviation from the mean of each "independent" scale show the data pattern presented in Figure 4. As can be seen, the intention to behave aggressively against foreigners is highest for high prejudice-high anger subjects, with only a small additional moderation by different degrees of fear. Thus, the data support an expectation that intergroup aggression is especially high if high prejudice is accompanied by a feeling of anger about the outgroup in question.

Taken together, the results of the survey studies demonstrate the importance of the proximal variables prejudice and intergroup emotions as predictors of intergroup aggression, as proposed in the social psychological kernel of our heuristic model.

Resume and Outlook

The societal relevance of research on intergroup aggression is self-evident. In this chapter, we presented a heuristic model that allows for the integration of concepts from different disciplines such as sociology, history, political sciences, and social psychology focusing on different levels of explanation for intergroup aggression. A real, i.e., externally valid, explanation of intergroup aggression presupposes an inter- and cross-disciplinary perspective, using models and theories from different disciplines and the interaction of the relevant predictors they propose. This should also include a multi-method empirical access, including the analysis of historical data, survey results, interviews with convicted intergroup aggression perpetrators, experimental studies, etc.

The social psychological core of the heuristic model was further elaborated. Here the model focuses on different kinds of categorization relevant in intergroup aggression: On the one hand, categorization within the societal context (society level categorization), that normatively presents outgroups that can be stigmatized, and on the other hand, a categorization on the level of the peer- or gang-ingroup and respective outgroup(s). Different mediators and moderators of the categorization-prejudice-intergroup aggression link are considered. A research example from survey research showed that intergroup emotions are mediators and moderators of the prejudice-behavior relationship.

The results presented here are preliminary. They urgently need additional experimental analyses to provide detailed information on the relationship of different kinds of categorization and additional relevant processes, especially intergroup emotions and arousal. Of special interest in this context could also be the controlled analysis of prevention programs against intergroup aggression and violence (Wagner, Christ, & van Dick, 2002). The empirical demonstration of the effectiveness of a theoretically derived prevention program is comparable to an experimental testing of explanatory theories about mediators and moderators and thus also delivers information on relevant background processes.

Acknowledgement

We are grateful to Frank Asbrock for his helpful comments on a first draft of this paper.

References

American Psychological Association (APA). (1998). *Hate crime today: An age-old foe in modern dress*. Retrieved October 4, 2006, from http://www.apa.org/releases/hate.html.

Asbrock, F., Wagner, U., & Christ, O. (2006). Diskriminierung. Folgen der Feindseligkeit [Discrimination. The consequences of hostility]. In W. Heitmeyer (Ed.), *Deutsche Zustände. Folge 4* (pp. 156–175). Frankfurt/Main, Germany: Suhrkamp.

Bandura, A. (1999). Moral disengagement in the perpetration of inhumanities. *Personality and Social Psychology Review, 3*, 193–209.

Baron, R. S., Kerr, N. L., & Miller, N. (1992). *Group process, group decision, group action*. Pacific Grove, CA: Brooks/Cole.

Brewer, M. B. (2001). Ingroup identification and intergroup conflict. In R. D. Ashmore, L. Jussim, & D. Wilder (Eds.), *Social identity, intergroup conflict, and conflict resolution* (pp. 17–41). Oxford, UK: Oxford University Press.

Brosius, H. B., & Esser, F. (1995). *Eskalation durch Berichterstattung* [Escalation through reportage]. Opladen, Germany: Westdeutscher Verlag.

Brown, R. (2000). *Group processes*. Oxford, UK: Blackwell.

Bundesminsterium des Inneren & Bundesminsterium der Justiz (2001). *Erster periodischer Sicherheitsbericht* [First periodical security report]. Berlin, Germany: Author.

Castano, E., & Giner-Sorola, R. (2006). Not quite human: Infrahuminzation in response to collective responsibility for intergroup killing. *Journal of Personality and Social Psychology, 90*, 804–818.

Christie, D. J., Wagner, R. V., & Winter, D. D. (2001). *Peace, conflict and violence.* Upper Saddle River, NJ: Prentice-Hall.

Craig, K. M. (2002). Examining hate motivated aggression. A review of the social psychological literature on hate crimes as a distinct form of aggression. *Aggression and Violent Behavior, 7*, 85–101.

Dunbar, E. (2003). Symbolic, rational, and ideological signifiers of bias-motivated offenders: Towards a strategy of assessment. *American Journal of Orthopsychiatry, 73*, 203–211.

Festinger, L. (1957). *A theory of cognitive dissonance.* Stanford, CA: Stanford University Press.

Fredrickson, G. M. (2002). *Racism. A short history.* Princeton, NJ: Princeton University Press.

Green, D. P., Abelson, R. P., & Garnett, M. (1999). The distinctive political views of hate crime-perpetrators and white supremacist. In D. A. Prentice & D. T. Miller (Eds.), *Cultural divides: Understanding and overcoming group conflict* (pp. 429–464). New York: Russel Sage.

Green, D. P., Glaser, J., & Rich, A. (1998). From lynching to gay bashing: The elusive connection between economic conditions and hate crime. *Journal of Personality and Social Psychology, 75*, 82–92.

Green, D. P., Strolovitch, D. Z., & Wong, J. S. (1998). Defended neighbourhoods, integration and racial motivated crime. *American Journal of Sociology, 104*, 372–404.

Hamner, K. M. (1992). Gay-bashing: A social identity analysis of violence against lesbians and gay men. In G. M. Herek & K. T. Berrill (Eds.), *Hate crime. Confronting violence against lesbian and gay men* (pp. 179–190). Thousand Oaks, CA: Sage Publications.

Hatfield, E., Cacioppo, J. T., & Rapson, R. L. (1994). *Emotional contagion.* Paris: Cambridge University Press.

Hess, U., & Kirouac, G. (2000). Emotion expression in groups. In M. Lewis & J. M. Haviland-Jones (Eds.), *Handbook of Emotions.* New York: Guilford.

Hoffmann, C., Bergmann, W., & Walser Smith, H. (Eds.). (2002). *Exclusionary violence. Antisemitic riots in modern German history.* Ann Arbor, MI: The University of Michigan Press.

Horowitz, R. (1987). Community tolerance of gang violence. *Social Problems, 34*, 437–450.

Horowitz, D. L. (2001). *The deadly ethnic riot.* Berkeley, CA: University of California Press.

Hovland, C. I., & Sears, R. R. (1940). Minority studies in aggression: VI. Correlation of lynching with economic indices. *Journal of Psychology, 9*, 301–310.

Huesmann, L. R., & Guerra, N. G. (1997). Children's normative beliefs about aggression and aggressive behavior. *Journal of Personality and Social Psychology, 71*, 408–419.

Jaffe, Y., Shapiro, N., & Yinon, Y. (1981). Aggression and its escalation. *Journal of Cross-Cultural Psychology, 12*, 21–36.

Jaffe, Y., & Yinon, Y. (1979). Retaliatory aggression in individuals and groups. *European Journal of Social Psychology, 9*, 177–186.

Koopmans, R., & Olzak, S. (2004). Discursive opportunities and the evolution of right-wing violence in Germany. *American Journal of Sociology, 110*, 198–230.

Krahe, B. (2001): *The social psychology of aggression.* Hove, UK: Psychology Press.

Levin, J., & McDevitt, J. (1993). *Hate crimes: The rising tides of bigotry and bloodshed.* New York: Plenum.

Mackie, D. M., Devos, T., & Smith, E. R. (2000). Intergroup emotions: Explaining offensive action tendencies in an intergroup context. *Journal of Personality and Social Psychology, 79*, 602–616.

Marsh, P., Rosser, E., & Harre, R. (1978). *The rules of disorder.* London: Routledge and Kegan Paul.

McDevitt, J., Levin, J., & Bennett, S. (2002). Hate crime offenders: An expanded typology. *Journal of Social Issues, 58*, 303–317.

Moscovici, S., & Zavalloni, M. (1969). The group as a polarizer of attitudes. *Journal of Personality and Social Psychology, 12*, 125–135.

Oakes, P. J. (1987). The salience of social categories. In J. C. Turner, M. A. Hogg, P. J. Oakes, S. D. Reicher, & M. S. Wetherell (Eds.), *Rediscovering the social group* (pp. 117–141). Oxford, UK: Blackwell.

Ohlemacher, T. (1994). Public opinion and violence against foreigners in the reunified Germany. *Zeitschrift für Soziologie, 23*, 222–236.

Pettigrew, T. F. (1996). *How to think like a social scientist*. New York: Harper Collins.

Scarpa, A., & Raine, A. (2000). Violence associated with anger and impulsivity. In J. Borod (Ed.), *The neurophysiology of emotions* (pp. 320–329). New York: Oxford University Press.

Schachter, S. (1951). Deviation, rejection and communication. *Journal of Abnormal and Social Psychology, 46*, 190–207.

Schneider, H. J. (2001). *Kriminologie für das 21. Jahrhundert* [Criminology for the 21st century]. Münster, Germany: Lit.

Short, J. F., & Strodtbeck, F. L. (1965). *Group process and gang delinquency*. Chicago: University of Chicago Press.

Sidanius, J., & Pratto, F. (1999). *Social dominance: An intergroup theory of social hierarchy and oppression*. Cambridge, UK: Cambridge University Press.

Simon, B. (1992). The perception of ingroup and outgroup homogeneity. Reintroducing the intergroup context. In W. Stroebe & M. Hewstone (Eds.), *European Review of Social Psychology* (Vol. 3, pp. 1–30). Oxford, UK: Wiley.

Smith, E. R. (1993). Social identity and social emotions: Toward new conceptualizations of prejudice. In D. M. Mackie, & D. L. Hamilton (Eds.), *Affect, cognition, and stereotyping: Interactive processes in group perception* (pp. 297–315). San Diego, CA: Academic Press.

Smith, E. R., & Mackie, D. M. (2005). Aggression, hatred, and other emotions. In J. F. Dovidio, P. Glick, & L. A. Rudman (Eds.), *On the nature of prejudice* (pp. 361–376). Malden, MA: Blackwell.

Sommer, G., & Fuchs, A. (2004). *Krieg und Frieden* [War and peace]. Weinheim, Germany: BeltzPvu.

Spergel, I. A. (1964). *Racketville, Slumtown, and Haulberg*. Chicago: University of Chicago Press.

Staub, E. (1989). *The roots of evil: The origins of genocide and other group violence*. New York: Cambridge University Press.

Tajfel, H., Billig, M. G., Bundy, R. P., & Flament, C. (1971). Social categorization and intergroup behaviour. *European Journal of Social Psychology, 1*, 149–177.

Tajfel, H., & Turner, J. C. (1979). An integrative theory of intergroup conflict. In W. G. Austin & S. Worchel (Eds.), *The social psychology of intergroup relations* (pp. 33–47). Monterey, CA: Brooks/Cole.

Turner, J. C., Hogg, M. A., Oakes, P. J., Reicher, S. D., & Wetherell, M. S. (1987). *Rediscovering the social group*. Oxford, UK: Blackwell.

Vanbeselaere, N. (1987). The effects of dichotomous and crossed social categorizations upon intergroup discrimination. *European Journal of Social Psychology, 17*, 143–156.

Waddington, D., Jones, K., & Critcher, C. (1987). Flashpoints of public disorder. In G. Gaskell & R. Benewick (Eds.), *The crowd in contemporary Britain*. London: Sage.

Wagner, U., Christ, O., & Pettigrew, T. F. (2006) *Prejudice and group-related behavior in Germany*. Manuscript in preparation.

Wagner, U., Christ, O., & van Dick, R. (2002). Die empirische Evaluation von Präventionsprogrammen gegen Fremdenfeindlichkeit [The empirical evaluation of primary prevention programs against xenophobia]. *Journal für Konflikt- und Gewaltforschung, 4*, 101–117.

Wagner, U., & van Dick, R. (2001). Fremdenfeindlichkeit „in der Mitte der Gesellschaft:" Phän-
omenbeschreibung, Ursachen, Gegenmaßnahmen [Prejudice in the "middle of society:" Description, causes, countermeasures]. *Zeitschrift für Politische Psychologie, 9*, 41–54.

Wagner, U., & Ward, P. L. (1993). Variation of out-group presence and evaluation of the in-group.
British Journal of Social Psychology, 32, 241–251.

Willems, H. (2002). Rechtsextremistische, antisemitische und fremdenfeindliche Straftaten in
Deutschland: Entwicklung, Strukturen, Hintergründe [Extreme rightwing, antisemitic, and
xenophobic crime in Germany]. In T. Gumke & B. Wagner (Eds.), *Handbuch Rechtsradika-
lismus* (pp. 141–157). Opladen, Germany: Leske & Budrich.

Willems, H., Eckert, R., Würtz, S., & Steinmetz, L. (1993). *Fremdenfeindliche Gewalt: Einstel-
lungen, Täter, Konflikteskalationen* [Violence against foreigners: Attitudes, offenders, escalation of conflict]. Opladen, Germany: Leske & Budrich.

Wolf, C., Stellmacher, J., Wagner, U., & Christ, O. (2003). Druckvolle Ermunterungen. Das Mei-
nungsbild fördert menschenfeindliche Gewaltbereitschaft [Pressurized encouragement: The
public opinion supports misanthropist violence]. In W. Heitmeyer (Ed.), *Deutsche Zustände.
Folge 2* (pp. 142–158). Frankfurt, Germany: Suhrkamp.

Zillmann, D. (1979). *Hostility and aggression*. Hillsdale, NJ: Erlbaum.

Zimbardo, P. (1969). The human choice: Individuation, reason, and order versus deindividuation,
impulse and chaos. *Nebraska Symposium on Motivation, 17*, 237–307.

9

Emotions in Negative Intergroup Relations: An Affective Route to Outgroup Derogation

Kerstin Schütte and Thomas Kessler

Matthew Shepard died on October 12, 1998. He was a 21-year old student. Shepard had been brutally beaten by two men he had met in a bar. They had driven him out of town, tied him to a fence, and left him behind in freezing temperatures. Shepard was found after 18 hours and died 5 days later. He had never regained consciousness. Supposedly, Matthew Shepard was murdered because he was gay.

Aggressive acts are performed for various reasons, sometimes even without a clearly discernible cause, without an obvious behavior of the target person that triggered the aggressive response. In the present example, the group membership of the victim seems to be the only instigating reason for the perpetrators' actions. Matthew Shepard's murderers may have held a negative attitude towards homosexuals; maybe they had already been angry before they met their later victim. Matthew Shepard may have disclosed his sexual orientation. Matthew Shepard's murder case appears to be a prime example of what is called a hate crime, that is, a crime based on a certain group membership of the victim (see e.g., McDevitt, Levin, & Bennett, 2002).

Hate crimes are but one example of aggressive acts in intergroup relations. Other examples of extremely severe manifestations of intergroup aggression are warfare, genocide (e.g., in Rwanda or the Jewish extermination in Nazi Germany), ethnic cleansing (e.g., in the former Yugoslavia or in Darfur, Sudan), and the continued conflicts between Israelis and Palestinians or between Protestants and Catholics in Northern Ireland. The increase of anti-Muslim attitudes enhances the risk for even merely Arab-looking persons to be exposed to mistrust, social exclusion, hostility, or unwarranted criminal prosecution in Western countries since 9/11. Less conspicuous forms of intergroup aggression include malevolently intended derisive remarks towards outgroup members such as overweight people or those speaking with a certain accent. Age discrimination, gender discrimination, or discrimination of the disabled can also take the form of explicitly harmful treatment of the respective group. Targets of intergroup aggression may have committed no other transgression than simply being a member of a particular group. They may be treated aggressively without having individually provided a cause for any aggressive response. At the same time, aggressors may act upon provocations directed at their ingroup without themselves necessarily being personally affected by the provocation. Therefore, negative treatment based on the target's membership in a certain social group cannot fully be grasped by theories of interpersonal aggression. This chapter focuses on intergroup aggression as well as outgroup derogation and proposes as a particular process that group-based emotions can explain negative behavior toward an outgroup or its members.

The next section differentiates outgroup derogation from other forms of intergroup bias. The particular process explaining aggressive behavior, triggered displaced aggression, is delineated and transferred to the intergroup level. A further group-level concept, group-based emotion, is subsequently elucidated and proposed as a determinant of out-group derogation. Finally, we present some data from our own research on an affective route to outgroup derogation.

Outgroup Derogation – A Group Level Phenomenon

Every individual belongs to a number of social groups. Individuals that share member-ship in a certain social group constitute an *ingroup*, whereas all other individuals are noningroup members and belong to an *outgroup*. Typical group memberships are based, for example, on nationality, gender, age, race, or religious affiliation.

Conceiving of an individual as a member of a particular social group is an act of categorization. This cognitive process is fundamental to all group level phenomena. How we categorize ourselves and how we are categorized by others is not necessarily identical. Kurdish people living in Germany, for example, are occasionally categorized as Turks. Furthermore, Germans of Kurdish descent who self-categorize as Germans may still frequently be categorized by others as Kurds, or even as Turks.

Some group memberships are easily discernable because of the high visibility of qualifying features like, for example, skin color. Visible features may, however, be false indicators of a person's group membership as when a German of Kurdish descent is categorized as not German. Such errors of categorization are less frequent when indi-viduals intentionally display symbols indicating their group membership (e.g., national flags or the paraphernalia that fans of sports teams wear). Membership in some groups is self-chosen (e.g., membership in a political party), membership in other groups is involuntary and not easy – sometimes impossible – to change (e.g., membership in an ethnic group).

Of course, a particular group membership becomes salient only under certain condi-tions. The salience of a particular group membership depends on its accessibility and fit (Oakes, 1987). *Accessibility* refers to an individual's readiness to use a particular social categorization, it reflects the person's motivational state and chronic and recent activa-tion of knowledge structures. Highly religious people are more frequently aware of their religious affiliation than people who assign less significance to this particular group membership. *Fit* of a particular social categorization has two distinguishable aspects: (a) perceived intragroup differences relative to perceived intergroup differences within the comparative frame (comparative or structural fit), and (b) the consistency of the per-ceived intra- and intergroup differences with stereotypical beliefs about the content of a particular social categorization (normative fit). The salience of social categories is thus dependent on their normative appropriateness and their suitability to provide meaning in a given social context. Living in a foreign country, for example, a person's national identity is likely to be frequently salient.

Group memberships may guide our behavior when we interact with other people (e.g., Bushman & Bonacci, 2004; Gaertner & Bickman, 1971) and they impact how we feel about others belonging to either the ingroup or a particular outgroup (e.g., Cottrell & Neuberg, 2005; Dijker, 1987; Fiske, Cuddy, Glick, & Xu, 2002; Gordijn, Wigboldus, & Yzerbyt, 2001). A necessary condition for group membership to gain influence on a person's emotions and actions is that the person not only self-categorizes as a member of the group (i.e., sees herself as formally belonging to the group) but also identifies with that group. Identification with a group entails attachment, emotional involvement, and valuing of the group membership (Tajfel & Turner, 1979, 1986). People identifying with a particular social category will be affected emotionally by events happening to that group (even if they are not individually affected) and they will likely act on behalf of that group. Identification with the groups one belongs to is hence seen as a precondition of derogating a corresponding outgroup, but – as we will illustrate below – it is not a sufficient explanation (Brewer, 2001). For a person to be *treated* as a member of its respective group, it is sufficient that the other party categorizes the person as a member of that group. Many detainees in the Guantanamo Bay camps are kept imprisoned without trial on the basis of being categorized as unlawful combatants, which is a categorization that the imprisoned are quite unlikely to share.

In all of the examples of explicitly negative group-based treatment listed above, the aggressor does not have a specific interpersonal relationship to the individual target person. Suicide bombers do not intend to kill precisely those persons who happen to be around when the bomb detonates; group-level aggression is directed indiscriminately against members of the respective outgroup. Generally, intergroup behavior is distinguished from interpersonal behavior by the fact that single members of the same group are perceived as almost interchangeable (Tajfel, 1978). Whenever an interaction is based on the group memberships of the parties involved rather than on the person's unique selves – while it might still take place between two individuals only – it qualifies as intergroup behavior (Tajfel & Turner, 1986).

In analogy to the definition of aggression (e.g., Baron & Richardson, 1994), outgroup derogation is defined as any behavior intentionally performed with the explicit aim to harm the target group (or members of the group), while the target group is motivated to avoid such behavior. Outgroup derogation is one manifestation of the well-established tendency to relatively favor the ingroup over the outgroup, termed intergroup bias (Hewstone, Rubin, & Willis, 2002). Quite surprisingly, when viewed from the perspective of an aggression researcher, outgroup derogation was in the beginning of intergroup research not recognized as a phenomenon separate from other intergroup bias strategies such as ingroup favoritism which is preferential treatment of ingroup members and maximization of differences between ingroup and outgroup. Although different strategies of intergroup bias were distinguished, the measures used could not clearly differentiate between outgroup derogation and ingroup favoritism. In classical allocation matrices, for instance, both groups' outcomes were interdependent (see e.g., Tajfel, Billig, Bundy, & Flament, 1971), a relatively more positive outcome for the ingroup necessarily brought about a relatively more negative outcome for the outgroup and vice versa. More generally, ratings obtained for ingroup and outgroup lacked a standard (e.g., ratings for an uncategorized target) to discern whether ratings for the ingroup were relatively increased or ratings for the outgroup were relatively decreased. An observed systematically more favorable treatment of the ingroup relative to an outgroup might thus have been produced by quite different underlying psychological processes. Distinguishing between the intergroup bias strategies was not considered because they were assumed to represent a single dimension. The insightful research on intergroup behavior pioneered by Tajfel is thus not particularly informative as to why people intend to explicitly harm outgroup members.

Further research suggests that different underlying processes are involved in the intergroup bias strategies outgroup derogation and ingroup favoritism, they may be differentially motivated (Brewer, 1999; Mummendey & Otten, 1998). Predictors for explicitly negative behavioral intentions towards the outgroup were at best very weak predictors of the evaluation of one's own group as more strongly characterized by positive traits than the outgroup, and they did not at all predict relative evaluative outgroup negativism on negative traits (Struch & Schwartz, 1989). Distancing from outgroups was likewise not negatively correlated with positive evaluations of one's ingroup (Brewer & Campbell, 1976). Moreover, research on the positive-negative asymmetry in social discrimination[1] revealed that even the valence of resources or evaluations impacts on the readiness to differentiate along group lines (see Mummendey & Otten, 1998, for a review). Experimental conditions that elicit ingroup favoritism with regard to allocations or evaluations of positive stimuli were insufficient to produce the same pattern for negative stimuli. Hence, already the mechanism underlying ingroup favoritism is not exactly identical when positive versus negative stimuli are concerned. In light of the result that participants prefer a fairness strategy over ingroup favoritism when dealing with negative stimuli unless aggravating conditions apply, it is reasonable to assume that explicitly negative treatment of outgroup members implies the operation of other psychological processes than preferential treatment of ingroup members.

Inherent in the proposition of different underlying processes (Brewer, 1999, 2001) is the consequence that an explanation of aggressive tendencies towards outgroups cannot simply be derived by drawing inferences from the large body of research on ingroup favoritism. Explanations of outgroup derogation have to be put to an explicit test, thus research explicitly addressing outgroup derogation is warranted. However, with the exception of Struch and Schwartz (1989), research explicitly addressing outgroup derogation is still largely missing. Which factors drive outgroup derogation is therefore not well understood to date.

The Triggered Displaced Aggression Paradigm

One classical explanation of aggression, the frustration-aggression hypothesis (Dollard, Doob, Miller, Mowrer, & Sears, 1939), holds that people act aggressively whenever they have been frustrated. At the same time, frustration was conceived of as a necessary antecedent of aggressive behavior. Frustration is defined as a blockage of goal attainment. While the strong relation between frustration and aggression had to be relaxed,

---

[1] Social *differentiation* is any unequal treatment based on group membership comprising preferential treatment of one group as well as disadvantageous treatment of another group. Social *discrimination* denotes such social differential behavior that is perceived as illegitimate (Mummendey & Otten, 2001). Aggressor and target of the aggressive action (or a noninvolved observer) may diverge regarding their perspectives on the legitimacy of the action. In other words, the evaluative judgment of the differential treatment as illegitimate is pivotal. Social discrimination is hence not objectively ascertainable.

the general idea is still present in more recent theories. The cognitive-neoassociationistic model of emotional aggression (Berkowitz, 1990, 1993) conceptualizes aggression as one possible action tendency following from aversive stimulation, which could, for example, have been a frustrating incident. However, aversive stimuli can also result from nonhuman sources like hot temperatures.

Sometimes an appropriate target for aggression is not available. Thus, frustration because of getting stuck in a traffic jam has no tangible source that would pose a target for an aggressive response. In other cases, the target is not available for direct retaliation, as when one is upset about a politician, or an aggressive response to the source of the aversive stimulation may be suppressed because the person enjoys considerable power. The aggressive response may then be displaced to another target. A recent meta-analysis found displaced aggression to be a robust effect with a mean effect size of $d = 0.54$ (Marcus-Newhall, Pedersen, Carlson, & Miller, 2000). Participants who had been provoked but were unable to retaliate were more aggressive towards an innocent target than nonprovoked participants.

Displaced aggression can be further distinguished from triggered displaced aggression (Miller & Marcus-Newhall, 1997; Miller, Pedersen, Earleywine, & Pollock, 2003; Pedersen, Gonzales, & Miller, 2000). Whereas the aggression target in displaced aggression is assumed innocent, the target in triggered displaced aggression itself committed a minor transgression. Triggered displaced aggression is conceptualized to result when the aggressor, prior to the interaction with the aggression target, experienced a provocation that precluded an aggressive response. The aggressive response is *displaced* in the sense that it is not directed towards the original source of the provocation that instigated an aggressive behavioral tendency in the first place. The aggressive response is *triggered* in the sense that it is not invariably directed towards any target (as displaced aggression) but only towards such a target that subsequently provides a minor provocation. Triggered displaced aggression hence denotes a disproportionately aggressive response towards a target that committed a minor transgression. Supposedly, triggered displaced aggression has greater ecological validity than nontriggered displaced aggression; it seems more likely that an aggressive reaction is displaced to a target that commits a minor transgression itself than to a completely innocent target (Miller & Marcus-Newhall, 1997). Yet, it is impossible to determine the actual influences on persons' behavior in real-life episodes. The constant stream of events and emotional states cannot be cleanly separated and referred to the sources from which they originated.

In triggered displaced aggression, the initial strong provocation and the subsequent minor provocation interact to produce the disproportionately aggressive response to the triggering provocation. The aggressiveness of the response exceeds the amount of aggression that would be expected based on the intensity of the trigger alone or based on simple additive effects of both provocations. For such an interactive effect of both provocations, it is crucial that the second provocation is trivial, that is, of low intensity (Vasquez, Denson, Pedersen, Stenstrom, & Miller, 2005). Low intensity triggers are more ambiguous with respect to whether or not they constitute a provocation. Ambiguous triggers might thus simply be dismissed as not demanding an aggressive response by persons not previously provoked. If, however, a strong provocation preceded the triggering provocation, it might function as a priming event so that the trigger might be more easily noticed and/or it might be more readily attributed to malevolent intent. This explanation potentially accounts for triggered displacement of aggression with considerable temporal distance from the initial provocation (cf. Bushman, Bonacci, Pedersen, Vasquez, & Miller, 2005). Nontrivially strong "triggering" provocations are not subject to such attributional distortion so that the interactive effect of both provocations would not be expected to occur. At the same time, nontrivially strong "triggering" provocations are unlikely to go unnoticed or to be ignored by nonprovoked participants.

The process of rumination (Martin & Tesser, 1996) may account for the prolonged effect of an initial provocation. Persistent and recurring worrying and brooding may lead to the formation and maintenance of cognitive representations of the subjective state instigated by the initial provocation. This ruminatively-based explanation of triggered displaced aggression is in line with both the cognitive-neoassociationistic model of emotional aggression (Berkowitz, 1990, 1993) and the general aggression model (Anderson & Bushman, 2002).

A personality variable serving a similar function as the initial provocation is narcissism. Persons high in narcissism reacted aggressively towards targets that provided a bad evaluation whereas persons low in narcissism were less likely to aggress against that target (Bushman & Baumeister, 1998). Interestingly, persons low in narcissism were also less likely than persons high in narcissism to perceive a bad evaluation as threatening, suggesting that the evaluation-threat-aggression network is chronically activated in narcissists.

An explanation complementary to this cognitive process suggests that the aggressive response towards the triggering target reflects persisting negative affective arousal caused by the initial provocation (Miller et al., 2003). The still present arousal may combine with the arousal induced by the triggering target. The aggressor may misattribute the negative affective arousal stemming from the initial provocation to the triggering source. The ruminatively-based explanation and the arousal-based explanation may apply under differential circumstances. The arousal-based explanation is, however, confined to situations in which the triggering event follows up on the initial provocation within a couple of minutes, because physiological arousal dissipates rather quickly.

Triggered displacement of aggression might occur on a group level in much the same way as it does on the interpersonal level. If experienced subsequent to a strong provocation (whether that be person-based or group-based), a trivially mild triggering group-based provocation might suffice to elicit disproportionately aggressive treatment of the respective outgroup. Empirically, results from a longitudinal study conducted within the context of the German reunification (Kessler & Mummendey, 2001) fit a triggered displaced aggression explanation, thus hinting at the ecological validity of the concept of triggered displacement of explicitly harmful behavior toward outgroups. Xenophobia expressed by East Germans who self-categorized on the superordinate level (i.e., German) was significantly predicted by resentment elicited by the relationship between East and West Germans.

While ingroups are generally assigned positive valence, outgroups are not necessarily per se assigned negative valence (Otten & Moskowitz, 2000; Otten & Wentura, 1999). Hence, merely being an outgroup member should not convert an innocent target into a triggering target. Although the ingroup/outgroup distinction moderates the effect of a triggering action following a moderately strong provocation on displaced aggression, the moderation hinges on the buffering effect of ingroup membership, not on further augmentation of triggered displacement when the target was an outgroup member (Pedersen, Bushman, Vasquez, & Miller, 2006, Study 2). Inasmuch as outgroups are conceived of as sources of conflict and competition or are associated with negative stereotypical expectations, though, the mere appearance or thought of an outgroup (member) might indeed function as a triggering event. Possibly, displaced outgroup derogation is triggered more easily than displaced interpersonal aggression. The interindividual-intergroup discontinuity effect repeatedly demonstrated by Insko, Schopler, and colleagues (Schopler & Insko, 1992) illustrates that intergroup contexts promote competitiveness compared with interpersonal contexts. Furthermore, the interindividual-intergroup discontinuity effect was demonstrated to extend to aggressive behavior; groups were significantly more aggressive than individuals, and higher levels of aggression were directed at groups than at individuals (Meier & Hinsz, 2004).

In interpersonal aggression research, negative affective reactions to the triggering incident have been shown to mediate the effect of the trigger on displaced aggression among initially provoked participants (Pedersen et al., 2000, Study 2; Vasquez et al., 2005). Our own research sought to establish an analogous affective route to explicitly harmful behavior towards outgroup members. Since the behavior to be explained is an intergroup phenomenon, the emotions involved should likewise be group-based. We propose that specifically group-based anger serves an important function in the elicitation of disproportionately aggressive responses to target outgroups. Other group-based emotions are not expected to be associated with explicitly harmful action tendencies.

Affect in Intergroup Relations – Group-Based Emotions

One potential route to outgroup derogation was tested in our own work. We suggest that group-based emotions (E. R. Smith, 1993, 1999) are likely to be involved in the generation of outgroup derogation. Emotions have been demonstrated to be potent and consistent predictors of attitudes towards outgroups (Esses, Haddock, & Zanna, 1993; Stangor, Sullivan, & Ford, 1991), and the importance of affect for positive consequences of intergroup contact has been recognized (Tropp & Pettigrew, 2004).

The proposition of the concept of group-based emotion followed from an integration of appraisal theories of emotion (Frijda, 1986; Roseman, 1984; Scherer, 1988; Smith & Ellsworth, 1985) with social identity theory (Tajfel & Turner, 1979, 1986) and self-categorization theory (Turner, 1985; Turner, Hogg, Oakes, Reicher, & Wetherell, 1987). According to appraisal theories of emotion, the perceiving individual plays an active role in the elicitation of emotions. The person constructively appraises the environmental situation in relation to its needs and goals (Frijda, 1986; Lazarus, 1991; Roseman, 1984). The constructive role of the appraising person accounts for differentiated emotional reactions towards the same object or situation in different contexts or at different points in time.

Appraisal theorists view emotions as adaptive responses where specific emotions are assumed to be associated with specific action tendencies (Frijda, 1986; Frijda, Kuipers, & ter Schure, 1989; Roseman, 1984; Smith & Ellsworth, 1985). Emotions serve as indicators, evoking a psychological readiness for specific behaviors that are warranted under particular circumstances. Thus, the constructive role of the appraising person also accounts for differential behavior towards identical interaction partners over time and changing contexts.

Primarily, cognitive appraisal processes are viewed as antecedents of emotions. Additionally, however, the emotional experience itself consists, in part, of the perception of a particular appraisal pattern (Frijda, 1993; Lazarus, 1991). The actual antecedent appraisals need not be accurately represented by the perceived appraisal structure. Emotional experiences themselves summon cognitive consequences like attributions or attentional changes, and these secondary elaborations modulate and more fully determine the emotional experience (Berkowitz, 1990; Frijda, 1993). An elaborated model which integrates insights from neuroscience demonstrating how affect and cognition are inextricably linked through recursive processes was proposed by Lewis (2005).

Social identity theory and self-categorization theory hold that through identification with a social group, the group can become part of a person's self. The various affiliations with one's ingroups constitute a person's social identity. Like any other part of the self, the social identity takes on motivational and affective significance. The experience of group-based emotions is thus predicated on identification with the respective group. Situations or events with affective significance for an ingroup elicit group-based emotions among group members identified with the particular group. Group members appraise objects and situations in relation to an ingroup's needs and goals provided that the particular group membership is psychologically active. Group-based emotions are then experienced on behalf of one's ingroup, the individual person need not be affected personally.

Research on group-based emotions corroborates the fundamental importance assigned to identification with the respective group. Stronger anger responses to unfair treatment of persons that participants categorized as ingroup members emerged for participants highly identified with that group than for participants with low identification (Gordijn, Yzerbyt, Wigboldus, & Dumont, 2006; Yzerbyt, Dumont, Wigboldus, & Gordijn, 2003). On the other hand, anger towards either an in- or outgroup impacts the level of identification (Kessler & Hollbach, 2005). Whereas anger towards the outgroup increased identification with the ingroup, anger towards the ingroup decreased identification with that same group.

Empirical research further demonstrated the regulatory function of group-based emotions for intergroup behavior. Successful implementation of emotion-appropriate behavior leads to a decrease of the subjective experience of the respective emotion, whereas no such dissipation occurs when the implementation is unsuccessful or the intergroup behavior performed is emotion-inappropriate (Maitner, Mackie, & Smith, 2006).

Anger is the emotion that aggression researchers as well as appraisal theorists conceptualize and empirically find to be associated with approach, moving against tendencies, or, most specifically, with aggression[2] (e.g., Anderson & Bushman, 2002; Berkowitz, 1983; Frijda et al., 1989; Geen, 1990; Mackie, Devos, & Smith, 2000; Yzerbyt et

---

[2] The relationship between anger and aggression is not exclusive, however. Anger can lead to various behavioral responses and aggression can occur without the experience of anger (e.g., Averill, 1983).

al., 2003). Mackie and collaborators (2000) provided empirical evidence that *group-based* anger can have specific behavioral consequences. Group-based anger was demonstrated to be a potent predictor of the tendency to move against an outgroup. In the context of the current topic it has to be noted, however, that their dependent variable cannot be equated with outgroup derogation. Groups had been created on the basis of participants' opinions; items then primarily tapped disputatious inclinations. Instead of aggressive tendencies, Mackie and colleagues may have assessed the motive to convince the outgroup of one's own opinion.

Mackie et al. (2000, Studies 2 and 3) manipulated perceived ingroup strength via information about the collective support the ingroup ostensibly enjoyed. Consistent with conceptualizations of individual-based anger (e.g., Roseman, 1984), perceived strength (ingroup strength in that case) significantly predicted group-based anger. All else being equal, people that perceive their ingroup to have no power are expected to experience helplessness and apathy rather than anger (Abramson, Seligman, & Teasdale, 1978). Aggression towards outgroup members is highly unlikely given a perception of low ingroup strength. However, this important appraisal dimension was not varied in our own research.

Empirical Evidence on the Affective Route to Outgroup Derogation

We sought to demonstrate that outgroup derogation can result from triggered displacement of an aggressive reaction and further utilized the triggered displaced aggression paradigm to address the question of whether group-based emotions contribute to the occurrence of outgroup derogation. In a series of studies, we tested whether participants who were exposed to two orthogonal provocations, the initial one comparatively strong, the second trivially mild, would display higher levels of outgroup derogation than participants who had been exposed to only one or none of those provocations. Two of these studies are delineated below. We examined the role of group-based anger as compared to group-based dejection and an index of positive group-based emotions in the relationship of intergroup behavior and both experimental provocations.

In a vignette study relating to naturally occurring groups (Schütte & Kessler, 2006, Study 1) outgroup derogation was indeed significantly stronger in the provocation-trigger condition than in the other 3 conditions (see Figure 1).

Specifically, two different intergroup contexts were established in two parts of the study. German student participants were addressed as Europeans as opposed to U.S.-Americans in the first part of the study and as members of the younger generation as opposed to the elderly in the second part of the study. Participants who had initially read a provoking report about U.S. measures in the so-called "war against terror" and were then informed about a rather luxurious home for the elderly expressed higher agreement with statements demanding forfeit for the elderly compared to all other participants. The nonprovoking condition reproduced the events on and surrounding D-Day, the invasion of Normandy by the Allied Forces on June 6, 1944, emphasizing the U.S. contribution to these events and the importance for European history. The nontriggering description of the residential home for the elderly pictured a nice but comparatively modest institution.

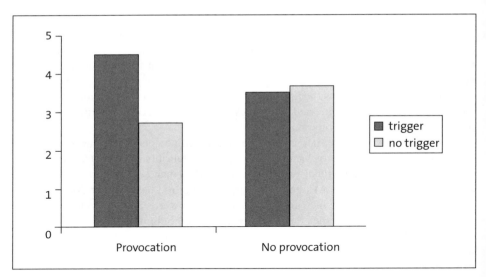

Figure 1. Outgroup derogation as a function of initial strong provocation and trivial triggering provocation (Schütte & Kessler, 2006, Study 1).

Trigger-elicited anger significantly predicted outgroup derogation. Furthermore, provocation-elicited anger moderated the relationship between trigger-elicited anger and outgroup derogation (see Figure 2). Trigger-elicited anger predicted outgroup derogation when provocation-elicited anger was high, but not when provocation-elicited anger was low. Neither dejection-related emotions nor positive emotions significantly predicted outgroup derogation, thus empirically supporting the proposition that specifically group-based anger was associated with outgroup derogation. Outgroup derogation has thus been demonstrated to be a result of triggered displacement. Group-based emotions

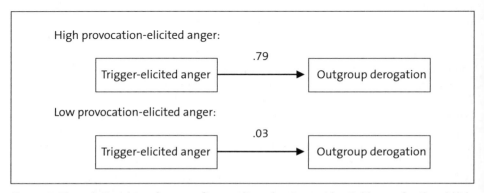

Figure 2. The relationship of anger after reading about a residential home for the elderly and derogation of the elderly separately for participants that reported high and low levels of anger elicited by the initial provocation (Schütte & Kessler, 2006, Study 1). Beta weights resulted from simple slope analysis following Aiken and West (1991).

and specifically group-based anger predicted the disproportionately negative treatment of the elderly.

The appraisal of how threatening[3] the elderly were did not differ across conditions as a consequence of the experimental manipulation. However, trigger-elicited anger significantly predicted perceived threat. Provocation-elicited anger again moderated the association. Trigger-elicited anger perceived threat derogation only when provocation-elicited anger was high, but not when it was low. Besides, perceived threat strongly predicted outgroup derogation. The disproportionately aggressive response to the triggering incident will potentially not be conceived of as out of proportion by the aggressor; it is in line with the aggressor's appraisal of the intergroup situation. Dejection and positive emotions were also less potent predictors than anger for perceived threat.

The statistically significant prediction of outgroup derogation by trigger-elicited anger was conceptually replicated with a new dependent measure and in other intergroup contexts with an availability sample of the general population of Jena, East Germany (Schütte & Kessler, 2006, Study 2). The initial provocation targeted participants' East German identity; it was set in the context of election campaigns for the German national parliament. The triggering provocation introduced foreigners as an outgroup allowing but not necessarily demanding recategorization at the more inclusive level "German." Anger that East German participants experienced after reading a report from the German Foreign Office (i.e., the trigger) predicted tendencies to engage in behavior derogating foreigners. The threat perceived to be posed by foreigners was also significantly predicted by trigger-elicited anger. As in the first study, the trigger-elicited anger determined the cognitive appraisal of how threatening the respective outgroup was as well as behavioral inclinations towards that outgroup. Consequently, cognitive appraisal and behavior are consistent; the affective route to outgroup derogation also adjusted corresponding appraisals of the intergroup relationship. Furthermore, the anger reaction to the initial provocation – like in the first study – moderated the effect of the anger reaction to the triggering event on perceived threat, though only marginally significantly this time. When anger-reactions to the initial provocation were strong, the level of anger after reading the German Foreign Office report highly significantly predicted the level of threat participants perceived. On the other hand, when anger-reactions to the initial provocation were weak, trigger-elicited anger and perceived threat were not significantly related.

Conclusions

Theoretical analyses as well as preliminary results support the proposition that negative group-based emotions and specifically group-based anger constitute an affective route to outgroup derogation. Cognitive appraisals of intergroup relations, namely threats perceived to be posed by the outgroup, as well as behavioral intentions towards naturally

---

[3] Perceived threat tapped exploitation of resources by the elderly and is therefore, although the variable name seems to suggest otherwise, perfectly compatible with anger and aggressive behavioral tendencies.

occurring outgroups have been shown to deteriorate as a consequence of group-based anger. It is conceivable that rumination and further minor triggers perpetuate negative intergroup relations. Particularly to the extent that anger emotions are experienced by the actor, triggered displacement has to be regarded as highly consequential for intergroup relations.

Acknowledgment

Support for the research reported in this chapter was provided by the DFG grant KE 792.

References

Abramson, L. Y., Seligman, M. E., & Teasdale, J. D. (1978). Learned helplessness in humans: Critique and reformulation. *Journal of Abnormal Psychology, 87*, 49–74.

Aiken, L. S., & West, S. G. (1991). *Multiple regression: Testing and interpreting interactions.* Thousand Oaks, CA: Sage Publications.

Anderson, C. A., & Bushman, B. J. (2002). Human aggression. *Annual Review of Psychology, 53*, 27–51.

Averill, J. R. (1983). Studies on anger and aggression: Implications for theories of emotion. *American Psychologist, 38*, 1145–1160.

Baron, R. A., & Richardson, D. R. (1994). *Human aggression* (2nd ed.). New York: Plenum Press.

Berkowitz, L. (1983). The experience of anger as a parallel process in the display of impulsive, "angry" aggression. In R. G. Geen & E. I. Donnerstein (Eds.), *Aggression: Theoretical and empirical reviews* (pp. 103–133). New York: Academic Press.

Berkowitz, L. (1990). On the formation and regulation of anger and aggression: A cognitive-neo-associationistic analysis. *American Psychologist, 45*, 494–503.

Berkowitz, L. (1993). *Aggression: Its causes, consequences, and control.* New York: McGraw-Hill.

Brewer, M. B. (1999). The psychology of prejudice: Ingroup love or outgroup hate? *Journal of Social Issues, 55*, 429–444.

Brewer, M. B. (2001). Ingroup identification and intergroup conflict: When does ingroup love become outgroup hate? In R. D. Ashmore, L. Jussim, & D. Wilder (Eds.), *Social identity, intergroup conflict, and conflict reduction* (pp. 17–41). New York: Oxford University Press.

Brewer, M. B., & Campbell, D. T. (1976). *Ethnocentrism and intergroup attitudes: East African evidence.* Oxford, UK: Sage.

Bushman, B. J., & Baumeister, R. F. (1998). Threatened egotism, narcissism, self-esteem, and direct and displaced aggression: Does self-love or self-hate lead to violence? *Journal of Personality and Social Psychology, 75*, 219–229.

Bushman, B. J., & Bonacci, A. M. (2004). You've got mail: Using e-mail to examine the effect of prejudiced attitudes on discrimination against Arabs. *Journal of Experimental Social Psychology, 40*, 753–759.

Bushman, B. J., Bonacci, A. M., Pedersen, W. C., Vasquez, E. A., & Miller, N. (2005). Chewing on it can chew you up: Effects of rumination on triggered displaced aggression. *Journal of Personality and Social Psychology, 88*, 969–983.

Cottrell, C. A., & Neuberg, S. L. (2005). Different emotional reactions to different groups: A sociofunctional threat-based approach to "prejudice." *Journal of Personality and Social Psychology, 88*, 770–789.

Dijker, A. J. M. (1987). Emotional reactions to ethnic minorities. *European Journal of Social Psychology, 17*, 305–325.

Dollard, J., Doob, L. W., Miller, N. E., Mowrer, O. H., & Sears, R. R. (1939). *Frustration and aggression*. New Haven, CT: Yale University Press.

Esses, V. M., Haddock, G., & Zanna, M. P. (1993). Values, stereotypes, and emotions as determinants of intergroup attitudes. In D. M. Mackie & D. L. Hamilton (Eds.), *Affect, cognition, and stereotyping: Interactive processes in group perception* (pp. 137–166). San Diego, CA: Academic Press.

Fiske, S. T., Cuddy, A. C., Glick, P., & Xu, J. (2002). A model of (often mixed) stereotype content: Competence and warmth respectively follow from perceived status and competition. *Journal of Personality and Social Psychology, 82*, 878–902.

Frijda, N. H. (1986). *The emotions*. Cambridge, UK: Cambridge University Press.

Frijda, N. H. (1993). The place of appraisal in emotion. *Cognition and Emotion, 7*, 357–387.

Frijda, N. H., Kuipers, P., & ter Schure, E. (1989). Relations among emotions, appraisal, and emotional action readiness. *Journal of Personality and Social Psychology, 57*, 212–228.

Gaertner, S., & Bickman, L. (1971). Effects of race on the elicitation of helping behavior: The wrong number technique. *Journal of Personality and Social Psychology, 20*, 218–222.

Geen, R. G. (1990). *Human aggression*. Milton Keynes, UK: Open University Press.

Gordijn, E. H., Wigboldus, D., & Yzerbyt, V. (2001). Emotional consequences of categorizing victims of negative outgroup behavior as ingroup or outgroup. *Group Processes and Intergroup Relations, 4*, 317–326.

Gordijn, E. H., Yzerbyt, V., Wigboldus, D., & Dumont, M. (2006). Emotional reactions to harmful intergroup behavior. *European Journal of Social Psychology, 36*, 15–30.

Hewstone, M., Rubin, M., & Willis, H. (2002). Intergroup bias. *Annual Review of Psychology, 53*, 575–604.

Kessler, T., & Hollbach, S. (2005). Group-based emotions as determinants of ingroup identification. *Journal of Experimental Social Psychology, 41*, 677–685.

Kessler, T., & Mummendey, A. (2001). Is there any scapegoat around? Determinants of intergroup conflicts at different categorization levels. *Journal of Personality and Social Psychology, 81*, 1090–1102.

Lazarus, R. S. (1991). Cognition and motivation in emotion. *American Psychologist, 46*, 352–367.

Lewis, M. D. (2005). Bridging emotion theory and neurobiology through dynamic systems modeling. *Behavioral and Brain Sciences, 28*, 169–245.

Mackie, D. M., Devos, T., & Smith, E. R. (2000). Intergroup emotions: Explaining offensive action tendencies in an intergroup context. *Journal of Personality and Social Psychology, 79*, 602–616.

Maitner, A. T., Mackie, D. M., & Smith, E. R. (2006). Evidence for the regulatory function of intergroup emotion: Emotional consequences of implemented or impeded intergroup action tendencies. *Journal of Experimental Social Psychology, 42,* 720–728.

Marcus-Newhall, A., Pedersen, W. C., Carlson, M., & Miller, N. (2000). Displaced aggression is alive and well: A meta-analytic review. *Journal of Personality and Social Psychology, 78*, 670–689.

Martin, L. L., & Tesser, A. (1996). Some ruminative thoughts. In R. S. Wyer (Ed.), *Advances in social cognition* (Vol. 9, pp. 1–47). Hillsdale, NJ: Erlbaum.

McDevitt, J., Levin, J., & Bennett, S. (2002). Hate crime offenders: An expanded typology. *Journal of Social Issues, 58*, 303–317.

Meier, B. P., & Hinsz, V. B. (2004). A comparison of human aggression committed by groups and individuals: An interindividual-intergroup discontinuity. *Journal of Experimental Social Psychology, 40*, 551–559.

Miller, N., & Marcus-Newhall, A. (1997). A conceptual analysis of displaced aggression. In R. Ben-Ari & Y. Rich (Eds.), *Enhancing education in heterogeneous schools: Theory and application* (pp. 69–108). Ramat-Gan, Israel: Bar-Ilan University Press.

Miller, N., Pedersen, W. C., Earleywine, M., & Pollock, V. E. (2003). A theoretical model of triggered displaced aggression. *Personality and Social Psychology Review, 7*, 75–97.

Mummendey, A., & Otten, S. (1998). Positive-negative asymmetry in social discrimination. In W. Stroebe & M. Hewstone (Eds.), *European review of social psychology* (pp. 107–143). Chichester, UK: Wiley.

Mummendey, A., & Otten, S. (2001). Aversive discrimination. In R. Brown & S. L. Gaertner (Eds.), *Blackwell handbook of social psychology* (pp. 112–132). Oxford, UK: Blackwell.

Oakes, P. J. (1987). The salience of social categories. In J. C. Turner, M. A. Hogg, P. J. Oakes, S. D. Reicher, & M. S. Wetherell (Eds.), *Rediscovering the social group: A self-categorization theory* (pp. 117–141). Oxford, UK: Basil Blackwell.

Otten, S., & Moskowitz, G. B. (2000). Evidence for implicit evaluative in-group bias: Affect-biased spontaneous trait inference in a minimal group paradigm. *Journal of Experimental Social Psychology, 36*, 77–89.

Otten, S., & Wentura, D. (1999). About the impact of automaticity in the minimal group paradigm: Evidence from affective priming tasks. *European Journal of Social Psychology, 29*, 1049–1071.

Pedersen, W. C., Bushman, B. J., Vasquez, E. A., & Miller, N. (2006). *The moderating effect of target attributes on triggered displaced aggression.* Manuscript in preparation.

Pedersen, W. C., Gonzales, C., & Miller, N. (2000). The moderating effect of trivial triggering provocation on displaced aggression. *Journal of Personality and Social Psychology, 78*, 913–927.

Roseman, I. J. (1984). Cognitive determinants of emotion: A structural theory. *Review of Personality and Social Psychology, 5*, 11–36.

Scherer, K. R. (1988). Criteria for emotion-antecedent appraisal: A review. In V. Hamilton, G. H. Bower, & N. H. Frijda (Eds.), *Cognitive perspectives on emotion and motivation* (pp. 89–126). Dordrecht, Netherlands: Kluwer Academic Publishers.

Schopler, J., & Insko, C. A. (1992). The discontinuity effect in interpersonal and intergroup relations: Generality and mediation. In W. Stroebe & M. Hewstone (Eds.), *European review of social psychology* (pp. 121–151). Chichester, UK: Wiley.

Schütte, K., & Kessler, T. (2006). *On the role of group-based anger in outgroup derogation.* Manuscript in preparation.

Smith, C. A., & Ellsworth, P. C. (1985). Patterns of cognitive appraisal in emotion. *Journal of Personality and Social Psychology, 48*, 813–838.

Smith, E. R. (1993). Social identity and social emotions. Toward a new conceptualization of prejudice. In D. M. Mackie & D. L. Hamilton (Eds.), *Affect, cognition, and stereotyping: Interactive processes in group perception* (pp. 297–315). San Diego, CA: Academic Press.

Smith, E. R. (1999). Affective and cognitive implications of a group becoming part of the self: New models of prejudice and of the self-concept. In D. Abrams & M. A. Hogg (Eds.), *Social identity and social cognition* (pp. 183–196). Oxford, UK: Blackwell.

Stangor, C., Sullivan, L. A., & Ford, T. E. (1991). Affective and cognitive determinants of prejudice. *Social Cognition, 9*, 359–380.

Struch, N., & Schwartz, S. H. (1989). Intergroup aggression: Its predictors and distinctness from in-group bias. *Journal of Personality and Social Psychology, 56*, 364–373.

Tajfel, H. (1978). *Differentiation between social groups. Studies in the social psychology of intergroup relations.* London: Academic Press.

Tajfel, H., Billig, M. G., Bundy, R. P., & Flament, C. (1971). Social categorization and intergroup behaviour. *European Journal of Social Psychology, 1*, 149–178.

Tajfel, H., & Turner, J. (1979). An integrative theory of intergroup conflict. In W. G. Austin & S. Worchel (Eds.), *The social psychology of intergroup relations* (pp. 33–47). Monterey, CA: Brooks/Cole.

Tajfel, H., & Turner, J. C. (1986). The social identity theory of intergroup behavior. In S. Worchel & W. G. Austin (Eds.), *Psychology of intergroup relations* (2nd ed., pp. 7–24). Chicago: Nelson-Hall.

Tropp, L. R., & Pettigrew, T. F. (2004). Intergroup contact and the central role of affect in intergroup prejudice. In L. Z. Tiedens & C. W. Leach (Eds.), *The social life of emotions* (pp. 246–269). New York: Cambridge University Press.

Turner, J. C. (1985). Social categorization and the self-concept: A social cognitive theory of group behavior. In E. J. Lawler (Ed.), *Advances in group processes* (pp. 77–122). Greenwich, CT: JAI Press.

Turner, J. C., Hogg, M. A., Oakes, P. J., Reicher, S. D., & Wetherell, M. S. (1987). *Rediscovering the social group: A self-categorization theory.* Oxford, UK: Basil Blackwell.

Vasquez, E. A., Denson, T. F., Pedersen, W. C., Stenstrom, D. M., & Miller, N. (2005). The moderating effect of trigger intensity on triggered displaced aggression. *Journal of Experimental Social Psychology, 41*, 61–67.

Yzerbyt, V., Dumont, M., Wigboldus, D., & Gordijn, E. (2003). I feel for us: The impact of categorization and identification on emotions and action tendencies. *British Journal of Social Psychology, 42*, 533–549.

Part 5

Emotions and Aggression in a Developmental Perspective

10 Tight Bonds or Loose Associations? Crossroads of Emotion, Social Integration, and Aggression In Early Adolescence

Angela Ittel

Introduction

The development of aggressive behavior in childhood and adolescence has been of interest not only to social scientists, but also to teachers, educators, and parents. In the attempt to explain the factors that contribute to the development of aggression, studies have either examined biological (e.g., Rowe, 1994; Scarr, 1992), social (e.g., Dodge, Bates, & Pettit, 1990), or emotional (e.g., Fabes & Eisenberg, 1992) antecedents and correlates. Studies on *biological* correlates have for example examined hormonal variations and the expression of aggression (Inoff-Germain et al., 1988). Studies on *social* antecedents of aggression have identified aspects of peer and family interaction such as rejection or conflictual family interaction as contributing to the development of aggressive behaviors in children (Brendgen, Vitaro, Turgeon, & Poulin, 2002; Ittel, Kuhl, & Werner, 2005; Ramsden & Hubbard, 2002). Studies on *emotional* antecedents of aggression examined children's appraisal or understanding of emotions and how they coincide with aggressive behaviors (Bohnert, Crnic, & Lim, 2003; Hubbard, 2001). However, only a few studies have considered the simultaneous impact of social and emotional factors in the development of aggression (Arsenio, Coopermann, & Lover, 2000). In this chapter we attempt to shed light on this issue by focusing on the individual and simultaneous contributions of social and emotional factors to the expression of aggressive behavior in early adolescence.

In the model that guides our work we consider several affective attributes such as level of depression, loneliness, self-worth, and social anxiety to indicate children's emotional disposition as a predictor of their aggressive behaviors. In a second step, we will examine the additional contribution of social integration by considering the quality of peer- and family relationships as mediators of emotional disposition and aggression. Recently, research on the development of aggression has convincingly argued for the need to describe gender-specific expression of aggression (Crick & Grotpeter, 1995) but only a few models are available that describe gender-specific pathways towards aggression (Watson, Fischer, Burdzovic Andreas, & Smith, 2004). Hence, a special aim of this paper is to delineate gender-specific patterns in the associations of emotional disposition, social integration and aggressive behavior in a longitudinal study for early adolescent boys and girls. The identification of these gender-specific pathways contributing towards the development of aggression is essential in the design of effective intervention programs for early adolescent boys and girls.

Emotional Disposition and Aggression

The tendency to engage in aggression[1] has clearly been linked to individual emotional attributes (Dumas, Neese, Prinz, & Blechman, 1996; Kolko & Kazdin, 1991; Lochman & Dodge, 1994). For example, there is evidence that children who display higher levels of aggression also display higher levels of depression (Edelbrock & Achenbach, 1980), social anxiety (Johnson, LaVoie, Spenceri, & Mahoney, 2001), and loneliness (Crick & Ladd, 1993), and lower levels of self-esteem (Parker, Low, Walker, & Gamm, 2005).

- *Self-worth* refers to the emotion and thoughts that a child describes in evaluating him- or herself as a person. It is based on one's own emotional appraisal and cognitive evaluation and on one's perception of other people's appraisal and evaluation of the self.
- *Depression* (nonclinical) is characterized by feelings of inadequacy, self-efficacy, sadness, and low motivation.
- *Loneliness* is the feeling of being disconnected from the outside world.
- *Social anxiety* refers to the fear of socially interacting with other people.

(cf. Zimbardo & Gerrig, 2004)

Figure 1. Working definitions of emotional attributes.

However, these affective attributes are not disparate emotions but concomitant rudiments of a person's general emotional framework (Arsenio et al., 2000). Hence, in this paper we view the often distinctly examined emotional antecedents of aggression as expressions of someone's general emotional disposition. That is, we assume a high intercorrelation between these emotions and, rather than examine the individual contribution of each emotional attribute towards aggression, examine their simultaneous predictive validity of aggression within our model of prediction of self-assessed aggression.

The emotional dispositions of a person can be described as a global pattern of his or her emotional responsiveness to certain situations. For example, a person with a negative emotional disposition (e.g., low levels of self-esteem, low competence, and high levels of depression) exhibits behaviors that get in the way of the formation of positive interpersonal relationships. That is, a child who demonstrates low levels of self-esteem and a high degree of depressive thoughts also often feels lonely and less socially integrated and in turn more often reports feeling rejected than a person who exhibits high self-esteem and exhibits no symptoms related to depression (Arsenio & Killen, 1996). These negative interpersonal experiences in turn lead to the avoidance of interpersonal interactions and, as a consequence, due to an increasing fear of rejection, these children more often avoid interaction with other people and are more likely to report malevolent and jealous feelings towards other people (Parker et al., 2005; Johnson et al., 2001). An inadequate experience in social interactions might be a result of learned helplessness which stems from a deficiently developed repertoire of socially competent behaviors

---

[1]   We use the term aggression referring to aggressive norm-breaking behaviors only.

(Seligman, 1999). That is, a negative emotional disposition is hypothesized to fuel interpersonal difficulties, such as maladaptive coping, poor affect regulation, interpersonal conflict, and the self-generation of stress which perpetuates the core risk factors of rejection by peers (Hayes, Harris, & Carver, 2004). Rejected children, however, commonly report feeling threatened by people in their immediate social environment. This defensive conviction leads to a greater likelihood of engaging in defensive aggression (Greenier et al., 1999). In other words, a negative emotional disposition can set off a vicious cycle in which negative emotions lead to more frequent rejection and result in lower levels of social integration and fewer opportunities to develop social skills, in turn leading to increased levels of aggressive behaviors (cf. Hodges & Perry, 1999).

However, while some studies convincingly delineate the association of aggression and negative emotional disposition, other studies do not support this notion (Treuting & Hinshaw, 2001). For example, some studies found that aggressive children often describe themselves as more positive and narcissistic than nonaggressive children (Björkvist, Ekman, & Lagerspetz, 1982; Baumeister, Bushman, & Campbell, 2000). In addition, Sippola, Epp, Buchanan, and Bukowski (2005), in examining the development of relational aggression in early adolescent girls, found that those girls who were identified as relationally aggressive report higher self-worth and are perceived to be more socially competent than girls who do not exhibit relationally aggressive behaviors. Hence in this study we want to reexamine the longitudinal association of negative emotional disposition and the tendency to exhibit aggressive behavior in early adolescent boys and girls. We expect that negative emotional disposition as indicated by low levels of self-worth, high depression, social anxiety, and loneliness, is related to higher levels of aggression for boys and girls.

Social Integration and Aggression

The explanation of why some children act aggressively and others do not should not only include individual antecedents but also look into factors that pertain to a child's social context (Moffit & Caspi, 2001). As previous research has shown, the degree to which a person is integrated into his or her immediate social context might serve as a protective factor in the development of negative outcomes such as aggression (Olson, Bond, Burns, Vella-Brodrick, & Sawyer, 2003). For example, Patterson, Reid, & Dishion (1992) developed a model that describes direct links between family interaction and aggression such that children who experienced harsh parenting at home are at greater risk for later interpersonal difficulties with peers or teachers. In addition, many studies report that a negative family climate fosters the development of aggression in children. That is, children who report lower family cohesion and more conflictual communicative patterns exhibit more aggressive behaviors than children growing up in families characterized by a harmonious interpersonal climate (Dodge et al., 1990; Sanders, Dadds, Johnston, & Cash, 1992). However, the results of other studies do not support the association between family climate and aggression in early adolescence. For example, while Malti (2005) found positive associations between negative psychological and emotional constructs and the degree of aggression for early adolescent girls and boys, her results did not reveal any associations between family climate and aggression. Moreover, research has not been able to delineate a coherent picture of the gender-specific significance of family factors on developmental outcomes (Davies & Windle, 1997). Whereas some studies show that boys are more affected by family-context variables than girls (McFadyen-Ketchum, Bates, Dodge, & Pettit, 1996; Storvoll & Wichstrom, 2002), other results suggest that family-context variables have greater effects on the adjustment of girls (Ittel & Rosendahl, 2007). However, often studies do not examine these gender specific associations at all (Hops, Davis, Leve, & Sheeber, 2003). In this paper we will examine to what extent the degree of social integration into the family influences the development of aggression over and above the impact of a child's emotional disposition. Also, we want to describe the gender-specific impact of family cohesion on these processes.

The inconsistent findings concerning the role of the family in the development of aggression in early adolescence might be partially explained by the increasing impact of peer relations in the lives of early adolescent boys and girls (Coie, Dodge, & Kupersmidt, 1990; Hartup, 1993). There are numerous studies that have delineated the influence of family processes on peer integration, psychosocial adjustment, and aggression (Brendgen et al., 2002). Results show that children who are rejected by peers are more aggressive than children that report good quality relations with their peers (Hubbard & Coi, 1994; Shortt, Capaldi, Dishion, Bank, & Owen, 2003). Furthermore, similar to the function of a high degree of integration into the family, high quality peer relations might also serve as a protective factor in the development of aggression (Engels & Ter Bogt, 2001) and mediate the above-described associations of emotional disposition and aggression. That is, if a child lacks in his or her emotional adjustment but at the same time reports a functioning peer network or high peer quality, the unfavorable associations between his or her emotional adjustment and aggression might be mitigated (Arsenio et al., 2000). Surprisingly little attention has been paid to gender-specific processes in the association between emotional adjustment, peer integration, and aggression. Due to the salience of peer relationships for early adolescents we assume that the integration into the peer context will mediate the association between emotional disposition and aggression for both girls and boys.

The research on the association of family processes and peer quality with the development of aggression has resulted in inconsistent findings concerning the impact of social integration on aggression, especially regarding gender-specific processes. Even though the crossroads of these social contexts have been convincingly demonstrated (Parke & Ladd, 1992), the impact of family and peer integration has mostly been studied independently. However, already a decade ago, Dishion and colleagues described the benefits of considering these contexts simultaneously when trying to understand psychosocial adjustment difficulties throughout adolescence (Dishion, Patterson, Stoolmiller, & Skinner. 1991). Early adolescence is an especially relevant age period for the simultaneous consideration of peer and family contexts due to the emerging importance of peers. Hence, in this study we want to explore the relative contribution of family and peer integration in the prediction of aggression in early adolescence.

Next to interpersonal processes, factors that pertain to the greater social context such as socioeconomic status (SES) and living environment can function as risk or protective factors in the psychosocial development of a child (Olson et al., 2003). An important finding from Conger's and Elder's work (1994) is that the experienced socioeconomic pressures of a family leads to children's greater tendency to engage in aggressive behavior (see also Beyers, Loeber, Wikstrom, & Stouthamer-Loeber, 2001). Dodge, Pettit, & Bates (1994) support this view and argue that low SES is associated with several negative psychosocial outcomes that enhance the risk of developing aggressive behaviors. However, others did not find this relationship between the SES of the family (and neighborhood characteristics) and the tendency to engage in aggressive behavior (Olweus, 1991). In this study, we will include measures of SES of the family and neighborhood characteristics to control for possible effects on aggressive behaviors.

In sum, the current study investigates the longitudinal associations of emotional dispositions and aggressive behavior in early adolescence. Most research conceptualizes social context factors and individual psychosocial factors as being an important source in the development of aggressive behavior (Slaby & Guerra, 1988). However, many studies consider individual factors (i.e., emotional disposition) as a mediating factor in the association of social context and aggression (Boivin, Hymel, & Bukowski, 1995; Guerra, Huesemann, & Spindler, 2003). In this study we take a different approach by examining the effect of social integration (i.e., family cohesion and peer integration) over and above the association of emotional disposition and aggression. That is, we assume that the quality of the social context moderates the association of emotional disposition and exhibition of aggression for early adolescent boys and girls. A special focus of this study is to examine the gender-specificity of the described associations. From the review of the literature we have developed several major hypotheses. Because we include a measure of behavioral aggression and norm-breaking behavior, we expect that boys are more aggressive than girls (Crick & Dodge, 1994). We also expect that a negative emotional disposition is associated with higher levels of aggression and lower levels of family cohesion and peer quality (Arsenio et al., 2000). Furthermore, we assume that positive social integration into the family and high quality of peer relationships moderates the longitudinal association of emotional disposition and aggression. Because of the importance of establishing gender-specific patterns for these associations, we will delineate these associations for boys and girls separately.

Method

We acquired the data from a larger longitudinal study conducted in 23 elementary schools in Berlin, Germany, with two measurement points (t1 and t2). Data were collected in the fall of 2004 (t1) and in the fall of 2005 (t2). "t1" and "t2" will be used thereafter to refer to the two measurement points that occurred approximately one year apart. A series of ANOVAs was conducted on all study variables to analyze mean level differences between the group of children ($N = 484$) who participated in both measurement points (t1 and t2) compared to the children ($N = 844$, retention rate 54.8%) who only participated in t1. There were no significant differences between children who participated in t1 and t2 and who participated in t1 only. Because in this study we examined longitudinal associations of emotions and aggression, only the children who participated at both measurement points were considered for the current analysis.

Participants

A total of 484 children participated at both measurement points of the study. The early adolescents' ages ranged from 8 to 14 years ($M = 10.36$) at t1 and from 9 to 15 years ($M = 11.26$) at t2 . The sample contained 55.5% girls resulting in a slightly significantly larger proportion of girls over boys, $\chi^2(2, N = 480) = 4.53, p < .03$. The schools were selected with the intention of providing a sample of diverse ethnicities and SES. Seventy and two-tenths percent of the participants indicated that they were German, 6.4% participants had a Turkish background, and 12.6% of the sample were of some other ethnic background. Ten and eight-tenths percent did not provide information concerning their nationality. Thus, the sample was comprised of more children with German background than with any other ethnic background, $\chi^2(4, N = 455) = 28.40, p < .001$. To indicate the SES of the participants, children were asked to estimate the number of books their families owned. This indicator of familial cultural capital is commonly used in samples with children and early adolescent participants (cf. Baumert & Schümer, 2001). This indicator ranges from 1 through 5, with 1 indicating a *low cultural capital* and 5 indicating a *high cultural capital*. The sample contained more children with higher cultural capital (categories 3–5) than with lower cultural capital (categories 1–2), $\chi^2 (4, N = 455) = 72.30, p < .000$.

Procedure

Before filling out the questionnaire, parents were asked to provide their active consent. Only children returning the signed consent form participated in the study. At the first measurement point the questionnaires were administered at school within a two-hour class period. One or two trained research collaborators were present at all times to answer any questions the children might have. Before children responded to the questionnaire they were informed that the survey was anonymous and that no one would know how they answered the questions. Children received a small gift after completing the questionnaire. At the time of the second data collection, for those children who were still enrolled at the same school, questionnaires were again administered at school within a two-hour class period. All other children received the questionnaire through the mail. Again, children received a small gift after completing the questionnaire.

Measures

Measures included questionnaire data concerning (1) children's aggression as dependent variable, (2) emotional disposition and (3) social integration as independent and/or mediator variables, and (4) social background variables as control variables.

Dependent variable
Aggression[2] (1): The Misconduct Scale (Feldman, Rosenthal, Mont-Reynaud, Leung, & Lau, 1991). This 8-item scale measures the frequency, ranging from 0 (*never*) to 3 (*often*), of misconduct behaviors that the adolescent has engaged in. A sample item is "Have you ever gotten into fights with a classmate?" Scores are averaged so that a higher score indicates a higher level of aggression. Internal consistency of the scale was good with $\alpha = .81$ (girls) and .79 (boys).

Independent Variables
Emotional disposition (2): *Social Anxiety for Children – Revised* (La Greca & Stone, 1993). This 18-item scale measures social anxiety and fear of negative evaluation from peers. Sample items are "I worry about being teased" and "I'm afraid other kids will not like me." Participants respond on a 5-point scale ranging from 1 (*strongly disagree*) to 5 (*strongly agree*). Responses are averaged, so that a higher score indicates greater social anxiety. Internal consistency of the scale was good with $\alpha = .88$ (boys) and .87 (girls).

Coopersmith Self-Esteem Inventory – School Short Form (Coopersmith, 1967). This is a widely used and well-validated 25-item measure of global self-esteem. Participants indicate whether statements such as "I'm a lot of fun to be with" and "I find it hard to talk in front of the class" are "Like Me" or "Unlike Me." Negative items were recoded and a total sum score was then used in further analysis. Kuder-Richardson reliability estimates (KR20s) for this sample were found to be acceptable with $\alpha = .79$ (boys) and .81 (girls).

Children's Depression Inventory (CDI; Kovacs, 1985, 1992). This widely used 10-item scale measures symptoms of depression from emotional, cognitive, and behavioral domains. Each item has three questions of varying levels of different symptoms of depression, such as "I am sad once in a while," "I am sad a lot of the time," or "I am sad all of the time." Respondents are asked to indicate which sentence best describes how they have felt for the past one or two weeks. Each sentence is given a point value (0, 1, or 2) with higher scores indicating higher levels of depressive symptoms. Responses are averaged, so that a higher score indicates a higher level of depression. Internal consistency of the scale was good with $\alpha = .81$ (boys) and .84 (girls).

Revised UCLA Loneliness Scale-8 (ULS-8; Hays & DiMatteo, 1987). This 8-item short form of the original 20-item UCLA Loneliness Scale measures the discrepancy between achieved and desired levels of social contact and was chosen for its sufficient psychometric properties when used with adolescents. Respondents indicate the extent to which they agree with statements such as "I feel isolated from others" using a scale of 1 (*never*) to 4 (*often*). Positive items such as "I am an outgoing person" and "I can find companionship when I want it" were reverse-coded. The mean score was calculated so that a higher score indicates more loneliness. Internal consistency of the scale was acceptable with $\alpha = .71$ (boys) and .74 (girls).

---

[2] This scale was used as the dependent variable (t2) and as a control variable (t1) to control for children's initial level of aggression.

Mediator Variables

Social Integration (3): *Family Cohesion* (Olson, Portner, & Bell, 1982; Olsen, Sprenkle, & Russell, 1979). This 16-item family cohesion subscale from the Family Adaptability and Cohesion Evaluation Scales II (FACES-II) measures the degree of separation or connection family members have with one another. A sample item is, "Family members feel very close to each other." The response format ranges from 1 (*almost never*) to 5 (*almost always*). Internal consistency of this scale was acceptable with $\alpha = .70$ (boys) and .72 (girls).

Quality of Peer Relationship (Hudson, 1982). The Index of Peer Relations (IPR) subscale of the Clinical Measurement Package will be used to measure the perceived quality of friendships. Sample items are "I get along very well with my peers" and "My peers seem to like having me around." Participants respond on a 7-point scale from 1 (*none of the time*), 4 (*some of the time*), and 7 (*all of the time*). Negatively worded questions are reverse-coded and all responses are summed, meaning that a higher score indicates a higher quality of peer relationships. Internal consistency of this scale was good with $\alpha = .82$ (boys) and .82 (girls).

Social Context Variables

Control Variables (4): *Cultural Capital* (Baumert & Schüber, 2001). Children were asked to indicate how many books their family owned. Answers ranged from 1 to 5, with a high score indicating a large number of books (i.e., high cultural capital) and a low score indicating a small number of books or none (i.e., low cultural capital).

Socioeconomic context (Statistisches Landesamt Berlin, 2003). The location of children's schools was coded according to its location in a traffic cell (a small district).[3] Coding ranged from 1 to 7 and was based on information concerning proportion of employment, status of employment, migration, income, age, and gender of each person registered in each district. A low number indicates a poor living environment and a high number indicates a favorable living environment.

Results

The results section is structured as follows: We will first provide descriptive information on all study variables and discuss significant gender differences. Then we will provide information on the intercorrelations between pairs of study variables and present the results of our hierarchical regression analysis examining (a) the longitudinal effects of emotional disposition and aggression, and (b) the mediating role of social integration for the longitudinal associations of emotional disposition and the development of aggression for boys and girls.

An ANOVA with gender as a group variable was performed with each of the 10 primary study variables. As can be seen in Table 1, girls showed higher levels of depression, $F(1, 478) = 5.39$, $p < .05$, higher levels of social anxiety, $F(1, 467) = 12.97$, $p < .001$, and reported higher levels of family cohesion $F(1, 476) = 4.93$, $p < .05$. Boys

---

[3]   See http://www.statistik-berlin.de/pms2000/sg03/2003/03-08-12a.html for further information.

Table 1. Descriptive Data for All Measures

		Boys			Girls		
		N	M	SD	N	M	SD
1. Dependent variables	Aggression (t2)	208	1.71	.48	260	1.63	.42
2. Emotional disposition	Self-esteem (t1)	214	16.9	4.78	268	16.49	4.53
	Depression (t1)	213	1.33	.29	265	1.39**	.29
	Loneliness (t1)	209	1.74	.52	261	1.76	.55
	Social anxiety (t1)	208	2.38	.71	261	2.62***	.72
3. Social integration	Family cohesion	211	3.60	.52	267	3.71**	.51
	Peer quality	208	5.55	1.0	259	5.68	.96
4. Control variables	Aggression (t1)	215	1.65	.48	266	1.51***	.34
	Cult. capital (t1)	201	3,26	1.25	252	3.57***	1.15
	SES context (t1)	178	4.53	2.12	221	4.32	2.0

Note: Significant differences in means between boys and girls are indicated by $* p < .05; ** p < .01; *** p < .001$

exhibited higher levels of aggression, but only at t1, $F(1, 478) = 12.77, p < .001$. Surprisingly, the mean scores of aggression did not differ between girls and boys in t2. We also found significant gender differences in the family cultural capital for boys and girls. Girls noted that their families owned more books than boys' families did, $F(1, 451) = 5.58, p < .01$.

A t test for dependent samples comparing the degree of aggression across measurement points showed that girls and boys exhibited significantly more aggression at t2 (M girls = 1.63; M boys = 1.71) than at t1 (M girls = 1.52; M boys = 1.63) with $t(1, 451) = 8.34, p < .001$.

Variable Intercorrelations

The correlations between the central variables in our study are provided in Table 2. Due to our interest in gender-specific variations we present the correlations for boys and girls separately. Coefficients appearing above the diagonal apply to girls ($N = 251$), and coefficients appearing below the diagonal apply to boys ($N = 214$). Stability coefficients (i.e., test-retest reliabilities over a one year interval) for the measure of aggression were significant ($r = .59$ for boys and $r = .41$ for girls).

The analysis confirmed our assumption that the measure indicating the child's emotional disposition and his or her social integration were related to aggression at t2. That is, except for the scales of social anxiety and cultural capital for boys, and loneliness and peer integration for girls, all variables were significantly associated with the degree of

Table 2. Intercorrelations of All Study Variables

	A	B	C	D	E	F	G	H	I	J
1. A Aggression (t2)		−.20**	.21**	.22**	.10	−.16**	.01	.41**	−.21**	.14*
2. B Self-esteem	−.23*		−.63**	−.44**	−.55**	.39**	.41**	−.29**	.30**	.01
C Depression	.14*	−.53**		.41**	.59**	−.39**	−.40**	.32**	−.27**	.04
D Social anxiety	.03	−.30**	.29**		.50**	−.19*	−.28**	.17**	−.15*	.02
E Loneliness	.25*	−.50**	.48**	..49**		−.39**	−.52**	−.25**	−.20	.06
3. F Family cohesion	−.15*	.38**	−.27**	−.03	−.26**		.31**	−.24**	.11*	.18**
G Peer integration	.12**	.49*	−.54**	−.34**	−.59**	.23**		−.16*	.10*	.16**
4. H Aggression (t1)	.59**	−.16*	.20**	.07	.22**	−.15*	−.22*		−.10*	.14**
I Cult cap. (t1)	.09	.15*	−.04	.02	−.13	.12	.09	−.12		.06
J SES context (t1)	.17*	.03	−.03	−.05	−.09	−.03	.06	.09	−.20**	

Note: * $p < .05$; ** $p < .01$; below the diagonal: boys; above the diagonal: girls; 1 = DV, 2 = Emotional disposition, 3 = Social integration, 4 = Control variables. Underlined correlations are stability coefficients. t1 = Time 1; t2 = Time t2

aggression at t2.[4] The moderately high multicollinearity between the scales measuring the emotional dispositions is of special interest, especially for girls. Furthermore, the scales indicated some interesting differences between boys and girls in the associations between emotional disposition at t1 and aggression at t2. While self-esteem, depression, and social anxiety are more strongly associated with aggression for girls than for boys (Fisher z-scores ranged from −1.62 through 1.78, $p < .05$), loneliness (t1) was significantly more highly associated with aggression (t2) for boys than for girls ($z = 1.6$, $p < .05$).

Longitudinal Prediction of Aggression

The previous correlational analysis confirmed that our study variables were sufficiently associated to conduct regression analyses. To clarify the predictive gender-specific value of these contributors to aggression in early adolescence, we conducted hierarchical regression analyses for boys and girls separately to examine the longitudinal contribution to the exhibition of aggression by variables indicating emotional disposition and social integration for adolescent boys and girls. To account for the different response ranges of

---

[4] The correlation coefficients showed similar patterns for the degree of aggression at t1.

the scales, all scores entered into the regression were converted into z-scores. In keeping with procedures for testing mediational models outlined by Baron and Kenny (1986), we tested the model in three steps. A first condition of mediation is that the predictors (emotional disposition) must be related to the mediator (social integration). A second condition is that there must be a significant link between the predictors (emotional disposition) and the dependent variable (aggression). A third condition specifies that a significant link should exist between the mediator (social integration) and the dependent variable (aggression), when the predictors (emotional disposition) are included in the model. In this third and final step, the direct relationships of the predictors to the dependent variable should then disappear (i.e., the regression coefficient should drop to zero for full mediation or decrease and become nonsignificant for partial mediation).

Hierarchical Regression
Aggression (t1) and the variables pertaining to the social context (i.e., cultural capital and ocioeconomic context) were entered first as control variables. Then we entered the variables pertaining to emotional disposition (i.e., self-esteem, depression, social anxiety, and loneliness). In the last step we entered the variables measuring social integration (i.e., family cohesion and peers) to measure whether they mediated the association of emotional disposition and aggression. We calculated the regression analysis separately for boys and girls to be able to describe gender-specific pathways to aggression.

Table 3. Regression Analyses Predicting Boys' and Girls' Aggression (Based on Z-Scores)

	Boys			Girls		
	Model 1	Model 2	Model 3	Model 1	Model 2	Model 3
	β	β	β	β	β	β
Control Variables						
Aggression (t1)	.48**	.51***	.51***	.36***	.36***	.35***
Social capital	−.10	−.09	−.09	−.15**	−.16**	−.16**
SES context	−.01	−.01	−.01	−.12*	−.12*	−.16*
Emotional Disposition						
Self-esteem		−.02	−.02		−.14*	−.01
Depression		.12*	.20*		.12*	.09
Loneliness		−.00	−.03		−.13*	−.07
Social anxiety		−.00	.02		.11*	.08
Social Integration						
Family cohesion			−.19**			.08
Peer integration			.08			−.16**
R^2 (adjusted)	.35***	.36***	.39***	.17**	.18**	.19**
Δ R (change)		.03*	.04*		.06**	.03**

Note: *** $p < .001$, ** $p < .01$, * $p < .05$

As can be seen in Table 3, in the first model (Model 1 $R^2 = .35, p < .01$ for boys; $R^2 = .17, p < .05$ for girls) aggression at t1 was a significant predictor of aggression at t2 for boys ($\beta = .48, p < .001$) and girls ($\beta = .36, p < .001$). The variables entered to delineate social context (i.e., cultural capital and socio-economic context) only contributed to the prediction of girls' aggression in all three models. That is, there is a negative association between the degree of cultural capital ($\beta = -.15, p < .01$) and favorable neighborhood characteristics ($\beta = -.12, p < .05$) and aggression. For boys, these variables did not contribute significantly to the prediction of aggression at t2.

In Model 2 (Model 2 $R^2 = .36, p < .001$ for boys; $R^2 = .18, p < .01$ for girls) we entered all variables pertaining to the emotional disposition of the boys and the girls. For boys, depression (t1) predicted the exhibition of aggression (t2) in this model ($R^{2\triangle} = .03, p < .05$). That is, boys who were more depressed at t1 also showed more depression at t2 ($\beta = .12, p < .05$). In contrast, all variables depicting girls' emotional disposition (self-esteem; $\beta = -.14, p < .05$, depression; $\beta = .12, p < .05$, loneliness; $\beta = .13, p < .05$, social anxiety, $\beta = .11, p < .05$) at t1 made a significant contribution to the explanation of the level of aggression at t2 ($R^2 = .06, p < .01$).

In the next step (Model 3) we wanted to examine whether integration in the social context contributed uniquely to the prediction of aggression in boys and girls over and above their emotional disposition. An interesting gender-specific pattern emerged. For boys the final model accounted for 39% of the variance predicting aggression ($R^2 = .39, p < .001$). Only the degree of family cohesion (t1) predicted the degree of aggression (t2), ($\beta = -.19, p < .01$) such that boys who report lower levels of family cohesion at t1 also report higher levels of aggression at t2 ($R^2 = .04, p < .05$). However, family cohesion did not mediate the association of depression at t1 and aggression at t2. That is, family integration did not change the predictive validity of emotional disposition (t1) (i.e., depression) for aggression (t2) in boys. A different pattern emerged for girls. The final model accounted for 19% of the variance predicting aggression ($R^2 = .19, p < .01$). Only the perceived peer quality (t1) predicted the exhibition of aggression at t2 ($\beta = -.16, p < .01$) ($R^{2\triangle} = .03, p < .01$). Family cohesion was not a significant predictor in this model. Furthermore, peer quality totally mediated the associations for emotional disposition at t1 and aggression t2 for girls. That is, all regression coefficients of the variables indicating emotional disposition (t1) dropped close to zero and became nonsignificant when entering the measure of peer quality into the model predicting aggression (t2) from emotional disposition (t1).

Discussion

Coming back to our initial question, our results reveal that there are tight bonds between emotions, social integration, and the development of aggression, especially for girls. For boys these associations are less clear. The central analysis revealed that the proposed mediational model examining the effects of social integration over and above the longitudinal associations between emotional dispositions on aggression was supported for girls only. We will first summarize the results for boys and girls and then discuss the implications of these findings.

For boys, aggression at t1 was a strong predictor of the exhibition of aggression at t2 in all three models. Variables indicating the external social context (i.e., cultural capital and socioeconomic context) did not make a significant contribution to the prediction of aggression. For boys only, depression – as one variable indicating adolescents' emotional disposition – was a significant predictor of aggression (t2). This association did not change, however, when entering the variables of social integration (family cohesion and peer integration). That is, whereas family cohesion (t1) was a significant predictor of aggression at t2, it did not change the association of depression and aggression for boys. The perceived peer quality did not predict aggression for boys significantly.

For girls, aggression at t1 was also a strong predictor of aggression at t2. In contrast to boys, variables entered to indicate the external social context did make a significant contribution to the prediction of aggression at t2, such that girls who go to schools in less favorable neighborhoods and who live in families with little cultural capital exhibit greater aggression than girls who go to school in more favorable neighborhoods and who grew up in families with higher cultural capital. Furthermore, in contrast to boys, all four emotional attributes measured at t1 contributed significantly to the prediction of aggression at t2. Girls with lower self-esteem and higher levels of depression, social anxiety, and loneliness at t1 exhibit greater aggression at t2. Finally, also in contrast to boys, peer quality (t1) emerged as a significant predictor of aggression (t2). Furthermore, the degree to which girls feel integrated into the peer contexts totally mediated the association of emotional disposition (t1) and aggression (t2). Family cohesion (t1) did not emerge as a significant predictor of aggression (t2) for girls.

The results of this study clearly highlight the importance of delineating gender-specific patterns in the prediction of emotional disposition, social integration and aggression. For example, the variables indicating social context were significant predictors of aggression only for girls. While we cannot examine this assumption with data from this study, these findings might point to the fact that for girls, external context variables are more influential, whereas for boys, intrapersonal factors are more decisive in the explanation of norm-breaking behavior and aggression.

Another interesting gender-specific pattern emerges by looking at the predictive validity of emotional disposition and aggression. Clearly, emotional attributes seem to predict development of aggression in more complex ways for girls than for boys. Whereas for girls, all indicators of their emotional disposition predict aggression, for boys, only depression significantly adds to the explanation of aggressive behavior. The co-occurrence of depression and aggression has been supported in many studies (Brendgen et al., 2002), however the gender-specific patterns of their comorbidity are still unclear. Other studies (Bohnert et al., 2003) found that the association between aggression and emotional expression did not differ between boys and girls. Alas, in their study only a single variable indicating emotional disposition (i.e., reported happiness) was used to predict aggression. The results of this study indicate the need to include a wider variety of positive and negative emotions to examine the predictive validity of emotional disposition on aggressive behavior in boys and girls.

Next to examining the associations of emotions and aggression, this study aimed to examine the role of social integration and aggression. Again, a clear gender-specific pattern emerged. Whereas for boys, negative family cohesion functions as a risk factor (i.e., lower family cohesion predicts higher exhibition of aggression), for girls, integration into the peer context emerges as a protective factor in the development of aggression. In turn, the integration into the peer context and the integration into the family did not reach a significant predictive value for boys and girls, respectively. That is, our results suggest that different social contexts are important for the development of aggression for boys and girls. These results are interesting considering the ongoing debate concerning the significance of social context processes for boys and girls (Storvoll & Wichstrom, 2002) and highlight the importance of considering the impact of several social contexts simultaneously when predicting psychosocial outcomes in adolescence.

Furthermore, a central aim of this study was to examine whether social integration changes the association of emotional disposition and aggression. Results show that for girls, the degree to which they feel integrated into the peer context buffers the associations of girls' negative emotional dispositions on aggression. That is, the degree to which girls are integrated into their peer network explains the variance in expression of aggression over and above their emotional disposition. For boys the social integration does not change the predictive validity of the emotional disposition for aggression.

Of course this study has several limitations. For example, results might be further differentiated if measures of different forms of aggression and internalizing behaviors had been included. We are currently examining the question of the comparative development of different psychosocial outcomes in a study investigating the impact of gender-specific family processes in the development of aggression and depression. Results of that study show that family-related processes have more impact on the development of depression in girls than in boys. These findings point to the fact that social context variables might vary when considering different psychosocial outcomes. Furthermore, our models cannot explain the strong predictive validity of the baseline aggression at t1 for aggression at t2, which might point to the importance of including additional predictive factors such as biological and hormonal correlates of the development of aggression. While further studies need to confirm the suggested gender-specific patterns, the presented results demonstrate – in line with arguments of Dishion and colleagues (1991) – the importance of placing different foci in intervention programs for girls and for boys. Whereas for boys the strengthening of interpersonal family processes seems to be central in the development of aggression, for girls the processes improving their peer integration seem to have positive effects on the inhibition of aggression. In addition, the strengthening of girls' general emotional dispositions needs to be at the center of prevention and intervention, including improvement in self-esteem and social skills to prevent the perception of loneliness and social anxiety. For boys, the recognition of symptoms of depression needs to be of special interest. While this study clearly demonstrates gender-specific antecedents of aggression, further work needs to convey these findings to guide the development of gender-specific intervention and prevention programs for aggression.

Acknowledgments

We are grateful to the adolescents who participated in this study and to the many undergraduate and graduate student assistants who helped collect and analyze the data. A special thank you goes to the school principals and the teachers who allowed us to conduct our research in their classrooms. This project was funded by a grant from the Alexander von Humboldt Foundation to the first author and the coprincipal investigator Prof. Linda Juang, San Francisco State University, USA. I also want to thank Lars Kuring for his valuable support in preparing this manuscript.

References

Arsenio, W. F., Cooperman, S., & Lover, A. (2000). Affective predictors of preschoolers' aggression and peer acceptance: Direct and indirect effects. *Developmental Psychology, 36,* 438–448.

Arsenio, W., & Killen, M. (1996) Conflict-related emotions during peer disputes. *Early Education and Development, 7,* 43–57.

Baron, R. M., & Kenny, D. A. (1986). The moderator-mediator variable distinction in social psychological research: Conceptual, strategic, and statistical considerations. *Journal of Personality and Social Psychology, 51,* 1173–1182.

Baumeister, R. F., Bushman, B. J., & Campbell, W. K. (2000). Narcissism, self-esteem, and aggression: Does violence result from low self-esteem or from threatened egotism? *Current Directions in Psychological Science, 9,* 26–29.

Baumert, J., & Schümer, G. (2001). Familiäre Lebensverhältnisse, Bildungsbeteiligung und Kompetenzerwerb [Family lifestyle, educational participation, and acquisition of competence]. In Deutsches PISA-Konsortium (Ed.), *PISA 2000, Basiskompetenzen von Schülerinnen und Schülern im internationalen Vergleich* (pp. 323–407). Opladen, Germany: Leske & Budrich.

Beyers, J. M., Loeber, R., Wikström P.-O., & Stouthamer-Loeber, M. (2001).What predicts violence in better-off neighborhoods? *Journal of Abnormal and Child Psychology, 29*(5), 369–381.

Bjorkqvist, K., Ekman, K., & Lagerspetz, K. M. (1982). Bullies and victims: Their ego picture, ideal ego picture and normative ego picture. *Scandinavian Journal of Psychology, 23*(4), 307–313.

Bohnert, A., Crnic, K., & Lim, K. (2003). Emotional competence and aggressive behavior in school-age children. *Journal of Abnormal Child Psychology, 31,* 79–91.

Boivin, M., Hymel, S., & Bukowski, W. M. (1995). The roles of social withdrawal, peer rejection, and victimization by peers in predicting loneliness and depressed mood in childhood. *Development and Psychopathology, 7,* 765–785.

Brendgen, M., Vitaro, F., Turgeon, L., & Poulin, F. (2002). Assessing aggressive and depressed children's social relations with classmates and friends: A matter of perspective. *Journal of Abnormal Child Psychology, 30,* 609–624.

Coie, J., Dodge, K. A., & Kupersmidt, J. (1990). Peer group behavior and social status. In S. R. Asher & J. D. Coie (Eds.), *Peer rejection in childhood.* New York: Cambridge University Press.

Conger, R. D., & Elder, G. H., Jr. (Eds.). (1994). *Families in troubled times.* New York: Aldine De Gruyter.

Coopersmith, S. (1967). *The antecedents of self-esteem.* San Francisco: W.H. Freeman & Company.

Crick, N. R., & Dodge, K. A. (1994). A review and reformulation of social information-processing mechanisms in children's social adjustment. *Psychological Bulletin, 115,* 74–101.

Crick, N. R., & Grotpeter, J. K. (1995). Relational aggression, gender, and social-psychological adjustment. *Child Development, 66,* 710–722.

Crick, N. R., & Ladd, G. W. (1993). Children's perceptions of their peer experiences: Attributions, loneliness, social anxiety, and social avoidance. *Developmental Psychology, 29,* 244–254.

Davies, P. T., & Windle, M. (1997). Gender-specific pathways between maternal depressive symptoms, family discord, and adolescent adjustment. *Developmental Psychology, 33,* 657–668.

Dishion, T. J., Patterson, G. R., Stoolmiller, M., & Skinner, M. I. (1991). Family, school, and behavioral antecedents to early adolescent involvement with antisocial peers. *Developmental Psychology, 27*, 172–180.

Dodge, K. A., Bates, J. E., & Pettit, G. S. (1990). Mechanisms in the cycle of violence. *Science, 250*, 1678–1683.

Dodge, K. A., Pettit, G. S., & Bates, J. E. (1994). Socialization mediators of the relation between socioeconomic status and child conduct problems. *Child Development, 65*, 649–665.

Dumas, J. E., Neese, D. E., Prinz, R. J., & Blechman, E. A. (1996). Short-term stability of aggression, peer rejection, and depressive symptoms in middle childhood. *Journal of Abnormal Child Psychology, 24*, 105–119.

Edelbrock, C., & Achenbach, T. M. (1980). A typology of child behavior profile patterns: Distribution and correlates for disturbed children aged 6–16. *Journal of Abnormal Child Psychology, 8*, 441–470.

Engels, R., & Ter Bogt, T. (2001). Influences of risk behaviors on the quality of peer relations in adolescence. *Journal of Youth and Adolescence, 30*, 675–695.

Fabes, R. A., & Eisenberg, N. (1992). Young children's coping with interpersonal anger. *Child Development, 63*, 116–128.

Feldman, S. S., Rosenthal, D. A., Mont-Reynaud, R., Lau, S., & Leung, K. (1991). Ain't misbehavin': Adolescent values and family environments as correlates of misconduct in a cross-national study of Chinese, Australian and American youth. *Journal of Research in Adolescence, 1*, 109–134.

Greenier, K. D., Kernis, M. H., McNamara, C. W., Waschull, S. B., Berry, A. J., Herlocker, C. E., et al. (1999). Individual differences in reactivity to daily events: Examining the roles of stability and levels of self-esteem. *Journal of Personality, 67*, 185–207.

Guerra, N. G., Huesmann, L. R., & Spindler, A. J. (2003). Community violence exposure, social cognition, and aggression among urban elementary-school children. *Child Development, 74*(5), 1507–1522.

Hartup, W. W. (1993). Adolescents and their friends. In B. Laursen (Ed.), *New directions for child development: Close friendships in adolescence* (pp. 3–22). San Francisco: Jossey Bass.

Hayes, A. M., Harris, M. S., & Carver, C. S. (2004). Predictors of self-esteem variability. *Cognitive Therapy and Research, 28*, 369–385.

Hays, R. D., & DiMatteo, M. R. (1987). A short-form measure of loneliness. *Journal of Personality Assessment, 51*, 69–81.

Hodges, E. V. E., & Perry, D. G. (1999). Personal and interpersonal antecedents and consequences of victimization by peers. *Journal of Personality and Social Psychology, 7*, 677–685.

Hops, H., Davis, B., Leve, C., & Sheeber, L. (2003). Cross-generational transmission of aggressive parent behavior: A prospective, mediational examination. *Journal of Abnormal Child Psychology, 31*, 9–161.

Hubbard, J. A. (2001). Emotion expression processes in children's peer interaction: The role of peer rejection, aggression, and gender. *Child Development, 72*, 1426–1438.

Hubbard, J. A., & Coie, J. D. (1994). Emotional correlates of social competence in children's peer relations. *Merrill-Palmer Quarterly, 40*, 1–20.

Hudson, W. (1982). A short-form scale to measure peer relations dysfunction. *Journal of Social Service Research, 13*(4), 57–69.

Inoff-Germain, G. E., Arnold, G. S., Nottelmann, E. D., Susman, E. J., Cutler, G. B., Jr., & Chrousos, G. P. (1988). Relations between hormone levels and observational measures of aggressive behavior of early adolescents in family interactions. *Developmental Psychology, 24*, 129–139.

Ittel, A., Kuhl, P., & Werner, N. E., (2005). Familie, Geschlechterrolle und Relationale Aggression [Families, gender role, and relational aggression]. In A. Ittel & M. von Salisch (Eds.). *Lügen, Lästern, Leiden lassen. Aggressives Verhalten in Kindheit und Jugend* (pp 135–172). Stuttgart, Germany: Kohlhammer.

Ittel, A., & Rosendahl, Y. (2007). Internetnutzung und Soziale Integration im frühen Jugendalter [Internet use and social integration in early adolescence]. In L. Mikos, D. Hoffmann, & R. Winter (Eds), *Mediennutzung, Identität und Identifikation. Die Sozialisationsrelevanz der Medien im Selbstfindungsprozess von Jugendlichen* (pp. 183–206). Weinheim and Munich, Germany: Juventa.

Johnson, H. D., LaVoie, J. C., Spenceri, M. C., & Mahoney, M. A. (2001). Peer conflict avoidance: Associations with loneliness, social anxiety, and social avoidance. *Psychological Reports, 88,* 227–235.

Kolko, D. J., & Kazdin, A. E. (1991). Motives of childhood firesetters: Firesetting characteristics and psychological correlates. *Journal of Child Psychology and Psychiatry, 32,* 535–550.

Kovacs, M. (1985). The Children's Depression Inventory (CDI). *Psychopharmacology Bulletin, 21,* 995–998.

Kovacs, M. (1992). *Children's Depression Inventory Manual.* North Tonawanda, NY: Multi-Health Systems, Inc.

La Greca, A. M., & Stone, W. L. (1993). The Social Anxiety Scale for Children – Revised: Factor structure and concurrent validity. *Journal of Clinical Child Psychology, 22,* 17–27.

Malti, T. (2005). Einfluss familialer Merkmale auf Persönlichkeitsentwicklung und Aggression bei Kindern [Influence of family characteristics on the development of personality and aggression of children]. In A. Ittel & M. von Salisch (Eds.), *Lügen, Lästern, Leiden lassen. Aggressives Verhalten in Kindheit und Jugend.* Stuttgart, Germany: Kohlhammer.

McFadyen-Ketchum, S. A., Bates, J. E., Dodge, K. A., & Pettit, G. S. (1996). Patterns of change in early child aggressive-disruptive behavior: Gender differences in predictors from early coercive and affectionate mother–child interactions. *Child Development, 67,* 2417–2433.

Moffitt, T. E., & Caspi, A. (2001). Childhood predictors differentiate life-course persistent and adolescent-limited antisocial pathways among males and females. *Development and Psychopathology, 13,* 355–375.

Olson, C. A., Bond, L., Burns, J. M., Vella-Brodrick, D. A., & Sawyer, S. M. (2003). Adolescent Resilience: a conceptual analysis. *Journal of Adolescence, 26,* 1–11.

Olson, D. H., Portner, J., & Bell, R. (1982). *FACES II.* St. Paul, MN: University of Minnesota Press.

Olson, D. H., Sprenkle, D. H., & Russell, C. S. (1979). Circumplex model of marital and family systems I: Cohesion and adaptability dimensions, family types and clinical applications. *Family Process, 18,* 3–28.

Olweus, D. (1991). Bully/victim problems among schoolchildren: Basic facts and effects of a school-based intervention program. In D. Pepler & K. Rubin (Eds.), *The development and treatment of childhood aggression.* Hillsdale, NJ: Lawrence Erlbaum.

Parke, P. D., & Ladd, G. W. (1992). *Family-peer relationships: Modes of linkages.* Hillsdale, NJ: Erlbaum.

Parker, J. G., Low, C. M., Walker, A. R., & Gamm, B. K. (2005). Friendship jealousy in young adolescents: Individual differences and links to sex, self-esteem, aggression, and social adjustment. *Developmental Psychology, 41*(1), 235–250.

Patterson, G. R., Reid, J. B., & Dishion, T. (1992). *Antisocial boys: A social interactional approach* (Vol. 4). Eugene, OR: Castalia Publishing Company.

Scarr, S. (1992). Developmental theories for the 1990s: Development and individual differences. *Child Development, 63,* 1–19.

Ramsden, S. R., & Hubbard, J. A. (2002). Family expressiveness and parental emotion coaching: Their role in children's emotion regulation and aggression. *Journal of Abnormal Child Psychology, 30,* 657–667.

Rowe, D. C. (1994). *The limits of family influence: Genes, experience, and behavior.* New York: Guilford Press.

Sanders, M. R., Dadds, M. R., Johnston, B. M., & Cash, R. (1992). Childhood depression and conduct disorder: I. Behavioral, affective, and cognitive aspects of family problem-solving interactions. *Journal of Abnormal Psychology, 101*, 495–504.

Seligman, M. E. (1999). The president's address. *American Psychologist, 54*, 559–562.

Shortt, J. W., Capaldi, D. M., Dishion, T. J., Bank, L., & Owen, L. D. (2003). The role of adolescent friends, romantic partners, and siblings in the emergence of the adult antisocial lifestyle. *Journal of Family Psychology, 17*(4), 521–533.

Sipppola, L., Epp, L. Buchanan, C., & Bukowski, W. (2005). Relationale Aggression und Zusammenhalt sozialer Netzwerke frühadoleszenter Mädchen [Relational aggression and the cohesion of social networks of girls in early adolescence]. In A. Ittel & M. von Salisch (Eds.), *Lügen, Lästern, Leiden lassen. Aggressives Verhalten in Kindheit und Jugend.* Stuttgart, Germany: Kohlhammer.

Slaby, R. G., & Guerra, N.G. (1988). Cognitive mediators of aggression in adolescent offenders: 1. Assessment. *Developmental Psychology, 24*(4), 580–588.

Statistisches Landesamt Berlin (2003). *Arbeitslosen- und Einwohnerzahlen für Berlin; 31.12.2002* [Unemployment and inhabitation figures for Berlin; date: 31 December, 2002] Retrieved February 15, 2006, from http://www.statistik-berlin.de/pms2000/sg03/2003/03-08-12a.html.

Storvoll, E. E., & Wichstrom, L. (2002). Do the risk factors associated with conduct problems in adolescents vary according to gender? *Journal of Adolescence, 25*, 183–202.

Treuting, J., & Hinshaw, S. P. (2001). Depression and self-esteem in boys with attention-deficit/hyperactivity disorder: Association with comorbid aggression and explanatory attributional mechanisms. *Journal of Abnormal Child Psychology, 29*, 23–39.

Watson, M. W., Fischer, K. W., Burdzovic Andreas, J., & Smith, K. W. (2004). Pathways to aggression in children and adolescents. *Harvard Educational Review, 74*, 404–430.

Zimbardo, Z., & Gerrig, R. (2004). Psychologie [Psychology] (16th ed.). München, Germany: Pearson.

11 Moral Emotions and Aggressive Behavior in Childhood

Tina Malti

Many researchers assume that the attribution of negative (moral) emotions in a moral dilemma situation implies the internalization of a moral norm and reflects children's moral motive strength (Keller, 1996; Montada, 1993; Nunner-Winkler, 1999). The motivation to act morally may express the end of a process of internal conflict resolution, in the way that an individual is willing to follow an internalized moral rule, even so he or she is aware of opposing motives in a moral dilemma, such as hedonistic or pragmatic interests (Hoffman, 2000). Moral motivation may thus constitute an important basis for children's moral behaviors, or, conversely, provide an impediment for immoral behaviors (Eisenberg, 2000). And although not all immoral behaviors can be considered aggressive behaviors, many can, given that both refer to an intention to harm someone (Tisak, Tisak, & Goldstein, 2006).

Theoretically, the role of moral emotions in children's (im)moral behaviors has been discussed in moral internalization theory (Hoffmann, 2000; cf. Gibbs, 2003). Considering the neglected role of moral emotions in cognitive-developmental theory (Edelstein & Schröder, 2000), moral internalization theory elaborated on the role of moral emotions with regard to the gap between moral understanding and moral action. Besides the cognitive understanding of a moral conflict, a willingness to consider the needs of other children is also necessary in order to act morally (Hoffmann, 2000; see Arsenio & Lemerise, 2001). This willingness, or moral motivation, is reflected in children's moral emotions. Guilt and empathy as the prototypical moral emotions are considered to be central prosocial motives in moral rule transgression (Hoffman, 1982, 2000).

Theories on the development of moral identity and moral motivation have emphasized that moral motivation and cognitive aspects of morality are continuously interrelated across development and codetermine moral action (Blasi, 1995, 1999). These theories have the advantage that they not only take into account emotional processes, e.g., empathic emotions such as guilt, in the genesis of (im)moral action, but also consider the idea from cognitive-developmental theory that moral behavior is related to cognitive decentration as well as differentiation in perspective-taking ability (Keller & Edelstein, 1991; Kohlberg & Candee, 1984; Piaget, 1965). Nonetheless, we still do not know much about the relative influence of cognitive and affective components on related social behaviors in childhood (Arsenio, Gold, & Adams, 2006; but see Arsenio & Lover, 1995).

In the following, we give an overview of the previous research on moral emotions and their relations with children's aggression. Moral emotions have frequently been studied in the so-called *happy-victimizer paradigm*. This research paradigm has been used to investigate the attribution of emotions to hypothetical wrongdoers after moral transgressions, and has revealed a gap between young children's moral rule understanding (Turiel, 1983) and the attribution of positive emotions to victimizers. Four-year-old kindergarten children appear to attribute predominantly positive (immoral) emotions to hypothetical wrongdoers, but there seems to be a shift to a greater number of negative (moral) attributions among 6- to 8-year-old children (e.g., Arsenio & Kramer, 1992; Lourenco, 1997; Nunner-Winkler & Sodian, 1988).

To date, little research has been conducted on the relationship between moral emotions and aggression in childhood (Arsenio & Lemerise, 2004). The following case study illustrates the idea of a relationship between moral motivation and aggression by describing how the attribution of moral emotions can be helpful as a diagnostic tool for exploring aggressive children's moral motive strength.

> L., a 6-year-old girl, attends psychotherapy to reduce her highly aggressive behavior at home. The parents report that L. insults them, does not follow rules, and destroys objects in the house. Moreover, she has been continually involved in fights with her siblings. The diagnostic sessions of the psychotherapy included an interview on L.'s socio-moral development. L. was asked about the emotions she would attribute to a hypothetical victimizer, who had stolen another child's chocolate in the kindergarten hall, about the emotions she would attribute to herself in the role of the victimizer, and how she would justify the attributed emotions. The girl answered: "Mhm, I think that Lisa (the victimizer) feels just great, because she really loves chocolate, and (…) I would feel great as well, because I like chocolate very much, too. However, if the kindergarten teacher found out, I would get in trouble. But she won't (smiles)."

L.'s answers show a lack of guilt and regret when imagining having transgressed the moral rule. L.'s emotion attributions and justifications presumably relate to her real-life aggressive behavior and are thus helpful for diagnostics. In a next step, it would be interesting to explore the underlying motives for her aggressive behaviors at home. This may be useful not only for understanding, but for attempts to change the dysfunctional behaviors. But is the described phenomenon only a single case, or does it apply to other children with aggressive behaviors as well? And if so, how?

Previous research investigating moral emotions by hypothetical dilemmas showed that aggressive behavior is associated with a delayed understanding of the emotional consequences of rule violations, especially of those involving guilt and empathic feelings (Menesini et al., 2003; Orobio de Castro, Merk, Koops, Veerman, & Bosch, 2005). A study by Asendorpf and Nunner-Winkler (1992) documents that the attribution of immoral (positive) emotions, used as an indicator of moral motive strength, predicted children's antisocial behavior in a cheating situation. However, not all studies revealed a negative association between moral emotions and aggression. For example, Arsenio and Fleiss (1996) showed that clinically aggressive children attributed more negative (moral) emotions to victimizers than nonaggressive children. However, aggressive children referred more often to hedonistic reasons – and less often to moral reasons – than nonaggressive children. In contrast, a study by Malti (2003) found no differences between the emotions attributed to hypothetical victimizers by aggressive and nonaggressive children (see Hughes & Dunn, 2000). Furthermore, a study by Arsenio, Ramos-Marcuse, and Hoffman (2005) also did not document any differences between the emotion attributions of aggressive and nonaggressive preschoolers. In sum, the findings of previous research concerning the relationship between moral emotions, as attributed to a hypothetical rule violator, and aggression are rather inconsistent. One explanation for these inconsistencies may be the neglected differentiation between emotions attributed to hypothetical victimizers and emotions attributed to the self as victimizer. This differentiation is important though, because only the latter may be a salient indicator of a personal commitment to norms (Keller, 1996). Research has supported this view and revealed that even young children predominantly attribute negative (moral) emotions to themselves as victimizers, even if they do not attribute these emotions to hypothetical victimizers (Keller, Lourenço, Malti, & Saalbach, 2003; Keller & Malti, 1999; Keller, Schuster, Fang, Tang, & Edelstein, 1996; Malti, Gumerun, & Buchmann, in press; Malti & Keller, in press).

Research on self-attributed moral emotions and aggression is scant, however. Krettenauer and Eichler (2006) found that the intensity of self-attributed moral emotions is negatively related to delinquency in adolescence. Self-attributed positive (immoral) emotions predicted peer-reported aggressive behavior in first- and second-graders in a study by Gasser and Alsaker (2005). Likewise, Malti & Keller (2006) found that elementary-school children's observed aggression is predicted by diminished self-attributed moral emotions in a moral dilemma. To our knowledge, the relationship between other- and self-attributed moral emotions and aggression in kindergarten children has not often been studied to date. Against this background, the study at hand investigated the following research questions:

First, we examined the relationship between kindergarten children's aggressive behavior and the emotions they attribute to victimizers and to themselves as victimizers in moral transgressions and in a moral dilemma, as well as the corresponding justifications. We studied 6-year-old kindergarten children, given that this age group is especially interesting with regard to the attributions of moral emotions. As already described above, there seems to be a shift to moral emotion attributions among 6- to 8-year-old children. Based on the theory of moral internalization (Hoffmann, 2000) and previous research on the attribution of moral emotions, we expected that self-attributed emotions would be negatively associated with aggression, but that this would not necessarily apply to victimizer-attributed emotions. Moreover, in accordance with the assumption in cognitive-developmental theory that the quality of social behavior relates to decentration and differentiation in perspective-taking abilities, we assumed that hedonistic reasoning, as an expression of egocentric thinking, is positively related to aggression, whereas moral and empathic reasoning is negatively associated with aggression.

Second, we investigated the relationship between aggression and the consistency of emotion attributions across different moral dilemmas. There is not much previous research on this topic, but, in a study by Malti (2003), aggressive children more consistently attributed mixed (positive and negative) and neutral emotions across various moral dilemmas than nonaggressive children. Thus, we hypothesized that aggression is associated with less consistently negative (moral) emotion attributions to the self.

Moreover, we examined the influence of different types of moral dilemmas on the relationship between children's emotion attributions and aggression, i.e., rule transgressions as used in the happy-victimizer paradigm *and* a moral dilemma as used in Kohlberg's dilemma method (1984). In the happy-victimizer paradigm, children are asked how a hypothetical victimizer would feel after a moral transgression, which cognitively presupposes the ability to coordinate perspectives of the self and other (Harris, 1989; Keller, 2004; Selman, 1980). In contrast, in the "classical" moral dilemma method, the child has to reflect on the morally right choice in a situation of conflicting moral obligations, and attribute corresponding emotions (Keller, 2004, p. 271). This requires the cognitive ability of a general, third-person, observer perspective. The latter assessment method thus requires more complex cognitive abilities than the emotion attributions as assessed in the happy-victimizer paradigm. Due to these cognitive constraints, the emotions attributed in the dilemma method may, therefore, relate to children's aggression differently than those attributed in the happy-victimizer paradigm.

Last but not least, we investigated gender differences in the relationship between moral emotions and aggression. In previous research, the expression of moral emotions was associated with children's aggression and symptoms thereof, in a gender-specific way (Ferguson, Stegge, Miller, & Olsen, 1999). Based on these findings, we hypothesized that the relationship between moral emotions and aggression differs for boys and girls.

Method

Participants

The data of the present study were taken from the pilot study of the Swiss Longitudinal Survey of Children and Adolescents (COCON), a longitudinal study investigating inter- and intraindividual competence differences in relation to the most influential social contexts from a life course perspective (Buchmann & Fend, 2004).

A random sample of kindergarten children and their primary caregivers was drawn based on the resident population in the Canton of Zurich in Switzerland. Requests for participation were first sent by mail to the caregivers, and they were then phoned by interviewers asking for their participation. Eighty percent of the persons contacted by mail and phone gave their consent for participation. Two hundred seventeen children and their primary caregivers participated. Nine interviews were not completely realized due to technical problems, and thus, 208 complete child interviews were available.

Of the primary caregivers 89% gave their written consent to our contacting the kindergarten teachers, and 152 of the corresponding kindergarten teachers participated (78%). Complete data for the triads (child/primary caregiver/kindergarten teacher) were available for $N = 150$ children. The participating children were on average 6.4 years of age $(SD = 0.18)$ with 68 girls and 82 boys. With regard to the ethnic composition of the sample, 83% of the corresponding primary caregivers were of Swiss nationality, and 17% were of other nationalities, predominantly European.

The kindergarten teachers were predominantly female (95%) with a mean age of 38 years $(SD = 11.9)$. Their average teaching experience was $M = 13$ years $(SD = 10.4)$.

Procedure

The assessment was conducted during Spring 2005. The children and primary caregivers were individually interviewed at home via a computer-assisted personal interview (CAPI). The child and the primary-caregiver interviews lasted about 25–30 minutes each. At the end of the interviews, primary caregivers and children were thanked for their participation, and the child received a present. The primary caregiver filled in a supplementary questionnaire. Likewise, the corresponding kindergarten teachers received a questionnaire by mail, which they filled in and returned. The interviewers were professional interviewers who received intensive training in the interview technique.

Measures

Aggressive behavior. The children's aggressive behavior was assessed via ratings by primary caregivers and kindergarten teachers. The primary caregivers rated the aggressive behavior of their children using three items on the aggression subscale from the Strength and Difficulty Questionnaire with a four-point scale (SDQ; Goodman, 1997).
  The following items were used: (1) *my child often lies or cheats,* (2) *my child often has tantrums or has a hot temper,* and (3) *my child often bullies or teases other children.* A sum score was computed (M = 5.5, SD =1.6, Range = 3–9; α = .34). The kindergarten teachers completed the same three items and one additional item, taken from the aggression subscale of the Child Behavior Checklist CBCL 4/18 (*the child is defiant, hostile, or naughty towards me*; Achenbach & Edelbrock, 1983). A sum score was computed (M = 5.9, SD =2.4, Range = 4–15). The reliability of the scale was α = 0.79. The primary-caregiver and kindergarten-teacher ratings were significantly correlated (r = .27, p = .001). Moreover, the boys were rated as more aggressive than the girls by the kindergarten teachers (t = 2.51, p = .01).

Moral development: We assessed the children's moral development using three hypothetical moral dilemmas. The dilemmas are frequently used in the literature and have been validated in previous research (Keller, 1996; Keller et al., 2003; Nunner-Winkler & Sodian, 1988; Selman, 1980): The first two dilemmas, "pushing the child off the swing" and "stealing," confront the child with moral rule violations. In the third story, the child has to make an action choice in an interpersonal moral dilemma. The stories were illustrated by a three-frame sequence of cartoons. The cartoons were gender-matched.
  In the first story (pushing), a child (victim) swings, and the protagonist (victimizer) stands next to the swing (Cartoon 1). The corresponding text explains that the protagonist is desperate to swing, and pushes the first child (victim) off the swing. In the second story (stealing), a child (victim) leaves its jacket with a nice chocolate bar in the kindergarten hall (Cartoon 1). Another child (victimizer) takes the chocolate bar (Cartoon 2). In Cartoon 3, the first child (victim) realizes that the chocolate bar has been stolen. The child looks sad. In the third story, two children are presented as close friends. A third child is new in kindergarten and does not have any friends yet (Cartoon 1). When the friends talk about the new child, the protagonist requests his/her friend to understand

that it is a difficult situation when you are new in kindergarten, but the friend does not like the new child. The best friend asks the protagonist to meet him/her as usual on their special meeting day, and the protagonist promises the best friend to do so (Cartoon 2). The friend mentions new toys, but also wants to talk about an important problem. Later that day, the protagonist receives a phone call from the new child, who invites him/her to his/her house to watch an interesting DVD and eat pizza (Cartoon 3). The dilemma is that the invitation from the new child is at the very time of his/her meeting with the best friend.

After presenting the first two stories, children were asked the following questions:

1. *Moral judgment.* Is it right, what the protagonist did? Why/why not?
2. *Emotion attribution to victimizer.* How does he/she feel afterwards? Why?
3. *Emotion attribution to self.* How would you feel afterwards? Why?

After presenting the third story, the children were asked:

1. *Action choice.* Imagine that you are the protagonist. What would you decide to do in this situation? Why?
2. *Emotion attribution to self.* How would you feel afterwards? Why?

Coding of first and second story. In the first question, we assessed the moral judgment of the transgression. Answers were coded as "yes" and "no." Question 2 assessed the attribution of emotions to victimizers and Question 3 the emotions attributed to the self as victimizer (*moral emotions*). The attributed emotions were coded as "positive," "negative," and "mixed." The category "mixed" rarely occurred (2% victimizer; 6% self as victimizer) and was combined with the category "bad" for statistical analyses.

Coding of third story. The first question assessed the action choice in the dilemma. Answers were coded as "old friend," "new child," "other," and "don't know." The "other" category and the "don't know" category occurred only rarely (4% and 7% respectively) and were excluded from further analyses. Question 2 assessed the attribution of emotions to self (*moral emotions*). The attributed emotions were coded as "positive," "negative," "mixed," and "don't know." The "mixed" category rarely occurred (8%) and was combined with the "negative" category for statistical analyses. The "don't know" category, which occurred in 14% of cases, was excluded from the statistical analyses. Interrater agreement was 99%, all disagreements were discussed, and a consensus was found.

The reasons in the three stories were classified using a revised coding manual employed in previous studies (Keller et al., 2003; Keller, Edelstein, Schmid, Fang, & Fang, 1998; Lourenço, 1997). Three reasoning categories were defined:

- *Moral reasons.* Reasons concerning moral norms, rules, obligations (e.g., "he has promised to meet him").
- *Empathic concern.* Reasons related to the quality of the relationship or altruism/empathy (e.g., "the friend will be sad if he just doesn't come").
- *Hedonistic reasons.* Reasons of interest for an object or self-interest (e.g., "he wants to see the movie").
- *Other reasons.* Other reasons and unscoreable arguments.

The percentage of interrater agreement across categories was 95%, all disagreements were discussed, and a consensus was found. For further statistical analyses, moral and empathic reasons were summarized into one overall category and compared with hedonistic reasons in the friendship dilemma.

Results

Descriptive Analyses

Almost all children judged that it was not right to violate the rule in the two moral transgressions (97%), and gave corresponding moral or empathic justifications (91%). The frequencies of the emotion attributions to victimizers and self as victimizers in the first two stories and the corresponding justifications are reported in Table 1.

In both stories children attributed more negative (moral) emotions to themselves than to victimizers, pushing: $\chi^2 (1, N = 133) = 34.00, p = .000$; stealing: $\chi^2 (1, N = 127) = 10.28, p = .001$. No gender or story differences in the emotion attributions occurred. Concerning the reasons given for the emotion attributions, the results showed that 45% of the children referred to moral reasons, 15.5% referred to empathic reason, and 29.5% to hedonistic reasons when justifying their emotion attributions. Ten percent of the children referred to other reasons (e.g., sanction-oriented reasons). No gender or story differences occurred.

With regard to the friendship dilemma (third story), 42% of the children decided to go to the new child's house, and 58% decided to go with the old friend. For further statistical analyses, combined variables were created. First, a combined variable of action choice and justification was computed. Overall, 54% of the children decided in favour of the old friend and justified this choice with moral or empathic reasons. Only 1% of the children justified this choice with hedonistic reasons. This category was therefore dropped from further analyses. Thirty-one percent of the children decided to go to the new child's house and justified this with moral or empathic reasons. Fourteen percent of

Table 1. Frequencies (%) of Emotion Attributions to Victimizers and Self as Victimizer and Reasons by Story

Emotion attribution	Pushing	Stealing
Victimizer		
Negative (moral)	90 (66)	83 (59)
Positive (immoral)	46 (34)	57 (41)
Self as victimizer		
Negative (moral)	112 (84)	112 (84)
Positive (immoral)	21 (16)	22 (16)
Reasons*		
Moral	106 (44)	111 (46)
Empathic	37 (15)	39 (16)
Hedonistic	68 (28)	75 (31)
Other	32 (13)	17 (7)

* Reasons aggregated over other- and self-attributed emotions

the children decided to go to the new child's house and argued with hedonistic reasons. There was an overall gender difference in the combined variable, χ^2 (3, $N = 117$) = 11.05, $p = .01$. In particular, boys decided significantly more often in favour of the new child and justified this with hedonistic reasons compared to the girls, χ^2 (1, $N = 117$) = 5.94, $p = .02$. Girls also decided more often in favour of the new child but justified this with moral or empathic reasons, χ^2 (1, $N = 117$) = 5.95, $p = .02$. A further combined variable of action choice – emotion attribution – justification was created, thus indicating 2 × 2 × 2 possible combinations. If a child did not mention any justification, we categorized the pattern into the same category as moral/empathic justifications. The pattern "friend – positive-moral" occurred in 41% of cases, and the pattern "friend – negative-moral" in 10%. The pattern "new child – positive-moral" occurred in 20% of the cases, the pattern "new child – positive-hedonistic" in 14%, and the pattern "new child – negative-moral" in 10% of the cases. There were no significant gender differences in the pattern variable. The categories "friend – positive-hedonistic," "friend – negative-hedonistic," and "new child – negative-hedonistic" occurred rather infrequently or not at all (3%, 2%, and 0% respectively) and were therefore dropped from further analyses.

Moral Emotions and Aggression

Four univariate analyses of variance were computed to analyze the mean differences in aggression by the moral emotions attributed after moral transgressions (Story 1: stealing; Story 2: pushing off the swing). The aggression score (primary caregivers/kindergarten teachers) was specified as the dependent variable. As independent variables we used (a) the emotion attributions to victimizers and self in Story 1 and gender, and (b) the emotion attributions to victimizers and self in Story 2 and gender. The results show that the aggression as rated by the primary caregiver was significantly predicted by the first set of variables, $F(4, 130) = 3.22, p = .02$. Furthermore, there was a significant interaction between emotion attribution to self and gender: Girls who attributed positive emotions to themselves displayed higher aggression scores than girls who attributed negative emotions to themselves, whereas no difference was observed for boys (see Figure 1). Primary-caregiver-rated aggression was not significantly predicted by the second set of independent variables.

Aggression as rated by the kindergarten teachers was significantly predicted by both sets of independent variables, stealing: $F(4, 132) = 3.44, p = .01$; pushing off the swing: $F(4, 135) = 2.82, p = .01$. Children who made negative emotion attributions to the self displayed less aggression than children who made positive emotion attributions to the self. Moreover, boys were rated as more aggressive than girls in the second story (pushing off the swing).

Two further univariate analyses of variance were computed to analyze the mean differences in aggression using the combined pattern variable of action, emotion attribution, and justification in the friendship dilemma. The aggression score (primary caregivers/kindergarten teachers) was specified as the dependent variable. As the independent variable, the action – emotion attribution – justification variable was entered. The two models did not reach significance.

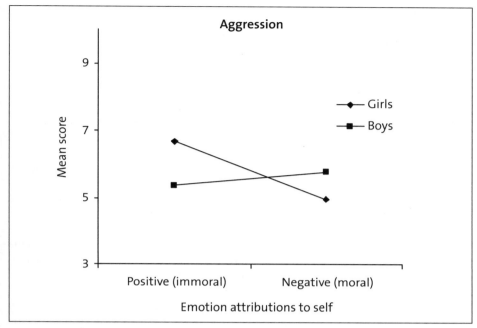

Figure 1. Aggression (primary-caregiver rating) by emotions attributed to self in stealing story by gender.

With regard to the relationships between aggression and the corresponding justifications, a correlational analysis was run. Aggression as rated by the primary caregivers was slightly negatively related to empathic reasons, $r = -.16$, $p = .06$, whereas aggression as rated by the kindergarten-teachers was positively associated with hedonistic reasons, $r = .19$, $p = .03$.

Consistency Patterns in Moral Emotion Attributions and Aggression

To analyze the relationship between moral emotions and aggression further, two consistency patterns in moral emotion attributions were computed across the two stories: The first pattern was the consistency in the emotions attributed to victimizers across the two stories. A consistently positive pattern implied the attribution of positive emotions to victimizers in both stories, a consistently negative pattern indicated the attribution of negative emotions in both stories, and an inconsistent pattern contained varying attributions across the two stories. The same pattern variable was created for the emotion attributions to the self as victimizer across the two stories.

In the next step, a consistency pattern variable for moral emotions as attributed to the self in the first two stories and the combined variable of action choice – emotion attribution – justification was created. A consistently positive pattern contained positive emotion attributions in the first two stories, and the pattern "new child – positive-

Table 2. Frequencies (%) of Consistency Patterns Across the Moral Dilemmas

Emotion attribution pattern	Victimizer[1]	Self[1]	Self[2]
Consistently positive	36 (27)	13 (9)	5 (4)
Inconsistent	26 (20)	32 (22)	89 (61)
Consistently negative	71 (53)	100 (69)	51 (35)

[1] Attributions across two moral transgressions; [2] Attributions across two moral transgressions and moral dilemma

hedonistic" or "new child – positive-moral" in the friendship dilemma. A consistently negative pattern contained the attributions of negative emotions in the first two stories, and the patterns "friend – positive-moral," "friend – negative-moral," or "new child – negative-moral" in the friendship dilemma. An inconsistent pattern contained all other combinations. The frequencies of the three pattern variables are displayed in Table 2.

Table 2 shows that the consistently negative pattern occurred more frequently in the victimizer and self attributions than the consistently positive and inconsistent pattern. Regarding the self attributions across the three stories, the inconsistent pattern occurred more frequently than the consistently negative and consistently positive patterns.

Four univariate analyses of variance were computed to analyze mean differences in aggression by the consistency patterns concerning the victimizer and the self across the two moral transgressions. The dependent variable was the aggression score (primary-caregiver/kindergarten-teacher ratings), the independent variables were (a) consistency in emotion attribution to victimizers and gender, and (b) consistency in emotion attribution to self as victimizer and gender.

Concerning the consistency pattern of emotion attributions to victimizers, no significant mean differences in aggression occurred. The results from the two ANOVAs regarding the consistency pattern of the emotions attributed to the self, however, were for the kindergarten-teacher related aggression, significant: $F(5, 144) = 3.85$, $p = .003$, and slightly significant for the primary-caregiver-rated aggression, $F(5, 142) = 2.17$, $p = .06$. Posthoc comparisons revealed that children who attributed consistently negative emotions to themselves displayed less aggression (as rated by the kindergarten teacher) than children who attributed positive or inconsistent emotions to themselves across the two stories (see Figure 2). Posthoc comparisons regarding primary-caregiver-rated aggression showed that children who consistently attributed positive emotions showed higher aggression scores than children who attributed inconsistent emotions.

Two further ANOVAs were computed to analyze the mean differences in aggression using the combined variable of emotions as attributed to the self in the first two stories and the variable of action choice – emotion attribution – justification. Primary-caregiver-rated aggression was not significantly predicted by the variable. However, children with consistently positive emotion attributions showed significantly higher aggression as rated by the kindergarten teacher than children with an inconsistent or consistently negative attribution pattern (see Figure 2).

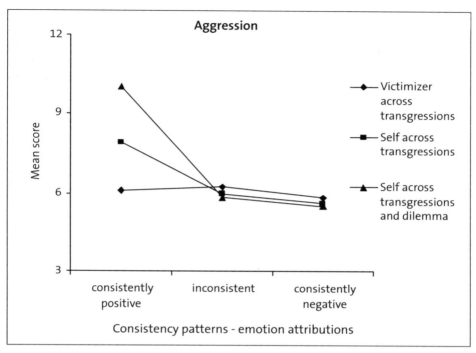

Figure 2. Mean differences in kindergarten-teacher rated aggression by consistency patterns.

Discussion

In the present study, two research questions were investigated: *First,* we examined the influence of self- and other-attributed moral emotions on kindergarten children's aggressive behavior, and *second,* we studied the association between consistency of patterns of emotion attributions in different moral situations and aggressive behavior.

Concerning the first research question, we assumed that self-attributed moral emotions are related to aggression, although this may not be true for emotions attributed to others, because previous research has revealed that even young children frequently attribute moral emotions to themselves, but not necessarily to hypothetical wrongdoers (e.g., Keller et al., 2003). The results predominantly confirmed this hypothesis: Aggression as rated by the kindergarten teachers was negatively associated with self-attributed negative (moral) emotions. The attribution of positive (immoral) emotions to the self after moral transgressions was related to aggression as rated by the primary caregivers. Likewise, self-attributed immoral emotions were associated with aggression as rated by the primary caregivers, but only in one of the two moral transgressions (stealing). The effect of the latter story is somewhat difficult to interpret and is possibly a sample artefact, but nonetheless, it may indicate that the context (e.g., psychological harm as described in the stealing story vs. physical harm as described in the pushing-off-the-swing story) influences emotion attributions as well as their association with aggression (Malti & Keller, 2006a). In sum, the results support the idea that self-attributed moral emotions after moral transgressions play an important role in children's aggressive behavior and thereby confirm theories on the influence of moral motive strength on aggressive behaviors (Arsenio & Lover, 1995; Hoffman, 2000).

With regard to the justifications, the results revealed that aggression as rated by the primary caregivers was negatively associated with empathic reasons, whereas aggression as rated by the kindergarten teachers was positively related to hedonistic reasons. These results are in line with previous studies that found children's aggressive behavior to be associated with hedonistic reasoning (e.g., Arsenio & Fleiss, 1996), and may confirm the assumption of moral internalization theory that immoral behavior is related to less empathic, and more egoistic, motives. However, the findings do not support the view that some aggressive children are well developed with regard to social-cognitive and socio-moral skills (Sutton, Smith, & Swettenham, 1999). Rather, the results may reflect a delay in the development of differentiation in perspective-taking (Piaget, 1965, 1981), which is expressed in hedonistic reasoning and a lack of empathic motives as well as a particular self-understanding (Malti, 2006). We did not differentiate between relational and physical forms of aggression however, and future research should clarify whether specific forms of aggression, e.g., relational aggression, are related to socio-moral competence in different ways from the others (e.g., Hawley, 2003).

With regard to the second research question regarding the relationship between aggression and the consistency patterns in moral emotion attributions, our hypothesis about the relationship between less negative consistency patterns of self-attributed emotions and aggression was predominantly confirmed by the findings. Children who attributed consistently negative emotions to themselves displayed less aggression (as rated by the kindergarten teachers and the primary caregivers) than children who attributed positive or inconsistent emotions to themselves across the two moral transgressions. Moreover, kindergarten-teacher-rated aggression was associated with a higher frequency of consistently positive emotions across the two transgressions *and* the moral friendship dilemma. The latter finding is very interesting, because it may indicate that children who (rather) consistently attribute positive (immoral) emotions to themselves across different moral rule violations also display the highest aggression level. Thus, it is possible that not only negative (moral) emotion attributions play a role in children's aggressive behavior, but also the strength of the moral motive, reflected in less variation across different moral dilemmas. It would be interesting to ascertain whether or not the level of the aggression relates differently to consistency patterns in emotion attributions to the self.

Moreover, the present study employed two different methods of assessing moral emotions and investigated the question of method-immanent differences in the relationship between self-attributed moral emotions and aggression. Concerning the method used in the happy-victimizer paradigm, the results revealed that children's positive (immoral) emotion attributions to the self relate to aggression. Regarding the dilemma method as used by Kohlberg (1984), the results did not reflect any influence of self-attributed moral emotions on aggression. This finding contradicts a previous study conducted by Malti & Keller (2006b), which explored the relationship between elementary-school children's self-attributed moral emotions in a moral friendship dilemma and their observed aggression. The latter study found that self-attributed moral emotions were predictive of lower aggression. Thus, the method used in the happy-victimizer paradigm seems to be valid for kindergarten children, whereas the dilemma method is possibly more valid for elementary-school children. The issue of age-adequate assessment methods of children's moral emotions needs further investigation.

With regard to gender differences in the relationship between moral emotions and aggression, we found that self-attributed moral emotions and gender had an interesting interaction effect on kindergarten-teacher-rated aggression: Girls who attributed immoral (positive) emotions showed higher aggression than girls who attributed moral (negative) emotions, whereas no difference was obtained for the boys. This result is rather surprising and not in line with previous research, which frequently reported gender differences in that highly aggressive boys displayed less guilt than nonaggressive boys (Orobio de Castro, Bosch, Veerman, Koops, 2003). Our finding may relate to the fact that we used a random, nonclinical sample of kindergarten children, which implies lower degrees of aggression and possibly different relationships to moral emotions (Eisenberg, 2000). Nonetheless, this result may indicate that the mechanisms by which moral emotions are associated with aggressive behaviors are different for boys and girls due, for example, to gender-specific parent-child interactions (McFadyen-Ketchum, Bates, Dodge, & Pettit, 1996).

In sum, this study is among the first to document that self-attributed moral emotions after moral transgressions and consistency patterns in the attributed emotions across different contexts influence kindergarten children's aggressive behaviors. Nonetheless, the study is not without limitations:

First, the reliability of the aggression scale as rated by the primary caregivers was not satisfactory, which indicates that homogeneity of the scale was rather low. The reliability of the kindergarten-teacher-rated aggression scale was good however, and many of the results did not greatly differ from the primary-caregiver ratings.

Second, we failed to differentiate between subgroups of aggression, e.g., reactive versus proactive forms of aggression (Vitaro, Brendgen, & Barker, 2006). Given that the *motives* to act aggressively may differ between subtypes of aggression, further qualitative research is needed to address this issue.

Third, the present study was cross-sectional focusing on one age group. Thus, we cannot make causal inferences from our findings, nor specify developmental effects, with regard to the relationship between emotion attribution and aggression.

Despite these limitations, the study demonstrates that aggression is associated with positive (immoral) self-attributed emotions and specific consistency patterns in emotion attribution. Future research could focus on the identification of the developmental pathways between the motives of children's aggressive behaviors and their self-attributed moral emotions. Furthermore, it would be very interesting to determine the influence that the quality of meaningful social relationships has on the growth of moral motivation and related moral behaviors in children (e.g., Kochanska, Padavich, & Koenig, 1996). Research in these areas could result in a valuable contribution to the prevention of aggressive developmental pathways (Noddings, 2002).

Acknowledgements

This research was funded by the Swiss National Science Foundation (SNF). I would like to thank all the children, parents, and kindergarten teachers for participating in the study. Moreover, I am grateful to the interviewers for their great work as well as to Richard Deppeler for his help in data coding.

References

Achenbach, T. M., & Edelbrock, C. S. (1983). *Manual for the child behavior checklist and revised child behavior profile*. Burlington, VT: University of Vermont.

Arsenio, W. F., & Fleiss, K. (1996). Typical and behaviourally disruptive children's understanding of the emotional consequences of sociomoral events. *British Journal of Developmental Psychology, 14*, 173–186.

Arsenio, W. F., & Kramer, R. (1992). Victimizers and their victims: Children's conceptions of the mixed emotional consequences of moral transgressions. *Child Development, 63*, 915–927.

Arsenio, W., & Lemerise, E. A. (2001). Varieties of childhood bullying: Values, emotion processes, and social competence. *Social Development, 10*, 59–73.

Arsenio, W., & Lemerise, E. A. (2004). Aggression and moral development: Integrating social information processing and moral domain models. *Child Development, 75*(4), 987–1002.

Arsenio, W., & Lover, A. (1995). Children's conceptions of sociomoral affect: Happy victimizers, mixed emotions, and other expectancies. In M. Killen & D. Hart (Eds.), *Morality in everyday life: Developmental perspectives* (pp. 87–198). Cambridge, UK: Cambridge University Press.

Arsenio, W. F., Gold, J., & Adams, E. (2006). Children's conceptions and displays of moral emotions. In M. Killen & J. Smetana (Eds.), *Handbook of moral development* (pp. 581–609). Mahwah, NJ: Lawrence Erlbaum.

Arsenio, W. F., Ramos-Marcuse, F., & Hoffman, R. (2005). *Young at risk children's emotionally-charged moral narratives: Relations with behavior problems, parental social support, and family disciplinary techniques.* Manuscript in preparation.

Asendorpf, J. B., & Nunner-Winkler, G. (1992). Children's moral motive strength and temperamental inhibition reduce their immoral behavior in real moral conflicts. *Child Development, 63*(5), 1223–1235.

Blasi, A. (1995). Moral understanding and the moral personality: The process of moral integration. In W. M. Kurtines & J. L. Gewirtz (Eds.), *Moral development: An introduction* (pp. 229–253). Boston, MA: Allyn & Bacon.

Blasi, A. (1999). Emotions and moral motivation. *Journal for the Theory of Social Behaviour, 29*, 1–19.

Buchmann, M., & Fend, H. (2004). *Context and competence: Swiss longitudinal survey of children and youth.* Research proposal, Swiss National Science Foundation.

Edelstein, W., & Schröder, E. (2000). Full house or Pandora's box? The treatment of variability in post-Piagetian research. *Child Development, 71*(4), 840–842.

Eisenberg, N. (2000). Emotion, regulation, and moral development. *Annual Review of Psychology, 51*, 665–697.

Ferguson, T. J., Stegge, H., Miller, E. R., & Olsen, M. E. (1999). Guilt, shame, and symptoms in children. *Developmental Psychology, 35*(2), 347–357.

Gasser, L., & Alsaker, F. D. (2005, June). *Implications of moral emotion attributions for children's social behavior and relationships.* Paper presented at the meeting of the Jean Piaget Society, Vancouver, Canada.

Gibbs, J. C. (2003). Moral development and reality: Beyond the theories of Kohlberg and Hoffman. Thousand Oaks, CA: Sage.

Goodman, R. (1997). The strengths and difficulties questionnaire: A research note. *Journal of Child Psychology and Psychiatry, 38*, 581–586.

Harris, P. L. (1989). *Children and emotion.* Oxford, UK: Basil Blackwell.

Hawley, P. H. (2003). Strategies of control, aggression, and morality in preschoolers: An evolutionary perspective. *Journal of Experimental Child Psychology, 85*, 213–235.

Hoffman, M. L. (1982). Development of prosocial motivation: Empathy and guilt. In N. Eisenberg-Berg (Ed.), *Development of prosocial behavior* (pp. 281–313). New York: Academic Press.

Hoffman, M. L. (2000). *Empathy and moral development. Implications for caring and justice.* Cambridge, UK: Cambridge University Press.

Hughes, C., & Dunn, J. (2000). Hedonism or empathy? Hard-to-manage children's moral awareness and links with cognitive and maternal characteristics. *British Journal of Developmental Psychology, 18*, 227–245.

Keller, M. (1996). *Moralische Sensibilität: Entwicklung in Freundschaft und Familie* [Moral sensibility: development in friendship and family]. Weinheim, Germany: Psychologie Verlags Union.

Keller, M. (2004). Self in relationship. In D. K. Lapsley & D. Narvaez (Eds.), *Moral development, self, and identity* (pp. 267–298). Mahwah, NJ: Lawrence Erlbaum.

Keller, M., & Edelstein, W. (1991). The development of socio-moral meaning making: Domains, categories, and perspective-taking. In W. Kurtines & J. Gewirtz (Eds.), *Handbook of moral behavior and development,* (Vol. 2, pp. 89–114). Hillsdale, NJ: Lawrence Erlbaum.

Keller, M., Edelstein, W., Schmid, C., Fang, F.-X., & Fang, G. (1998). Reasoning about responsibilities and obligations in close relationships: A comparison across two cultures. *Developmental Psychology, 34*(4), 731–741.

Keller, M., Lourenço, O., Malti, T., & Saalbach, H. (2003). The multifaceted phenomenon of 'happy victimizers:' A cross-cultural comparison of moral emotions. *British Journal of Developmental Psychology, 21*, 1–18.

Keller, M., & Malti, T. (1999, September). *Preschooler's friendship and fight relations: Links to sociomoral development and social behavior.* Paper presented at the European Conference of Developmental Psychology, Spetses, Greece.

Keller, M., Schuster, P., Fang F.-X., Tang, H., & Edelstein, W. (1996, November). *Cognition and motivation in the development of moral feelings in early childhood.* Paper presented at the Conference of the Association for Moral Education, Ottawa, Canada.

Kochanska, G., Padavich, D. L., & Koenig, A. L. (1996). Children's narratives about hypothetical moral dilemmas and objective measures of their conscience: Mutual relations and socialization antecedents. *Child Development, 67*(4), 1420–1436.

Kohlberg, L. (1984). *Essays on moral development: Vol. 2. The psychology of moral development: The nature and validity of moral stages.* San Francisco: Harper & Row.

Kohlberg, L., & Candee, D. (1984). The relationship of moral judgment to moral action. In W. M. Kurtines & J. L. Gewirtz (Eds.), *Morality, moral behaviour, and moral development* (pp. 52–73). New York: Wiley.

Krettenauer, T., & Eichler, D. (2006). Adolescents' self-attributed moral emotions following a moral transgression: Relations with delinquency, confidence in moral judgment, and age. *British Journal of Developmental Psychology, 24*(3), 489–506.

Lourenço, O. (1997). Children's attributions of moral emotions to victimizers: Some data, doubts, and suggestions. *British Journal of Developmental Psychology, 15*(4), 425–438.

Malti, T. (2003). *Das Gefühlsverständnis aggressiver Kinder* [Emotional understanding of aggressive children]. Doctoral dissertation, Free University Berlin (Electronic publication: http://www.diss.fu-berlin.de/2003/120/).

Malti, T. (2006). Aggression, self-understanding, and social competence in Swiss elementary-school children. *Swiss Journal of Psychology, 65*(2), 81–91.

Malti, T., & Keller, M. (in press). The relation of elementary-school children's externalizing behavior to emotion attributions, evaluation of consequences, and moral reasoning. *European Journal of Development Psychology.*

Malti, T., Grummerum, M., & Buchmann, M. (in press). Contemporaneous and one-year-longitudinal prediction of children's prosocial behavior from sympathy and moral motivation. *Journal of Genetic Psychology.*

Malti, T., & Keller, M. (2006). *Observed aggressive behaviour in elementary-school children: its relations with moral cognitions and moral emotions in close relationships.* Manuscript submitted for publication.

McFadyen-Ketchum, S., Bates, J., Dodge, K. A., & Pettit, G. A. (1996). Patterns of change in early childhood aggressive-disruptive behavior: Gender differences in predictions from early coercive and affectionate mother-child-interactions. *Child Development, 67*, 2147–2433.

Menesini, E., Sanchez, V., Fonzi, A., Ortega, R., Costabile, A., & Lo Feudo, G. (2003). Moral emotions and bullying: A cross-national comparison of differences between bullies, victims, and outsiders. *Aggressive Behaviour, 29*, 515–530.

Montada, L. (1993). Understanding oughts by assessing moral reasoning or moral emotions. In G. G. Noam & T. E. Wren (Eds.), *The moral self* (pp. 292–309). Cambridge, UK: MIT Press.

Noddings, N. (2002). *Educating moral people: A caring alternative to character.* New York: Teachers College Press.

Nunner-Winkler, G. (1999). Development of moral understanding and moral motivation. In F. E. Weinert & W. Schneider (Eds.), *Individual development from 3 to 12: Findings from the Munich longitudinal study* (pp. 253–290). New York: Cambridge University Press.

Nunner-Winkler, G., & Sodian, B. (1988). Children's understanding of moral emotions. *Child Development, 59*, 1323–1338.

Orobio de Castro, B., Bosch, J. D., Veerman, J. W., & Koops, W. (2003). The effects of emotion regulation, attribution, and delay prompts on aggressive boys' social problem solving. *Cognitive Therapy and Research, 27*(2), 153–166.

Orobio de Castro, B., Merk, W., Koops, W., Veerman, J. W., & Bosch, J. D. (2005). Emotions in social information processing and their relations with reactive and proactive aggression in referred aggressive boys. *Journal of Clinical Child and Adolescent Psychology, 34*(1), 105–116.

Piaget, J. (1965). *The moral judgement of the child.* New York: Free Press.

Piaget, J. (1981). *Intelligence and affectivity: Their relationship during child development* (T. A. Brown & C. E. Kaegi, Eds. & Trans.). Palo Alto, CA: Annual Reviews.

Selman, R. L. (1980). *The growth of interpersonal understanding: Developmental and clinical analyses.* New York: Academic Press.

Sutton, J., Smith, P. K., & Swettenham, J. (1999). Bullying and theory of mind: A critique of the social skills deficit view of anti-social behavior. *Social Development, 8*(1), 117–127.

Tisak, M. S., Tisak, J., & Goldstein, S. E. (2006). Aggression, delinquency, and morality: A social-cognitive perspective. In M. Killen & J. Smetana (Eds.), *Handbook of moral development* (pp. 611–632). Mahwah, NJ: Lawrence Erlbaum.

Turiel, E. (1983). Domains and categories in social cognitive development. In W. F. Overton (Ed.), *The relationship between social and cognitive development* (pp. 53–90). Hillsdale, NJ: Erlbaum.

Vitaro, F., Brendgen, M., & Barker, E. D. (2006). Subtypes of aggressive behavior: A developmental perspective. *International Journal of Behavioral Development, 30*(1), 12–19.

12

Emotion, Aggression, and the Meaning of Prevention in Early Childhood

Florian Juen, Doris Peham, Barbara Juen, and Cord Benecke

Introduction

Externalizing behavior problems cause untold difficulty for parents, teachers, children themselves, and society as a whole (Denham, Caverly, Schmidt, Blair, DeMulder, Caal et al., 2002). This is poignantly depicted by many occurrences of youth violence all around the world. Aggression and violence are social phenomena that are widely discussed in society. Increases in the scale and frequency of violent acts, accompanied by decreases in the ages of offenders, have led to higher levels of sensitivity to violence in society in general. Via the media we are horrified almost daily by tremendous acts of cruelty, including acts of terrorism, war, or cold-blooded murder. We are even more affected when the offenders of these crucial acts are children, always raising the question: "How can this happen?" Several authors describe the intensity of violence in the U.S. as a "public health epidemic" (Osofsky, 1995), and in Europe we seem to be headed in that direction. Each one of us is frequently overwhelmed by individual acts of violence, especially when they are committed by young people. But this is only the tip of the iceberg as we are continuously confronted with aggression and violence of lower levels of brutality in our every day lives. Teachers, in particular, report an increase of harshness in school, even among kindergarten caregivers. Due to this personal involvement, efforts are increased to solve these problems. The need for prevention therefore seems to be outstanding.

Attachment theory holds great promise as a framework for primary prevention and early intervention. Enabling and facilitating social competence, high self-esteem, and secure attachment is likely to create the conditions for a post-industrial society where relationships are based on mutual recognition and respect (Svanberg, 1998). A secure attachment organization will provide a substantial buffer against life requirements as we learn to make sense of a complex environment and learn to communicate in a highly interactive process. One of the crucial efforts in early life is to build up an internalized representational world that helps us to understand behavior of our own and others as meaningful. According to his concept of mentalization and his "playing with reality" theory, Peter Fonagy and colleagues illustrate the meaning of this reflective approach to the self and the process of achievement within the early attachment relationship (Fonagy, Gergely, Jurist, & Target, 2002). This also helps us to understand problems in early development that can potentially lead to aggressive and violent behavior in preschoolers, or to antisocial and delinquent behavior in adulthood. As Tremblay states that the best age to predict antisocial behavior is around five (Tremblay et al., 1999), this illustrates clearly the necessity of such (attachment related) understanding.

It seems that the violent movements and individual aggressive behavior of the last decades, which appear to have become more frequent in everyday life, have their origins in early childhood (Gauthier, 2003). Bowlby (1973) mentioned the importance of the close ties that anger and anxiety have with separation and loss of an attachment figure. Early interactive experiences of separation and loss have high impact on our developing representational system. Separation and loss mean instability of the self system, mainly in early childhood, which leads to higher arousal for increasing protection by retraction (anxiety) or higher tension (anger). Talking to prisoners arrested due to various outcomes of antisocial behavior, ranging from assault to murder, they almost systematically come to talk about their childhoods with a great majority of these individuals reporting that they grew up in a traumatic environment where they had been repeatedly violated and brutalized. Stunning support for this is described in a book by Gitta Sereny tracing early experiences made by a girl who murdered at age 10 (Sereny, 1999). Often it feels like a kind of yearning for emotional security while talking to offenders about their childhoods. In our opinion, aggression and violence cannot be understood without tracing their developmental origins to the very first years of life.

Along with the high variability of possible outcomes of aggressive behavior, we want to discuss underlying mental origins and developmental aspects that also lead us to the relationship of empathy and aggression as well as the often mentioned gender specifics before we try to draw a conclusion based on implications of our considerations for prevention. Our basic argument is to regard aggressive behavior as a result of a dynamic mental process caused by any kind of insecure or chaotic family environment in early childhood. In the development of these inner processes affects and their regulation play a major role. We assume that according to the attachment background of a child the experience of affects and the capacity to regulate them differs (e.g., Fonagy et al., 2002). Hence it is not primarily the behavior we are interested in but the role of underlying dysregulated affects and their ties to specific attachment experiences of children.

Outcomes of Aggression

Aggressive behavior is defined as a conduct problem according to the DSM-IV and ICD-10. This suggests that it is primarily an interactive phenomenon as aggressive behavior very often is directed towards others, although there is high variability. It seems to become manifest in an interactive setting, and as we will discuss later, also develops interactively. Auto-aggression, ranging from slight self injuries to committing suicide, might also be understood as a relationship problem in terms of withdrawal from social life, but we will not focus on auto-aggression specifically in the current paper. Various classifications of aggressive behavior are reported: hostile vs. instrumental, physical vs. indirect, and active vs. reactive, but all of the variations of aggressive behavior can be organized along one question: Who is victimized by whom in what way and to what extent? The *who* defines the victim that can either be a person, a group of persons, or an object (e.g., vandalism). *By whom* defines the offender that can either be a person or a group of persons. *The way* of the assault defines the behavior itself that can be direct or indirect, verbal or physical, and with or without assisting objects (like weapons). It is mainly the decision of the offender to choose what fits subjectively best to reach the goal. Finally, *the extent* defines the caused harm ranging from intimidation to the loss of life. Independent of these dimensions it is necessary that the act is intended to harm or at least that the harmful consequences are consciously hazarded. Therefore, the harm can be the target of the action itself or it is a crucial part on the path to reaching a goal. To kick a ball in a person's face by mistake therefore is not aggressive behavior. This shows the importance of the mental dimension in judging behavior as aggressive. An unwittingly caused harm may appear to be an aggressive act, it is not per definition, but can become so by the interpretation of others. Therefore, aggressive behavior covers a wide variety of different outcomes. Respect for this variability by analyzing individual motives and needs is important for the everyday dealing with aggressive behavior in order to understand and act appropriately. For research purposes this variability should be and is respected by working out specific similarities and differences in cognitive and emotional skills within different types of aggression. Is physical aggression accompanied by the same inner psychic structure as indirect forms of aggression? A better understanding of the *why* rather than the *how* of a behavioral outcome could lead to more specific intervention strategies (Persson, 2005a). Aggressive behavior can be seen as a result of any inner psychic process caused by external or internal stimuli that cannot be regulated in any other way. The main components in these inner psychic processes are affects and the close tie of specific affects to the attachment and the self system. Affect regulation does not mean only the reduction of affective intensity, but rather a modulation of intensity, quality, or duration of emotions. The interpreted intimidation of the (psychic) self could possibly bring about an emotional reaction that could lead to aggressive behavior. This of course is a highly subjective act of interpretation. Understanding this subjective view is our key to finding out more about the inner psychic dynamics underlying aggressive behavior. If the intimidation is elusive from the outside we focus on the maladaptive aggressive regulation of it; if the intimidation is not elusive we often interpret aggressive acts as cold blooded or ruthless. In the public view, aggression is often seen as the latter type because people do not understand the meaning of it and are therefore more highly affected by it. An adolescent who hits a schoolmate without any obvious reason is seen as rather cold blooded and we are likely to be negatively affected with hate and scorn. The same adolescent hitting a schoolmate who is always teasing him may inspire affection or appreciation although this is only a different subjective interpretation of the same observable behavior. It is mainly aggressive behavior for which people cannot find a meaning that causes helplessness in dealing with it, often seen in teachers or caregivers. Of course helplessness can also result when the meaning behind the act of violence is seen but is rather unspecific and hardly suggestive of a violent response. Let us give an example: Children often show aggressive behavior when a sibling is born. Imagine a three-year-old boy who is always trying to dump his six-month-old sister out of her crib. Like Bowlby, we would see these aggressive acts as motivated by being anxious about separation from the caregiver (Bowlby, 1973). A helpless mother is likely to primarily protect the little baby (which is obviously necessary) rather than to increase affection towards the older boy as she is likely to interpret the older boy's behavior as primarily harmful. Depending on her interpretation of the boy's intention and her subsequent reaction (e.g., soothing behavior vs. punishment) the boy will be able to cope with his anxiety in a way which enhances security again or feel rejected and hurt and regulate this narcisstic hurt by outward or inward aggression. This interpretation of mental states, which underlies behavior, is crucial for this process and again we are within the mentalization concept in Fonagy's terms. Mentalization implies the adequate attribution of mental states (intentions, feelings, etc.) to self and others, and therefore the basis for understanding the meaning of behavior. These mental states often are unconscious and therefore even more difficult to recognize. An inappropriate attribution of mental states is likely to lead to a misinterpretation of behavior. This wrong interpretation could then become the starting point of a vicious cycle as the intimidation is increased rather than reduced. Therefore, it is the understanding of the subjectively interpreted intimidation and consequently its reduction that should be efficient.

Aggression and Aggressive Behavior

Now we would like to explain our understanding of aggression as an essential part of the emotional system and aggressive behavior as a maladaptive regulation strategy, along with a brief discussion of several definitions. As will be described below, we understand aggression as an emotional reaction to a threatened self. Everybody knows what an emotion is until one is asked to give a definition (Fehr & Russell, 1984). This more than 20-year-old well-known citation illustrates a problem that can be easily adapted to aggression as it is an everyday phenomenon that is not yet clearly defined. Searching in various psychological textbooks, there are two major groups of definitions of the term aggression: One group describes aggression as a specific behavior that is directed to the intended harm of others or a kind of deliberately unfriendly behavior (Berk, 2004; Gerrig & Zimbardo, 2002). On the other hand, aggression is also defined as a mental dimension, either a primarily self protecting one (Fonagy, Moran, & Target, 1993), or an ability to show activity that can be expressed in forms ranging from self assertion to cruelty (Remschmidt, Schmidt, & Strunk, 1990). These differences accompany two major questions: First, is aggression a part of or an outcome of the individual inner world? As a mental dimension, it can become a reason for aggressive behavior; as an outcome, it is the behavior itself. The second question focuses on the distinction of constructive vs. destructive aggression: Does nondestructive aggression exist? If it is seen as a mental process, state or ability, this question is not asked, as aggression can only be expressed if defined as a behavior. Aggression as a behavior can be both constructive or destructive (Cierpka, 2002; Petermann, 2000) although sometimes aggression is not considered to be an appropriate term for the constructive part of it, so there are also terms like assertion for the constructive part (Dornes, 1997). Defining aggression as a behavior, we consequently would have to argue that individuals who do not show deliberately harmful behavior are not aggressive. In our opinion this causes confusion as our inner psychic experience is different. If we have the intention of harming an object (or person) but do not execute our intended action, we are not aggressive in behavioral terms. When we consider aggressive behavior as a maladaptive regulation strategy of an inner psychic process closely connected to our emotional system, we have a synergy of both definitions, as aggression now is an inner psychic dimension that can lead to harmful action, as well as to constructive acts of self assertion, and is linked to various emotions like anger, anxiety, and shame. Aggressive and violent behavior – both terms are often used synonymously – can now be seen as inappropriate interactive expressions of aggression rather than as aggression itself. Maybe it is time here to differentiate between aggression and other emotional states, mainly anger, to clarify our argument. If a person feels aggression, any part of his self can be affected. To differentiate, we would argue that it depends on the part of the self that feels intimidated for the person. Physical attack causes aggression that is related to fear, whereas psychic attack, like an insult, may cause anger instead, but both can lead to aggressive behavior if there are no strategies for behavioral regulation or if the person is unable to use them. Therefore, aggression is seen as an indicator, which leads to feelings appropriate to the situation. The appropriate emotional response or mixture of emotional responses can be seen as highly individual and therefore aggression can be accompanied by several emotional states. Moreover, the experience of a threat to any part of the self depends on the stability and flexibility of the self. A stable and flexible self – which is associated with a secure inner working model – is less likely to be affected and therefore is less likely to experience aggression. The person can feel angry, however, as anger also can be activated without aggression. Consequently, aggression itself is not pathologic per se but can also be part of a healthy mental system. Antisocial and delinquent behavior can also be seen as pathologic manifestations of aggression that lead to these behavioral patterns rather than as a simple reaction to frustration from the outer world. Fonagy et al. (2002) describe aggressive behavior as a maladaptive protection of the psychic self due to a lack of mentalizing capacities. This view could have high impact on intervention strategies, and, as we will discuss later, on prevention, as not the reduction of aggression itself is the focus, but rather the capacity to regulate one's own negative aggression-related feelings, an argument that we will take up again later.

We now have defined aggression and aggressive and violent behavior in short. Finally we want to add the term "aggressiveness" into our terminological discussion. Aggressiveness often is used to describe an inner disposition (Heinemann & Hopf, 2004) and therefore it seems to make sense to consider it as a part of temperament. So there is a system of aggressiveness, aggression, and aggressive behavior that can become a pathologic occurrence rather than being pathologic itself. Aggressiveness is a kind of trait of sensitivity of our aggression system, and aggression is closely connected to our emotional system. In the figure below we try to illustrate these connections. In a given situation, we interpret the meaning for ourselves and therefore this leads to an emotional reaction. When we see our psychic self threatened, aggression, fear, anger, anxiety, and so on might follow depending on our interpretation of the intensity and quality of the threat. This now can lead to aggressive behavior, but also to other regulating behavior as well. Mentalization and attachment (manifested in one's inner working model) has impact on this interpretation process as well as on the reflective choice of our regulating action.

Our emotional system is our only "sense organ" directed toward the internal world, whereas five sense organs are directed toward the outer world. Emotions tell us the meaning of outer world stimuli for ourselves (Solms & Turnbull, 2002; Tyson & Tyson, 1990) and thus cause action readiness (Frijda, 1986). Without emotions we would be blind to our motives. Feelings as a crucial part of our emotional system let us gain awareness of these meanings, although this awareness can be elusive. In Star Trek Mr.

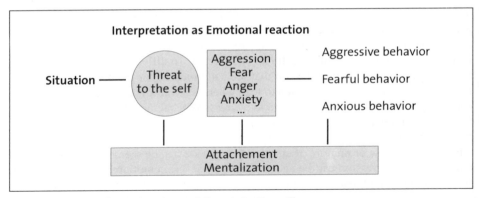

Figure 1. Emotional reactions toward threats to the self.

Spock once said: "Without emotions there is no reason for violence." He seems to be right, as we would not gain awareness of the meaning of stimuli (external or internal) for ourselves without emotions. So there would not be violence without emotions, but there would be no other kind of interactive behavior as well. Emotions thus play an important role in our action regulation and they not only screen our inner world, but they also let us recognize the inner worlds of others and influence our cognitive processes such as recognition, remembering, and so on (e.g., Frijda, 1986).

Let us consider aggression as a mental state or ability that is brought forth by a strong threat to our self system. As we illustrated above, threat to the self system can also yield fear and anxiety depending on the quality, intensity, and specificity of the intimidation. Aggression therefore can be seen as our inner psychic "threat indicating or regulating system." It judges the necessity of defending the self (physical and psychological) that can vary depending on the accompanying emotion. Consequently you can be angry or anxious without being aggressive as long as your psychic self is not affected as a whole. This view could possibly explain that the intensity of anger was not yet consistently found to be directly related to aggressive behavior (Orobio de Castro, Merk, Koops, Veerman, & Bosch, 2005). It also was demonstrated that the relationship between high emotionality and behavior problems depends on the quality of emotion regulation (Eisenberg et al., 1995). Therefore aggressive behavior becomes more likely when higher aggressiveness increases the frequency to interpret a situation as self affecting or when regulation capacities are reduced – or even both.

Developmental Aspects

Research on aggression in the past decades has been conducted mainly on school age and adolescent children, although aggression is already present in kindergarten (Tremblay, 2000). A study of Tremblay's research group in Montreal reveals that in 17-month-old children, physical aggression can be observed in a large number of children with a peak from 17 to 30 months (Tremblay et al., 1999). Interestingly, this is the same age at which the self is developing. Additionally, results on the relationship between low self esteem and externalizing problems in school age children are reported (Donnellan, Trzesniewski, Robins, Moffit, & Caspi, 2005), which might support the idea of aggression as an indicator of threat to the self. The reported evidence that between two and five years of age there is a marked decrease in aggressive behavior could possibly be seen as an outcome of increased regulation strategies. We would regard this development in emotion and self regulation as crucial for the manifestation of early childhood aggression from ages two to five. As emotional development can be seen as a highly interactive process within an attachment relationship (Fonagy, 1999; Nadel & Muir, 2005; Sroufe, Carlson, Levy, & Egland, 1999), family environment and attachment quality should have a strong impact on aggressive behavior. This is supported by results of Lyons-Ruth (Lyons-Ruth & Jacobvitz, 1999) who reports close ties between disorganized attachment classification at age 18 months and aggressive behavior at age five. In general, a family environment in early childhood where there is little warmth and support and a high degree of negativity and conflict shows high predictive value for aggressive behavior and even delinquency in adolescence (Fonagy et al., 1993; Gauthier, 2003). Moreover, studies on self-regulation and empathy have increasingly documented the importance of what is being played out between infants and their caregivers. Family climate and dyadic and triadic family interaction have impact on attachment (Ainsworth, 1985; von Klitzing, Bürgin, von Wyl, & Perren, 2001). Children from 18 months to 36 months of age are dealing with strong tendencies toward self assertion, opposition, and often physical aggression; thus, they have to develop internal control of those impulses. Internal control is gradually forming within the child under the influence of the interaction with parental milieu (Gauthier, 2003). The manner and quality of reaction of caregivers to these mentioned tendencies has strong impact on the developmental pathways of aggressive behavior (Keenan & Shaw, 1994) even if temperament is considered to be an influencing factor on gaining impulse control (Kochanska, 1995). Inappropriate emotion regulation strategies combined with maternal dominance are predictors of disruptive behaviors. Within the same period of time the moral emotions of shame and guilt develop and consequently play a major role in the internalisation of morally based impulse control strategies. We assume that above all the use of shame and humiliation as sanctioning strategies in the context of wrongdoing (which often includes aggressive behavior) has a tight link to the development of dysregulated aggression. Shame is inherently linked with weakening and threatening the self. Recapitulating this developmental stage is a major step in the acquisition of a capacity to control aggressive impulses as the self gains stability on the one hand and several regulation strategies develop on the other. Aggressive as well as prosocial behaviors are distinct parts of the children's behavioral repertoire from around two years of life (Coie & Dodge, 1998; Persson, 2005a; Zahn-Waxler, Radke-Yarrow, Wagner, & Chapman, 1992). Gauthier (2003) mentions a sequence of secure attachment, exploration, self assertion and aggression, prohibition and constraints, and control of aggression (or its opposite). Such control is often accompanied by empathy. Attachment theory allows us to understand this as it is fundamentally a regulatory theory (Shore, 2000).

Aggression and Empathy

Strayer and Roberts (2004) suggest two possible models for the association between empathy, anger, and aggression. In a so called "main effects model," empathy with the enhanced emotional and cognitive understanding of others inhibits both anger and aggression. In the so called "mediated model," the impact of empathy is on anger, and it is lower levels of anger that result in less aggression. They also argue that the understanding of the relationship between anger, empathy, and aggression has practical and theoretical implications for understanding aggression in children. The results reported in this study where assessment is based on direct observation rather than on reports by adults or teachers show support for a main effect model and give clear evidence of a complex relationship between anger and aggression. As in studies with school-aged children (Pepler, Craig, & Roberts, 1998) aggressive behaviors have been observed accompanied by neutral and even positive emotional expressions. This indicates that aggression also occurs in the absence of (visible) anger. Cognitive emotional processing models (Eisenberg, 2000; Roberts, 1999) also suggest that anger and aggression both result from an underlying difficulty in regulating emotions and the self in social interactions. Therefore, the expression of anger with words or gestures or physical aggression seems to be the outcome of individual dysregulation that is modified by additional factors caused by the situation. Therefore, this outcome should be explained by analyzing the operation of self regulation and empathy during episodes of conflict (Strayer & Roberts, 2004). Empathy plays a crucial role in moral and socio-emotional development (Eisenberg, 2005; Smith, 2006) and is thus an essential part of social behavior (Shamay-Tsoory, Tomer, Goldsher, Berger, & Aharon-Peretz, 2004). It is defined as "an affective response that stems from the apprehension or comprehension of another's emotional state or condition and is similar to what the other person is feeling or would be expected to feel in the given situation" (Eisenberg, 2005). Other definitions describe empathy as "sensitivity to, and understanding of the mental states of others" (Smith, 2006). According to these two definitions one can identify two underlying human abilities to which the term empathy refers: One is mental perspective taking described as cognitive empathy and the other is vicarious sharing of emotions described as emotional empathy (Smith, 2006). The cognitive aspect of these abilities has strong synonymy with theory of mind (Gopnik & Slaughter, 1991). Of course there is an ongoing discussion regarding whether these two aspects are inseparable aspects of a unitary system or if they are two separate systems that influence each other by mutually expanding or interacting (see Smith, 2006). For our purposes we see potential in this distinction for explaining the relationship between empathy and aggression as it provides a theoretical background for defining various types of empathic deficits. This might help to explain results that, for example, social intelligence (defined as cognitive capacity) is positively related to indirect forms of aggressive behavior (Kaukiainen et al., 1999) or that theory of mind abilities are positively related to forms of bullying and peer rejection in school (Sutton, Smith, & Swettenham, 1999; Villanueva Badenes, Estevan, & Bacete, 2000). This strengthens our suggestion that aggressive behavior is a maladaptive regulation strategy and that emotions play a crucial role in understanding its origins. This is supported by consistent results that a negative relationship exists between empathy (focusing emotional aspects) and aggressive behavior of either kind (Eisenberg, 2005; Kaukiainen et al., 1999). This concept of cognitive and emotional aspects of empathy shows agreement with Fonagy's description of mentalization that can be seen as a kind of emotionalized theory of mind (Fonagy et al., 2002). Even in the preschool years, limited emotional reflectiveness, which can be described as the capacity for perspective taking under emotional arousal, was shown to be related to aggressive behavior (Juen, 2005). Additionally, dysregulated aggressive and even traumatic themes in preschooler's narratives are related to both limited reflectiveness and more aggressive behavior (Juen, Benecke, von Wyl, Schick, & Cierpka, 2005).

Gender Differences

One of the most robust findings in the research literature is that boys are more aggressive than girls (Coie & Dodge, 1998). Former and recent typologies divide aggression into physical and relational aggression (Ostorov & Keating, 2004). Physical aggression implies intended harm to others through physical acts (e.g., hitting, kicking) or verbal threat of such acts, whereas relational aggression implies intended harm caused to others by damaging social relationships or feelings of peer acceptance. It is often reported that physical aggression is the domain of boys whereas relational aggression is girls' theatre (Crick, Casas, & Ku, 1999), but there is not much empirical observational data on either the conceptual distinction nor the relationship of these forms of aggression and gender, especially during the preschool years (Ostorov & Keating, 2004). Interestingly, even before children reach school age, they hold systematic beliefs about the relationship between gender and aggression according to the aforementioned results (Giles & Heyman, 2005). Reasons for these often reported gender differences are rather speculative at the moment. Sometimes it is mentioned that boys and girls may aggress differently in order to facilitate distinctly different gender-specific social goals such as boys seeking more physical dominance and girls seeking more secure social relationships (Crick & Grotpeter, 1995). Although these differences are of high relevance, we agree with Persson, who makes a distinction between the observable behavior (*the how*) and the underlying motivation (*the why*), that have not often been the focus of empirical research (Persson, 2005a). We would argue that the underlying inner psychic dynamics of aggressive behavior – namely its self-protecting function – are comparable for boys and girls. Differences in aggressive behavior that can be observed and have widely been reported might be due to the moderating effect of empathy which also varies between girls and boys (see Eisenberg, 2000). This affects regulation that can result in various types of observable behavior. As aggression is a highly interactive phenomenon it is worth analyzing the targets rather than the actors of both aggressive and prosocial behavior in peer interactions, an aspect that has gained scant respect although it can be expected that being targeted by peers has influence on the socio-emotional development of the victim as well. Stability of peer victimization has been considered during elementary school but the literature is scarce for preschooler's victimization stability (Persson, 2005b). There is some evidence that male victims of relational aggression were significantly less prosocial than their nonvictimized peers (Crick et al., 1999). Overall results on reciprocity of aggression and victimization are inconsistent, especially for preschool children (Persson, 2005b). A final remark in this section is worth mentioning as the amount of experienced victimization might have implications for intervention and even prevention as it is not only the outcome of aggressive behavior, but also a mediating factor for diverse problems. Being bullied (or victimized) may have serious short and long term consequences including depression, anxiety, low self esteem, and relationship problems (Fox & Boulton, 2006).

Aspects of Prevention

Because of this given developmental view on aggression and aggressive behavior, one may come to think in a rather pessimistic way. Aggressive behavior is transmitted in the early years where internal models are inscribed in a very sensitive brain (Gauthier, 2003). We only can observe the outcome and try to find solutions. If prevention is defined as an intervention that occurs before the onset of a disorder (Bor, 2004), we really seem to have a problem as the onset of a conduct disorder is often rather early – around five years of age. This implies on the one hand that preventive strategies have to be undertaken as early as possible, and on the other hand, that preventive strategies based on a universal approach should respect that the probability of having children in need of specific intervention in the group is likely, even within the preschool years, a fact that could have impact on the effectiveness of an intervention when it is not respected. These implications are important to increase effectiveness of so-called primary prevention by embedding specific programs within a package of measures also including additional support for children in need. For evaluation of programs this implies that the effects should not only be measured in general, but also detached for several subgroups like high or low risk samples. The effects of the same prevention strategies are expected to be different when comparing high risk and low risk groups. Therefore, we would like to introduce the question: "What works for whom?"

Implications for Intervention and Prevention

Prevention of aggressive behavior is a type of support for emotional development. As stated, we consider aggressive behavior as a regulation strategy for protecting the self (physical or psychic). Aggression is seen as an emotional indicator for a threatened (psychic) self. Aggression therefore is seen as an ability rather than as a deficit. We need it like we need anxiety, fear, or anger. We need our emotional system, and therefore aggression, to appraise the meaning of stimuli for ourselves. In our opinion you have to consider prevention across the life cycle. The major aim of any prevention should be the support for general developmental expenses. Aggressive behavior as an aggression-based regulation strategy therefore can be adaptive as long as the interpretation of stimuli as threatening is appropriate and there is no other effective strategy to deal with the situation. But this protection strategy can become maladaptive when either the interpretation is inappropriate or the strategy is ineffective. Both reading social situations and reflective action planning are crucially influenced by mentalizing capacities as we stated before. These mentalizing capacities develop within the first years of life embedded in attachment relationships. With regard to prevention we propose to put even more emphasis on the following two considerations:

First, in our view, attachment and self aspects have to become more central aspects in the prevention of aggressive behavior as a disorder. The primary "trigger" of a child's social competence and confidence is a secure attachment relationship, which provides the developing child with the resilience, trust, and ability to regulate emotions and to develop mentalizing and self reflective capacities which may be crucial when encountering adverse life events and hazards. Therefore the most effective general approach to prevention is the support of building secure attachment which can be done best from the very beginning of life from birth, or even during pregnancy. Efforts to help young families establish secure developmental environments for their children are increasingly given. This is an important additional step in dealing with the problem of aggressive behavior.

Second, the major aim of any prevention should be support of dealing with developmental tasks. Within this consideration we should furthermore differentiate between various groups of children. One group is at high risk of not adequately resolving forthcoming expenses. Another group – sometimes overlapping with the first group – already failed to resolve expenses, which increases the risk of failing in the future. A third group is likely to resolve forthcoming expenses and therefore does not even need support at that stage of life. As you can see in clinical research, almost any kind of psychic disorder can occur with any kind of emotional and self regulation deficits (Fonagy et al., 2002; OPD-Taskforce, 2001; Rudolf, 2002). Crucial in development is a stable self with stable capacities in regulation emotions. With several emphases this should be a key element of preventive intervention. A review of Yoshikawa (1995) clearly illustrates that most effective prevention focuses on very early family and early education support. Also, Svanberg (1998) reports clear benefits of early and prenatal involvement and even reports high economic benefits for the health system. The earlier prevention starts, the more effective it is. This does not indicate the reverse effect that later prevention is ineffective. Programs and provisions in primary and high school and even beyond are also highly important for two reasons. They are an essential addition for stabilizing positive effects and they are an effective tool for supporting development in the targeted ages. Basic skills for social life can also be learned after the (primary) sensitive phase for emotional development during the first three years of life. Other caregivers, such as teachers and nurses, can compensate for the lack of a stable emotional attachment that was not present in early childhood. Prevention and intervention should try to manipulate the origins rather than the outcomes. This means that the focus should lie on abilities not yet developed adequately like situation analyzing capacities (e.g., emotion recognition) as well as emotion regulation strategies. Consequently, violence prevention in the preschool years should focus on empathy rather than aggression. Moreover, this only can be fruitful in a productive surrounding. This means in short that it is not only the teaching of skills but also the application of these skills in daily life. If you teach alternative skills for problem solving, children have to get the opportunity to use them as well. Moreover, prevention means support of developmental tasks by creating resilience. With regard to intervention, we also suggest shifting the focus from behavior control and the improvement of cognitive capacities to a more emotion oriented approach where the recognition, understanding, and the regulation of emotion in affectively relevant contexts becomes a more central focus of intervention programs.

As a conclusion, we argue that preventive work should start early, last for a longer time and should be appropriate to the needs of specific age groups, always focusing on the retrieval of resources that have not been fully developed. This rather psychological task has to be accompanied by socioeconomic and socio-political provision that focus on the reduction of risks such as poverty, unemployment, and low education. With one sole step you will not reach the goal.

References

Ainsworth, M. D. S. (1985). Patterns of infant-mother attachments: Antecendents and effects on development. *Bulletin of the New York Academy of Medicine, 61*(9), 771–791.

Berk, L. E. (2004). *Development through the lifespan.* Boston, MA: Pearson Education.

Bor, W. (2004). Prevention and treatment of childhood and adolescent aggression and antisocial behavior: a selective review. *Australian and New Zealand Journal of Psychiatry, 38,* 373–380.

Bowlby, J. (1973). *Attachment and loss: Vol.2. Separation, anxiety and anger.* London: Hogarth Press.

Cierpka, M. (2002). *Kinder mit aggressivem Verhalten* [Children with aggressive behavior]. Göttingen, Germany: Hogrefe.

Coie, L. D., & Dodge, K. A. (1998). Aggression and antisocial behavior. In W. Damon & N. Eisenberg (Eds.), *Handbook of child psychology: Vol 3, Social, emotional and personality development.* New York: Wiley.

Crick, N. R., & Grotpeter, J. K. (1995). Relational aggression, gender, and social psychological adjustment. *Child Development, 66,* 710–722.

Crick, N. R., Casas, J. F., & Ku, H. (1999). Relational and physical forms of peer victimization in preschool. *Developmental Psychology, 35,* 376–385.

Denham, S., Caverly, S., Schmidt, M., Blair, K., DeMulder, E., Caal, S., et al. (2002). Preschool understanding of emotions: Contributions to classroom anger and aggression. *Journal of Child Psychology and Psychiatry, 43*(7), 901–916.

Donnellan, M. B., Trzesniewski, K. H., Robins, R. W., Moffit, T. E., & Caspi, A. (2005). Low self esteem is related to aggression, antisocial behavior and delinquency. *Psychological Science, 15*(4), 328–335.

Dornes, M. (1997). *Die frühe Kindheit* [The early childhood] (5th ed.). Frankfurt/Main, Germany: Fischer TB.

Eisenberg, N. (2000). Emotion, regulation, and moral development. *Annual Review Psychology, 51,* 665–697.

Eisenberg, N. (2005). The development of empathy-related responding. *Nebraska Symposium on Motivation, 51,* 73–117.

Eisenberg, N., Fabes, R. A., Murphy, B. C., Maszk, P., Smith, M., & Karbon, M. (1995). The role of emotionality and regulation in children's social functioning: A longitudinal study. *Child Development, 66,* 1360–1384.

Fehr, B., & Russell, J. A. (1984). Concept of emotion viewed from a prototype perspective. *Journal of Experimental Psychology: General, 113,* 464–486.

Fonagy, P. (1999). *Attachment and psychoanalysis.* New York: Other Press.

Fonagy, P., Gergely, G., Jurist, E. L., & Target, M. (2002). *Affect regulation, mentalization, and the development of the self.* Stuttgart, Germany: Klett-Cotta.

Fonagy, P., Moran, G. S., & Target, M. (1993). Aggression and the psychological self. *International Journal of Psycho-Analysis, 74*(3), 471–486.

Fox, C. L., & Boulton, M. J. (2006). Friendship as a moderator of the relationship between social skills problems and peer victimization. *Aggressive Behavior, 32,* 110–121.

Frijda, N. H. (1986). *The emotions.* Cambridge: Cambridge University Press.

Gauthier, Y. (2003). Infant mental health as enter the third millennium: Can we prevent aggression? *Infant Mental Health Journal, 24*(3), 296–308.

Gerrig, R., & Zimbardo, P. (2002). *Psychology and life.* Boston, MA: Pearson Education.

Giles, J. W., & Heyman, G. D. (2005). Young children's beliefs about the relationship between gender and aggressive behavior. *Child Development, 76*(1), 107–121.

Gopnik, A., & Slaughter, V. (1991). Young children's understanding of changes in their mental states. *Child Development, 62,* 98–110.

Heinemann, E., & Hopf, H. (2004). *Psychische Störungen in Kindheit und Jugend* [Psychic disorders in childhood and adolescence]. Stuttgart, Germany: Kohlhammer.

Juen, F. (2005). *Das Denken über das Denken und Fühlen – Psychische Realität, reflexive Kompetenz und Problemverhalten im Vorschulalter* [The thinking about thinking and feeling – psychic reality, reflexive competence, and problem behavior in preschool age]. Marburg, Germany: Tectum Verlag.

Juen, F., Benecke, C., von Wyl, A., Schick, A., & Cierpka, M. (2005). Repräsentanz, psychische Struktur und Verhaltensprobleme im Vorschulalter [Mental representation, psychic structure, and behavior problems in preschool children]. *Praxis der Kinderpsychologie und -psychiatrie, 54*(3), 191–209.

Kaukiainen, A., Björnkqvist, K., Lagerspetz, K., Österman, K., Salmivalli, C., Rothberg, S., et al. (1999). The relationships between social intelligence, empathy, and three types of aggression. *Aggressive Behavior, 28,* 81–89.

Keenan, K., & Shaw, D. S. (1994). The development of aggression in toddlers: A study on low income families. *Journal of abnormal Child Psychology, 22*(1), 53–77.

Kochanska, G. (1995). Children's temperament, mother's discipline and security of attachment: Multiple pathways to emerging internalization. *Child Development, 66,* 597–615.

Lewis, M. (2000). Self-conscious emotions: Embarrassment, pride, shame, and guilt. In M. Lewis & J.M. Haviland-Jones (Eds.), *Handbook of emotions* (2nd ed.). New York: Guilford.

Lyons-Ruth, K., & Jacobvitz, D. (1999). Attachment disorganization: Unresolved loss, relational violence, and lapses in behavioral and attentional processes. In J. Cassidy & P. Shaver (Eds.), *Handbook of Attachment.* New York: Guilford.

Nadel, J., & Muir, D. (Eds.). (2005). *Emotional development.* New York: Oxford University Press.

OPD Taskforce. (2001). *Operationalized psychodynamic diagnostics (OPD).* Cambridge, MA: Hogrefe.

Orobio de Castro, B., Merk, W., Koops, W., Veerman, J. W., & Bosch, J. D. (2005). Emotions in social information processing and their relations with reactive and proactive aggression in referred aggressive boys. *Journal of Clinical Child and Adolescent Psychology, 34*(1), 105–116.

Osofsky, J. D. (1995). The effects of exposure to violence on young children. *American Psychologist, 50*(9), 782–788.

Ostorov, J. M., & Keating, C. F. (2004). Gender differences in preschool aggression during free play and structured interactions: An observational study. *Social Development, 13*(2), 255–277.

Pepler, D., Craig, W., & Roberts, W. (1998). Observations of aggressive and nonaggresive children on the school playground. *Merill Palmer Quarterly, 44,* 55–76.

Persson, G. E. (2005a). Developmental perspectives on prosocial and aggressive motives in pre-schoolers' peer interaction. *International Journal of Behavioral Development, 29*(1), 80–91.

Persson, G. E. (2005b). Young children's prosocial and aggressive behaviors and their experiences of being targeted for similar behaviors by peers. *Social Development, 14*(2), 206–228.

Petermann, F., (2000). *Aggressionsdiagnostik* [Diagnosis of aggression]. Göttingen, Germany: Hogrefe.

Remschmidt, H., Schmidt, M. H., & Strunk, P. (1990). Gewalt in Familien und ihre Verhinder-ung. Zugleich ein Plädoyer für die Abschaffung des elterlichen Züchtigungsrechts [Violence in families and its prevention. Also a plea for abolishing the parental right to inflict physical punishment. A report of the "Violence Commission" of the federal government]. *Praxis der Kinderpsychologie und -psychiatrie, 39*, 162–167.

Roberts, W. (1999). The socialization of emotion expression: Relations with prosocial behavior and competence in five samples. *Canadian Journal of Behavioral Science, 31*, 72–85.

Rudolf, G. (2002). Gaining insight and structural capability as goals of psychodynamic psycho-therapy. *Zeitschrift für Psychosomatische Medizin und Psychotherapie, 48*(2), 163–173.

Sereny, G. (1999). *Cries unheard: Why children kill.* New York: Metropolitan Books.

Shamay-Tsoory, S. G., Tomer, R., Goldsher, D., Berger, D., & Aharon-Peretz, J. (2004). Impair-ment in cognitive and affective empathy in patients with brain lesions: Anatomic and cogni-tive correlates. *Journal of Clinical and Experimental Neuropsychology, 26*(8), 1113–1127.

Shore, A. N. (2000). Attachment and the regulation of the right brain. *Attachment and Human Development, 2*(1), 23–47.

Smith, A. (2006). Cognitive empathy and emotional empathy in human behavior and evolution. *The Psychological Record, 59*, 3–21.

Solms, M., & Turnbull, O. (2002). *The brain and the innerworld.* London: Other Press.

Sroufe, A., Carlson, E., Levy, A., & Egland, B. (1999). Implications of attachment theory for de-velopmental psychopathology. *Development and Psychopathology, 11*, 1–13.

Strayer, J., & Roberts, W. (2004). Empathy and observed anger and aggression in five year olds. *Social Development, 13*(1), 11–13.

Sutton, J., Smith, P. K., & Swettenham, J. (1999). Bullying and 'theory of mind:' A critique of the 'social skill deficit' view of antisocial behavior. *Social Development, 8*(1), 117–127.

Svanberg, P. O. G. (1998). Attachment, resilience, and prevention. *Journal of Mental Health, 7*(6), 543–578.

Tremblay, R. E. (2000). The development of aggressive behavior during childhood: What have we learned in the past century? *International Journal of Behavioral Development, 24*(2), 129–141.

Tremblay, R. E., Japel, C., Perusse, D., McDuff, P., Boivin, M., Zoccolollo, M., et al. (1999). The search for the 'onset' of physical aggression: Rousseau and Bandura revisited. *Criminal Behavior and Mental Health, 9*, 8–23.

Tyson, P., & Tyson, R. L. (Eds.). (1990). *Psychoanalytic theories of development.* New Haven, NJ: Yale UP.

Villanueva Badenes, L., Estevan, R. A. C., & Bacete, F. J. G. (2000). Theory of mind and peer rejection at school. *Social Development, 9*(3), 271–283.

von Klitzing, K., Bürgin, D., von Wyl, A., & Perren, S. (2001). Psychiatric symptoms and psy-chosocial strengths of kindergarten children: Dynamics and stability and change, associations with family and peer relationships. Unpublished research proposal. Basel, Switzerland: Uni-versity of Basel.

Yoshikawa, H. (1995). Long-term effects of early childhood programs on social outcomes and delinquency. *The Future of Children, 5*(3), 51–75.

Zahn-Waxler, C., Radke-Yarrow, M., Wagner, E., & Chapman, M. (1992). Development of con-cern for others. *Developmental Psychology, 28*(1), 126–136.

13 Preschool Prevention of Emotional-Social Disorders and Aggressive Behavior

Johannes Bach

Introduction: Emotional-Social Disorders in Childhood

Emotional-Social Disorders

Emotional-social disorders have a very high rate of prevalence in childhood and adolescence. In contrast to the presentations and impressions given by the mass media, there are not only externalizing disorders like aggression and use of force. Although aggressive behaviors and youth delinquency have a high rate of media presence, there exists a high rate of prevalence for internalizing behaviors like anxiety and depression in childhood and adolescence. It is rather difficult to compare the rates of prevalence in the different epidemiological studies because they are based on different definitions of disorders and systems of classifications (Petermann, 2005).

One of the largest surveys in recent years was the British child and adolescent mental health study (Ford, Goodman, & Meltzer 2003) in Great Britain with 10,438 children and adolescents between 5 and 15 years of age. It quickly became obvious that 9.47% of the participants had one or more disorder (DSM-IV). About 6% had an externalizing disorder and 3.77% had an anxiety disorder. One remarkable result showed that 20% of the children had a disorder which could not be characterized directly – they had severe impairments without fulfilling the criteria for one disorder completely. Furthermore, one third of the children and adolescents (29.7%) had more than one disorder: The comorbidity seems to be very high. Depression is particularly notable with a rate of 66%.

These phenomena raise the question of whether the categorical diagnostic approach is an appropriate way to describe emotional-social disorders. A dimensional description of disorders might be more appropriate because many disorders cannot be allocated to a specific category and the comorbidity between the disorders is remarkable high. Particularly in the child- and adolescent age groups, because the diagnostic criteria are not distinctly defined and/or are not based on empirical evidence (Petermann, 2005), it is very difficult to separate the clinical from the nonclinical disorders. In contrast, dimensional descriptions do not define several disorders, but rather sum across groups of them. Furthermore – as opposed to the categorical description – the difference between normality and pathology is considered in a special way (Rutter & Sroufe, 2000). Because of these reasons, we need more epidemiological studies that are oriented towards alternative criteria (e.g., psycho-social impairment) and that express the continuum between health and illness – as opposed to the categorical approach to diagnosis.

At the level of analysis, social-emotional disorders can be divided into the two domains of emotional and social disorders. In real life, these two domains often coexist.

Table 1. Central Domains of Emotional Disorders

1. Inability to perceive emotions (self/others).
2. Inability to express emotions.
3. Inability to regulate emotions (functional regulation).
4. Inability to react appropriately to an emotional occurrence/event (internal/external).

The term "disorder" can be defined or described as a nonsuccessful adaptation between person and environment which leads to an impairment of the person and/or the related persons (Rutter & Sroufe, 2000). In the following section, subdomains of these disorders are described to give a more detailed identification of the two domains of emotional and social disorders. The examples all relate to children and adolescents.

1. The inability to perceive emotions is the most important domain of emotional disorders and causes a lot of other problems concerning feelings (Table 1). On the one hand, these problems are related to one's self and can be described as an inability to perceive one's own emotions or to get entrance to one's own feelings. One example is a depressed person who is – in distinction to common beliefs – not able to feel sadness, and who is not able to perceive his or her own feelings. There is something like emptiness or nothing at all for the person. Similarly, for adolescents who are experiencing changes in moods and feelings – they have great difficulty gaining entrance to their own emotions and feelings. In extreme cases they try to feel their own bodies by hurting or scoring themselves. For these persons, pain is one possible means to get a feeling for themselves as individuals (Southam-Gerow & Kendal, 2002). Another domain is the inability to perceive the emotions of other persons. One consequence can be the misinterpretation of emotional states: Aggressive adolescents, for example, estimate neutral situations incorrectly (e.g., hostile and aggressive) and react because of this interpretation in an inadequate way (Orobio de Castro, 2005). The ability to perceive and understand the emotions of others is a necessary precedent to appropriate behavior (Denham & Burton, 2003).

2. In this context the expression of emotion is very important. It is especially difficult for children with a low speech level and intellectual deficits to express emotions. Some questions are very important for this age group: Does the child have a vocabulary for different emotions? Is the child able to express feelings like sadness or anxiety in difficult situations, and can it build emotional bonds to other persons? Furthermore, can the child express its emotions with facial expressions and gestures in an understandable way? The communication of emotions also depends on the receiver: There is a large difference between talking about feelings with peers or with adults, and with unknown persons or with one's own parents (Volling, McElwain, Notaro, & Herrera, 2002).

3. One more important field is the regulation of emotions. Emotional regulation refers to a person's ability to adequately control his or her emotional responses in arousing situations (Webster-Stratton, 2000). If a child chooses behaviors that are destructive and harmful for himself or for others, this represents a dysfunctional regulation of emotions. This refers to a person whose emotional responses are chronically out of control like a child with behavior problems. For example, expressing anger by spitting and hitting other children is not a functional regulation of emotion. The behavior has negative

consequences for the child himself as well as the other child. As another example, if the reaction to sadness is speechlessness, resignation, and withdrawal for a long time, a problematic pattern of behavior is established (von Salisch, 2002).

4. The functional regulation of emotion indicates that a person has an adequate repertoire of behavior that includes appropriate emotional responses for different situations. These contain both outside occurrences (e.g., an anxiety-generating situation in a new classroom) and intrapersonal conflicts or problems. The ability to find an adequate, controlled adaptation of one's own emotions in different social situations can be described as the modulation of emotion.

Table 2. Central Domains of Social Disorders

1. A disability in interacting in peer-groups.
2. A disability in consistently observing the rules of a group.
3. An inability to empathize with someone's position (cognitive and emotional).
4. A disability in accepting oneself and one's limitations.

1. The first domain of social disorders describes a very fundamental and severe disorder: An inability to interact in peer-groups at all means that the child is not able to find his position in the group or to give others a chance to talk and interact with him (Table 2). A lot of adolescents with these problems also have the same problems in interactions with adults. Relationships and daily interactions with peers are essential for social competence (Webster-Stratton, 2000).

2. An inability to interact with persons of the same age is very often connected with a second aspect of social disorders: problems in accepting and observing the rules of a group. This includes either specific agreements like rules for everyday life (e.g., to remove shoes inside the group) or unspecific agreements (e.g., group rituals).

3. The lack of empathy includes the domain of emotions and cognitions and has extensive consequences. Problems in perspective-taking can lead to incorrect evaluations of situations (e.g., the behavior of another child is interpreted as hostile, although he or she just wants to play alone and does not want to be disturbed). The consequences are inadequate behaviors in ambivalent or difficult situations, which lead to aggressive patterns of behavior or to a vicious circle of misunderstandings. The consequences of aggression are often not realized by the aggressor, and in many cases, neutral behaviors of other persons are misinterpreted as aggressions (Crick & Dodge, 1994). The same problems become obvious in the field of emotions and can lead to inappropriate feelings and behaviors like brutal force as a consequence for lack of empathy (Lemerise & Arsenio, 2000).

4. A last domain, which is rather important for children with mental handicaps, is the inability to accept oneself and one's limitations. As a result of comparing themselves to others, adolescents tend to focus on areas in which they have no or very little skill. In these situations, their expectations for success are rather bad. Perseveration in these problematic areas of behavior coupled with seeking social acceptance can inspire the choosing of inadequate action goals. This, in turn, can lead to poor indications for success, low self esteem, and rejection. The difficulty is fostered because people with

cognitive disabilities have problems abstracting from one single situation or skill and cannot apply their own knowledge and potential.

Risk-Factors and Protective Factors for Emotional-Social Disorders

In this section of the chapter, some risk factors and protective factors are described. These have an effect on emotional-social disorders and are in this respect important for prevention programs in this domain.

Table 3. Risk Factors for Emotional Development (Petermann & Wiedebusch, 2003, p. 96)

- Temperamental vulnerability, e.g., behavioral inhibition, hyperactivity.
- General developmental disorders, e.g., retardation.
- Increased physiological reactivity.
- Lack of readiness to take on responsibility.
- Limited repertoire of emotion regulation strategies.
- Problems in perception.
- Problems in information processing.

There are a lot of risk-factors that can negatively influence the emotional-social development of a child (Table 3). Central aspects are factors of temperament such as behavioral inhibition. They can lead to anxious behavior and withdrawal. They cause negative interactions and make anxiety disorders more likely to occur if these behavior patterns become more and more stable (Essau & Petermann, 2001). In equal measure, developmental retardation is a risk factor for developing an emotional-social disorder. Cognitive functions like perception or social information processing are key issues for emotional development. Mistakes in the perception of social situations very often lead to misunderstandings in interactions. Inadequate reactions in these ambivalent situations can cause general problems in social interactions (Orobio de Castro, 2005).

On the other hand, empirical research has shown a lot of clear and substantial protective factors for the emotional-social development of children which are rather important in the context of intervention and should be considered in planning a new program (Table 4). These are factors like positive temperament, emotional responsiveness and the ability to calm down quickly and to act independently, which is very rare for children with developmental disorders or retardation (Denham, 1998). Some more protective factors consist of self regulating systems for behavior and attention. Specifically, children with special needs often have problems in these domains, e.g., attention deficit hyperactivity disorder (Southam-Gerow & Kendal, 2002).

Achievement motivation is of further importance for children. It is necessary to find themes and topics in which the children are interested. They should be given the opportunity to gain mastery in one domain in order to create feelings of self-efficacy. Positive self-esteem and good marks in school are especially good protective factors, which, unfortunately, children with special needs cannot get.

Table 4. Protective Factors for Emotional Development (Katz et al., 1999)

- Positive temperament.
- Self-efficacy-regulation systems for attention, excitement, behavior.
- "Pleasure in..." – positive achievement motivation.
- Positive self-esteem, attractiveness.
- Abilities which are valued by society and self.
- Positive relationships with friends/peers.
- Good education.
- Spirituality and religious systems.

Simultaneously, it is very important to focus on risk factors as well as positive factors for parents of children with special needs, especially for children with cognitive and emotional-social handicaps who need special-educational treatment on a subclinical level.

The presence of a psychological disorder in parents is one important risk-factor, especially if one of the parents suffers from an emotional-social disorder like depression or a general anxiety disorder (Jones, Filed, Fox, Davalos, & Gomez, 2001; McClure, Brennan, Hammen, & Le Brocque, 2001). Furthermore, a lack of education that could result in inappropriate parental reactions to the behavior of the child can be problematic (Table 5). Low emotional parental sensitivity also poses a risk for the child: Insensitive treatment of the child can lead to deficiencies in emotional development and to a vicious circle of misunderstandings and punishment. There are also some indirect factors that can influence the emotional development of the child, e.g., a low level of parental relationship-satisfaction or a poor socio-economic situation. There may be a lack of resources for the child because the resources are needed in other domains.

On the other hand, however, there are important parental protective factors that can have a positive influence on the emotional development of a child (Table 6). Infants who habitually experience bad conditions, such as infants with unresponsive caregivers, exhibit difficulties in their regulation patterns. One important aspect is the responsiveness of the parents: To perceive the signals of the child and react in an appropriate and sensitive way in an adequate amount of time (Denham, Mitchell-Copeland, Standberg, Auerbach, & Blair, 1997; Saarni, Campos, Camras, & Witherington, 2006). In this context it is rather important that the parents are able to express their own emotions and have the necessary skills to provide an appropriate emotional model for the child (Garner, 1999; Saarni & Buckley, 2002).

Table 5. Parental Risk Factors for Emotional Development (Petermann & Wiedebusch, 2003, p. 97)

- Psychological disorder of one parent, e.g., depression of the mother.
- Inadequate parental education, e.g., overprotection.
- Social pressure in the family-system (low contentment in partnership, low socio-economic status).
- Lack of readiness to take on responsibility.
- Frequent expression of negative emotionality.
- Lack of assistance in child emotion-regulation.

Table 6. Parental Protective Factors for Emotional Development (Katz et al., 1999)

- Responsive parental behavior.
- Verbalizing of emotions: positive and negative emotions.
- Support in child's emotion-modulation (positive and negative emotions).
- Building a secure attachment system with the child.
- Positive relationships with other competent adults.
- Communal organizations and support systems.

Furthermore, it is of prime importance for the child to get support from the parents or other educators in order to develop strategies for emotion regulation. A necessary condition, therefore, is the development of a solid, stable, and trusting relationship with the child. With secure attachments to caregivers, the child can develop his or her exploration behavior and collect more experiences in interacting with the environment that will lead

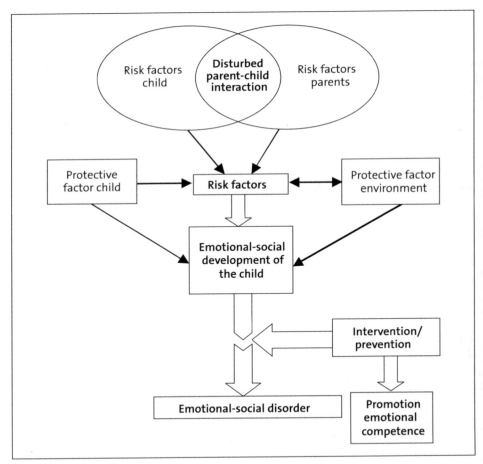

Figure 1. Prevention of emotional-social disorders.

to a larger repertoire of behavior. Volling et al. (2002) underline the importance of making and maintaining an emotional connection with the child; from their point of view the emotional connection is achieved through listening, validating, and understanding children's feelings.

Empirical studies have demonstrated the important influence of significant others in addition to the child's contact with the parents (Saarni, Campos, Camras, & Witherington, 2006). Interactions with other competent and caring adults provide a positive influence on the emotional development of the child. The same effect can be acquired from community organizations and support systems that can help the parents directly with money and social support and have a positive influence on the emotional development of a child (Katz, Wilson, & Gottmann, 1999).

Risk-factors for the child on the one hand and for the parents on the other hand have a cumulative effect and can increase the probability that the child will develop an emotional-social disorder. The probability is especially high if there are no protective factors to neutralize these risk factors and foster emotional competence. Therefore it makes sense to intervene as early as possible and give children with more risk-factors the opportunity to change their behavior and enlarge their repertoire of positive behavior before they find themselves in a vicious circle of negative interactions and inadequate reactions. They should be provided the opportunity to build emotional competence instead (Figure 1).

Program PESS (Prevention of Emotional-Social Disorders for Children with Special Needs)

Theoretical Framework

As discussed in Chapter 1, there is a very large need for effective prevention- and intervention-programs that are designed for emotional-social disorders and that focus on target-groups with cognitive and linguistic deficits. These programs are intended to help individuals build protective factors and corresponding competences (Figure 1) and to compensate for risk factors. Programs that focus on emotional-social disorders should keep their target group clearly in mind: They should also be designed for children with low cognitive abilities and speech deficits.

In the scientific literature there are many references to the importance of a good adaptation to the target group to succeed with the program (Durlak, 1997; Greenberg, Domitrovich, & Bumbarger, 2001). There are more universal programs designed and evaluated at the moment than programs for children at risk or programs designed for special target groups. The group-leader has to adapt the programs to the individual group, and there is a need to simplify the program if it is focused on children with special needs or developmental disorders. In most cases there aren't any hints or guidelines in the manuals for these simplifications, which poses extra challenges for the group-leaders. In planning the PESS program, we considered the needs of the target group in designing the concept and structure of the program and in an attempt to emphasize social and emotional exercises. The theoretical framework of the program is based on the model by Carolyn Saarni (1999) because she connects the important domains of social and emotional development in her concept of emotional competence (Saarni et al., 2006). She underlines the inseparability of emotional and social development in her model (1999). Additionally, Saarni focuses on the individual and his or her skills, but she hints in a special way at interactions with other persons and keeps in mind both the individual's own experiences and the influence of cultural and environmental factors.

Saarni (2000) proposes a working definition of emotional competence:

"...emotional competence is the demonstration of self-efficacy in emotion-eliciting social transactions. Self-efficacy is used here to mean that the individual believes that he or she has the capacity and skills to achieve a desired outcome."

In her definition Saarni hints at one of the most important concepts of developmental psychology: self-efficacy. Many empirical studies have confirmed the relevance of this construct from Bandura (1977, 1989) and its influence for development: The experience of self-efficacy can be described as the experience of self-control and can lead to emotional competence in social interactions.

Saarni divides emotional competence into different skills and describes the skills in a very precise way (Saarni 1999). The prevention program (PESS) focuses on the first six skills because they have a special meaning for the target group. The skills are described in Table 7.

Looking at the different skills it becomes obvious that Saarni's model, unlike biological models, considers the wide influence of socialization on emotions. Emotions as products of individual development are in an ongoing interaction with the environment, and are highly influenced by the experiences of the individual. The concept of emotional competence provides an opportunity to address the specific domains of emotional-social disorders. Furthermore, the theoretical framework allows for the operationalization of single skills, which is of great importance either for the intervention or for the evaluation of the program.

First, Saarni describes the awareness of one's own emotions or emotional state: The possibility of perceiving emotions at all. Secondly, her theory is about perceiving emotions of other persons and being able to understand the emotional undertones of a situation. The next two skills are parallel to the first one: Initially she describes the ability to

Table 7. Skills of Emotional Competence (Saarni, 1999, p. 77)

1. Awareness of one's emotional state.
2. Skill in discerning other's emotions.
3. Skill in using the vocabulary of emotion and expression terms commonly available in one's subculture.
4. Capacity for empathic and sympathetic involvement in others' emotional experience.
5. Skill in adaptive coping with aversive or distressing emotions by using self-regulatory strategies.
6. Capacity of emotional self-efficacy: The individual views herself or himself as feeling, overall, the way she or he wants to feel.

express one's own emotions with words, facial expressions, and gestures. Moreover, the development of a repertoire of expression is very important for achieving the ability to express one's own emotions.

Another important achievement is the ability to react appropriately to the emotions of other people. As a condition therefore a person must be able to empathize with another person (cognitively and emotionally). Furthermore, it is important to find a functional way of coping with aversive feelings and difficult situations. The individual has to learn to cope with situations by developing his or her own strategies such as the ability to calm one's self. The precondition for this skill is to have a broad repertoire of coping mechanisms.

The last skill contains the first five skills and can be considered to be a global goal of development. Self-efficacy is a precondition for healthy development: The person is able to achieve a desired outcome and to experience meaningfulness from the social context. It is only possible to develop these feelings in a social context (Saarni, 1999, 2000; Saarni et al., 2006).

Goals and Structure of the PESS Program

As described in the preceding paragraph, the PESS program is based on the theoretical conception and framework of Saarni (1999). The theoretical framework encompasses both the conceptual structure of the program and its goals. The combination of elements related to social development and elements related to emotional development are very strongly connected in the program (Figure 2). The PESS program focuses at each step on both social and emotional skills to foster emotional competence, which is a combination of these two aspects or domains of development.

In this context it is very important to start with some single skills such as the perception of emotions in an early part of the program to later develop the opportunity to repeat the lessons from the beginning and enhance the skills. Elements such as the perception of emotion and modulation of emotion have a very strong connection to each other. The repetition of these two steps of the program is essential for creating emotional competence. The participants come to know these two domains very well throughout the program. Like Saarni's model, on the one hand, the program focuses on the person himself ("How do I feel if I'm sad?"). On the other hand, it focuses on interactions with peers ("How can I react if somebody else is angry?").

In the domain of emotions the program zooms in on the central emotions: happiness, sadness, anxiety (fear), and anger. On the one hand, only these central emotions could be identified and differentiated in cross-cultural studies (Denham, 1998). It is possible to distinguish these emotions from each other, and they are of central importance for the emotional development of a child. On the other hand, it makes more sense to focus on a central view of emotion and work with these emotions very intensively (perception and modulation), rather than getting short time effects with a large number of emotions that can only be treated superficially.

Furthermore, the children get the opportunity to regard these central emotions as a medium to express their feelings. Later, they have the opportunity to speak about

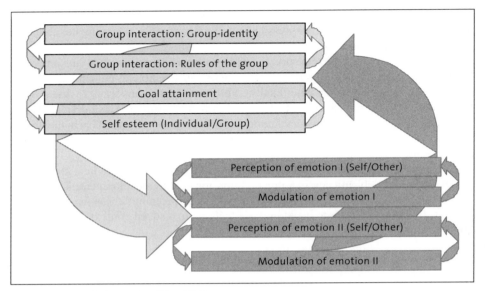

Figure 2. Central elements of the PESS program.

emotions on a more sophisticated level, but at the beginning they need a small number of tools to express their emotions. For example, if a child is able to show her feelings of happiness, the probability will be higher that she will be able to express other emotions such as pride, which is related to happiness. Focusing on these central emotions facilitates the development of a very broad repertoire of emotions. The perception and modulation of these central emotions is a first step or a foundation for developing more emotions and for developing the capacity to differentiate among them. However, it makes sense to focus on a few emotions in working with children with special needs – otherwise they would be overstrained because of their cognitive limitations.

The PESS program is designed as a group-program in preschool educational centers and focuses on secondary prevention (Table 8). Although most of the participating children are affected by many of the risk-factors mentioned in Section 1.2, in most instances there exists no clinical disorder at all. Very often the children endured negative social experiences, which can negatively impact their self-concept. In the preschool educational centers, the children are in a transitional phase between kindergarten and primary school. From a developmental psychology perspective, friendships and relationships with peers gain more and more in importance.

Table 8. Focus and Target Group of the PESS Program

- Middle childhood: 5–7 year old children (preschool level).
- Children with problems in emotional-social development (secondary prevention).
- Setting: educational centers (educator, special educator).
- Person-focused intervention (group program).
- Focus: children (primarily) and parents (for support).

PESS was conceived as a group program in the everyday life and everyday environment of the children. The advantage of being in normal environments makes it easier for the child. The setting is also helpful for the participants of the program: They can use their new knowledge and skills in everyday life. The group context has a central position, the participants of the program can learn with each other and from each other to cope with feelings in an appropriate way. Especially for the regulation of emotions and for emotional disorders the social context is very important. Some of the problems in the perception of emotion and regulation of emotion become obvious only in group contexts, for example, the lack of knowledge about different perceptions of social situations or socially inadequate ways of coping.

The program takes place once a week for two hours across three months of time (Table 9). The leaders of the program are the educators of the children in the preschool educational center because they have already established an emotional relationship with the children and can make the transfer to everyday life easier. All participating educators get the same intervention material and are trained before the program starts. Together with the children they create a workbook – the individual wishes of the participants are central for this.

The children can choose the colors and the way they create a jacket for the workbook. Furthermore, different photos of the child expressing different emotions are integrated into the workbook to show individual characters and to make the transfer easier. Moreover, the educators are requested to act as models for the children: The way they express their emotions and demonstrate a positive coping with aversive feelings in everyday life in addition to the program is very important for the positive emotional development of the children.

Table 9. Structure of the PESS Program

- Weekly group sessions with the children for three months.
- Parent's evening (at the beginning/at the end).
- Workbook to continue the contents after the program.
- Postcourse and lessons a half year later (refresher).

PESS is a person-focused program: The central aspect is to promote children's emotional and social skills. For support and transfer there is a parent's evening. The parents get information about emotional-social development, about the program and about possible ways to support their children. One aspect is the "parent-working book" with easy lessons for the parents and their children. The "parent-working book" is an endorsement of the lessons of the program in the preschool education centers. Conducting similar lessons in the family context, the children are supported in transferring their new skills and knowledge in the context of family. That way the transfer into everyday life is simplified and the possibility of long-term effects is enriched. In addition to that, the participants of the program get the opportunity to take part in a refresher course six months later. In the course they can reflect on their experience with the elements of the program and get a short training to refresh their abilities.

Table 10. Helpful Questions and Examples of the Modules of the PESS Program

1. **Awareness of one's emotional state.**
   - What makes me sad/angry/happy/anxious?
   - How do I feel, if I'm sad/angry/happy/anxious?
   - What is my facial expression if I'm sad/angry/happy/anxious?

Example "emotion-emblem lesson:"
The children paint one situation in each of four parts of an emblem, in which they have experienced one of the central emotions very intensely.

2. **Skill in discerning other's emotions.**
   - What are the feelings of the other persons?
   - How does a person look like if he or she is sad/angry/happy/anxious?

Example "pairs:"
The educator and the children are looking at a set of four pictures. The pictures show the same person in different emotional states. The children have to identify the different emotions and describe them in more detail.

3. **Skill in using the vocabulary of emotion and expression terms commonly available in one's subculture.**
   - How can I express my emotions?
   - How is it possible to describe feelings?

Example "funny and sad faces:"
The children create different faces with Play-Doh showing different emotions, e.g., happiness or anger. Afterwards they talk about their emotions.

4. **Capacity for empathic and sympathetic involvement in others' emotional experience.**
   - How can I react, if somebody is sad/angry/happy/anxious?
   - What is my feeling if another person is sad/angry/happy/anxious?

Example "blind-walk:"
The children come together in pairs and one child gets a blindfold. The other one has to lead his or her partner carefully through the room. After a few minutes they change their roles. Afterwards they describe their experiences in this situation.

5. **Skill in adaptive coping with aversive or distressing emotions by using self-regulatory strategies.**
   - What can I do if I'm sad/angry/happy/anxious?

Example "Playing conflicts:"
The educator portrays with two hand puppets a typical situation or conflict concerning a child's life. The educator and the children try to find different solutions for the conflict and talk about the consequences for both persons. In a role-play the children get the opportunity to find different solutions for this conflict.

6. **Capacity of emotional self-efficacy: The individual views herself or himself as feeling, overall, the way she or he wants to feel.**
   - Do I feel good?
   - Can I achieve my goals?

The goals and contents of each part of the program are discussed.

Example Exercises of the PESS Program

In the following, some exercises of the PESS program are described to provide information about the structure and the methods of the program. The lessons are often related to more than one dimension of emotional competence.

We developed several central questions to represent the central aspects of the skills mentioned in Saarni's theory. Some of these questions are guidelines for the educators conducting the program; others are used to talk with the children about their emotions (Table 10).

In Table 10, first, one skill of Saarni's theoretical framework is mentioned, secondly, there are some central questions referring to these skills, and finally, there is a description of an example from the PESS program. The capacity of emotional self-efficacy (Saarni VI) is a broader goal that is fostered in each part of the program and the program at large. For this reason there is no special lesson focusing on this goal.

At the moment the pilot study of the PESS Program has been completed in a few preschool educational centers. It became obvious that a few modifications of the program might be necessary to meliorate the program and adapt it optimally to the educational setting. The next step is the intervention phase to get further empirical results about the effectiveness of the program.

Conclusion

There are many possible ways and strategies to prevent emotional-social disorders in childhood. Single interventions like the PESS program, for example, are only one part of a puzzle to foster emotional development. The goal of the program is to support and to complement education inside and outside the family, but it cannot substitute for the development of emotional competence in these areas. There is a very huge need to develop and evaluate further programs. In this context it is very important to focus on a good adaptation between the program and the target groups. The preschool prevention of emotional-social disorders and aggressive behavior for children with special needs is in this meaning a desiderata desideratum for reasearchers and practicers.

References

Bandura, A. (1977). Self-efficacy. Toward a unifying theory of behavioral change. *Psychological Review, 84*, 191–215.

Bandura, A. (1989). Human agency in social cognitive theory. *American Psychologist, 44*, 1175–1184.

Crick, N. R., & Dodge, K. A. (1994). A review and reformulation of social information-processing mechanisms in children's social adjustment. *Psychological Bulletin, 115*, 74–101.

Denham, S. A. (1998). *Emotional development in young children.* New York: Guilford.

Denham, S. A., & Burton R. (2003). *Social and emotional prevention and intervention programming for preschoolers.* New York: Kluwer Academic/Plenum.

Denham, S. A., Mitchell-Copeland, J., Standberg, K., Auerbach, S., & Blair, K. (1997). Parental contributions to preschoolers' emotional competence: Direct and indirect effects. *Motivation and Emotion, 21*, 65–86.

Durlak, J. A. (1997). *Successful prevention programs for children and adolescents.* New York: Plenum.

Essau, C. A., & Petermann, F. (2001). *Anxiety disorders in children and adolescents. Epidemiology, risk factors and treatment.* Hove, UK: Brunner-Routledge.

Ford, T., Goodman, R., & Meltzer, H. (2003). The British child and adolescent mental health survey 1999: The prevalence of DSM-IV disorders. *Journal of the American Academy of child and Adolescent Psychiatry, 42*, 1203–1211.

Garner, P. W. (1999). Continuity in emotion knowledge from preschool to middle-childhood and relation to emotion socialization. *Motivation and Emotion, 23*, 247–266.

Greenberg, M. T., Domitrovich, C., & Bumbarger, B. (2001). The prevention of mental disorders in school-aged children: Current state of the field. *Prevention and Treatment, 4*(1).

Jones, N. A., Filed, T., Fox, N. A., Davalos, M., & Gomez, C. (2001). EEG during different emotions in 10-month-old infants of depressed mothers. *Journal of Reproductive and Infant Psychology, 19*, 295–312.

Katz, L. F., Wilson, B., & Gottmann, J. M. (1999). Meta-emotion philosophy and family adjustment: Making an emotional connection. In M. J. Cox & J. Brooks-Gunn (Eds.), *Conflict and cohesion in families: Causes and consequences. The advances in family research series* (pp. 131–165). Mahwah, NJ: Erlbaum.

Lemerise, E., & Arsenio, W. F. (2000). An integrated model of emotion processes and cognition in social information processing. *Child Development, 71*, 107–118.

McClure, E. B., Brennan, P. A., Hammen, C., & Le Brocque, R. M. (2001). Parental anxiety disorders, child anxiety disorders, and the perceived parent-child-relationship in an Australian high-risk sample. *Journal of Abnormal Child Psychology, 29*, 1–10.

Orobio de Castro, B. (2005). Emotionen bei der Verarbeitung sozialer Informationen von hochaggressiven Jungen [Emotions in social information processing in highly aggressive boys]. In A. Ittel & M. von Salisch (Ed.), *Lügen, Lästern, Leiden lassen. Aggressives Verhalten von Kindern und Jugendlichen* (pp. 33–44). Stuttgart, Germany: Kohlhammer.

Petermann, F. (2005). Zur Epidemiologie psychischer Störungen im Kindes- und Jugendalter: Eine Bestandsaufnahme [Epidemiology of mental disorders in children and adolescents. A critical review]. *Kindheit und Entwicklung, 14*(1), 48–57.

Petermann, F., & Wiedebusch, S. (2003). *Emotionale Kompetenz bei Kindern* [The emotional competence of children]. Göttingen, Germany: Hogrefe.

Rutter, M., & Sroufe, L. A. (2000). Developmental psychopathology: Concepts and challenges. *Development and Psychopathology, 12*, 265–296.

Saarni, C. (1999). *The development of emotional competence.* New York: Guilford.

Saarni, C. (2000). Emotional competence. A developmental perspective. In R. Bar-On & J. D. A. Parker (Eds.), *The handbook of emotional intelligence,* (pp. 68–91). San Francisco: Jossey-Bass.

Saarni, C., & Buckley, M. (2002). Children's understanding of emotion communication in family. *Marriage and Family Review, 34*, 213–242.

Saarni, C., Campos, J. J., Camras, L., & Witherington, D. (2006). Emotional development: Action, communication, and understanding. In W. Damon & R. M. Lerner (Eds.), *Handbook of child psychology (6th ed. Vol. 3*, pp. 226–299). New York: Wiley.

Salisch, M. v. (2002). Seine Gefühle handhaben lernen. Über den Umgang mit Ärger [Learning to handle one's emotions. About the regulation of anger]. In M. von Salisch (Ed.), *Emotionale Kompetenz entwickeln,* (pp. 135–156). Stuttgart, Germany: Kohlhammer.

Southam-Gerow, M. A., & Kendal, P. C. (2002). Emotion regulation and understanding. Implications for child psychology and therapy. *Clinical Psychology Research, 22*, 189–222.

Volling, B. L., McElwain, N. L., Notaro, P.C., & Herrera, C. (2002). Parents' emotional availability and infant emotional competence: Predictors of parent-infant attachment and emerging
self-regulation. *Journal of Family Psychology, 16*, 447–465.
Webster-Stratton, C. (2000). *How to promote children's social and emotional competence.* London: Chapman.

DATE DUE

Demco, Inc. 38-293